BEYOND
TODDLERDOM

BEYOND TODDLERDOM

Keeping five- to twelve-year-olds on the rails

Dr Christopher Green

VERMILION
London

First published in Great Britain in 2000

5 7 9 10 8 6 4

Text © Dr Christopher Green and Dr Hilary Green 2000
Illustrations © Roger Roberts 2000

Christopher Green has asserted his right to be identified as the author of
this work under the Copyright, Designs and Patents Act 1988.

First published in Australia and New Zealand in 2000 by Doubleday Australia,
an imprint of Transworld Publishers,
Division of Random House Australia Pty Ltd

First published in the United Kingdom in 2000 by Vermilion,
an imprint of Ebury Press
Random House, 20 Vauxhall Bridge Road, London SW1V 2SA

Random House South Africa (Pty) Limited
Endulini, 5A Jubilee Road, Parktown 2193, South Africa

The Random House Group Limited Reg. No. 954009

A CIP catalogue record for this book is available from the British Library.

ISBN 0 09 181624 6

Papers used by Vermilion are natural, recyclable products made from
wood grown in sustainable forests.

Printed and bound in the United Kingdom at

the University Press, Cambridge.

Contents

Appendices

Acknowledgements

Thanks to my wife, Hilary – without her this book would have been impossible. She supports and encourages and sees the humour in life.

Thanks are also due to Lorraine Partington, a secretary with the ability to bring order to my chaos, and a loyal friend; Dr John Coveney of the Department of Public Health, Flinders University – friend and dietitian who helped with *Toddler Taming* and brought the same good sense to this book; and Dr Kit Chee, who has worked with me and is now development and behavioural paediatrician at The Sydney Learning Clinic. I have learned much from parents, especially Gly Patrick.

And finally to colleagues and friends at the New Children's Hospital, Westmead for their sound advice, especially Dr Ted Beckenham, Professor Margaret Burgess, Dr Frank Martin, Professor Kim Oates, Dr Maureen Rogers and Professor Richard Widmer.

Introduction

I once wrote a book about toddlers, which sold a million copies around the world. *Toddler Taming* was practical, reassuring and based on reality. What's more, it could make mums laugh. After all, you can smile about toddlers because you know that most of their odd little behaviours will disappear when their brain discovers sense at the age of three years.

But five- to twelve-year-olds are much more complicated, which made this book a lot harder to write. These children are influenced by school, their friends, their families and their abilities, and their problems can easily deepen rather than disappear.

Beyond Toddlerdom looks at how primary school-age children feel, think and behave. The emphasis is on behaviour, with the aim of keeping parents close and in love with their children, so homes need never become a war zone.

I learnt the ideas you will read in this book from the thousands of parents and children I have attempted to help every day in my work. But I don't pretend to have all the answers: even after twenty-five years I still struggle to find ways to help some families I meet.

Hopefully, though, you will find lots of useful advice here. To help you find what you're looking for easily and quickly, *Beyond Toddlerdom* contains a clear index and plenty of tables that set out the main points.

Once I asked a mum how things were going. She said, 'It's like this, Doctor. Before we met you we were riding on a roller coaster completely out of control. Now we're still on a roller coaster but it's finally on the rails.'

This book is about keeping relationships between parents and children strong and happy. It's also about keeping children on the rails. I can't promise a smooth ride, but I hope I can help you avoid some of the bumps.

Christopher Green
January 2000

The secret of successful parenting: treat children the way you would like to be treated

This book is cram-packed with the latest child care information. But it is not a book about 'taming', 'compliance' and 'perfect behaviours'. Instead, *Beyond Toddlerdom* is about relationships: the art of keeping parents close and in love with their children. If we can achieve this, the rest usually falls into place.

Now, the key to a good relationship, whether it's between two adults or a parent and a child, is to treat the other person the way you would like to be treated. And that's what this book is all about: treat your children

1

the way you like to be treated and your relationship with them won't go far wrong.

As you skim through the chapters, you'll find that the same messages keep reappearing. These messages are the secret of successful parenting, but they could apply to any relationship. Here they are:

- Children need you to be available to admire, encourage and marvel.
- Children like routine, consistency and clear communication, but they also need flexibility and choice.
- Discipline is not about pain and punishment. In this new millennium we mould good behaviours through encouragement and reward.
- Confrontation, force and heavy discipline wreck many relationships. You may appear to win but at the cost of resentment, anger and hate.
- When things have gone badly, quickly forgive and restart with a clean slate. There is no place for grudges in a good relationship.
- Let unimportant behaviour pass. Take a step back and ask, 'Is this getting me anywhere?' If you are up a cul-de-sac, back off.
- Children do strange things and muck often hits the fan. Don't over-analyse. I have been at this for more than a quarter of a century and I still watch in wonderment.

Be available

Christopher Green is a busy man, but if I was always so busy that my wife never saw me, and when she did I told her I was way too busy to stop and talk, she may, quite rightly, start to feel as if she must be the least important person in my life.

Children don't need 'quality time'; they need a parent who is available to sit, listen, do things together and marvel at what they see.

Point 1: More than anything, children need you to be available.

Routine and structure

Everyone loves surprises, but if every day when you woke up you had no idea what was going to happen it would be very unsettling. Chaos makes us all feel as if we've got no control over the situation. Like adults, children are happiest when they know what's coming next.

Point 2: Children are happiest when they have a structured routine.

Consistent limits and rules

As I drive to the hospital I pass through three speed zones. I know each legal limit and the level of tolerance before I am booked. I cope because I know the stated limits and levels of tolerance. I would be very confused if either of these changed from day to day. Children may protest our limits but at least they know we care enough to care what they do. Unpredictability causes confusion, anger and emotional insecurity.

Point 3: Children are at their most secure when they know the rules and how far they can push these limits.

Flexibility and compromise

I don't cope well with rigid-minded people who insist that everything is done by the book. They quote council by-laws, can't compromise and never shift an inch.

I come up against schools who will only allow important medication to be given at 12.45pm because this is the one and only time they hand out tablets. But the child I care for falls apart without their 11am dose.

Here is another example. The rules state that the bus is designed to carry six people and the operator sees no difference between six sumos or six child-gymnasts. Adults with an almost autistic-like inflexibility need their rules, but a successful relationship won't work without compromise.

Parents need to adjust the rules to fit the individual situation: children sleep in their own beds, but during a thunderstorm everyone can sleep together; children must tidy away the dinner dishes, but tonight there is so much homework they can be excused.

Point 4: Rules and consistency are important for children, but there must be room for flexibility and compromise.

Choice and freedom

I wake up in the morning and am about to get dressed. 'Just wait a minute,' says my wife. 'Today you will wear a blue shirt, cream trousers and a red tie. For lunch you will have a gherkin and ham roll with a skim-milk cappuccino.'

'Hey, you wait a minute,' I think. 'Don't I have some say in my own life?'

A two-year-old can't cope with choice but a school-age child needs some freedom to decide their own destiny. Controlling parents create unhappy children who can't make a decision.

Point 5: School-age children respond best to choice.

Communicate clearly

Sometimes I enter a shop where the assistant doesn't bother to look up before asking coldly what I want. It seems as if my presence is an annoyance and they have no interest in me, the customer. Rude adults are immensely annoying; I like to be greeted with eye contact, interest and civility.

If you wish a child to respond, address them with interest and enthusiasm.

Point 6: To gain a child's attention, look them directly in the eye, talk simply and speak as though you mean it. Show them you're interested.

Ask, don't nag

Christopher Green hates being nagged. 'Have you done that yet? Why not? When will you do it? What's keeping you?' The more I am nagged, the more obstinate and angry I become.

If you want compliant children tell them what you wish them to do, encourage action, monitor results, then get off their backs.

Point 7: Children switch off and go deaf when parents nag.

Reward good behaviour

The rock concert has been spectacular and you wish it would never end. As the last note fades the audience spring to their feet and shriek their appreciation. The band responds to this show of enthusiasm and plays two more numbers.

The audience rewarded the band for their good playing. The band rewarded the audience for their enthusiasm. This was a win-win situation. If we had wanted the band to pack up and go home, we would have kept quiet.

With our children we mould their behaviour by ensuring the right (not the wrong) actions pay off.

Point 8: Encourage good behaviour by rewarding the good. Discourage bad behaviour by preventing any pay-off for the bad.

Subtle rewards are the best

How do you know that things are going well in your adult relationship? Does your partner give you a pound or a star? Of course not. We know that things are on track because we sense the positive vibrations between us. This subtle feedback is the main way we mould human beings of all ages.

Children know they are doing well by the way we look at them, the twinkle in our eyes, our tone of voice, our level of interest and the gentle reassuring touch as we brush by.

Point 9: Soft, subtle encouragement is the most powerful way to boost behaviour.

Notice the good

In my wish to be a domesticated dad, I go out to get the shopping. But when I return home it's all complaints: 'Could you not have got a larger loaf? Didn't they have redder apples? Why choose the dented can of dog food? Were there no straight bananas?' I busted myself but it seems everything is wrong. Soon I think, 'What's the point in bothering?'

Children often get this treatment from their parents. They set the table with great care: 'You've got the knives and forks the wrong way around.' They clean the dishes: 'There's egg on that plate.' They vacuum the lounge: 'You missed a bit.' When humans work hard and others only notice their faults and not the effort, it's a sure way to discourage and dishearten.

Point 10: Let children know when you are pleased. Change the focus from only seeing the bad. Catch them being good.

Confrontation causes resentment

When the first officer of the *Titanic* sees an iceberg ahead it is no time to ask nicely, 'I'd appreciate it if you could turn a little to the left.' He must issue a firm order. But when we are steaming in clear waters, humans are more receptive when asked rather than told.

We don't like being steamrollered and bullied: 'Just shut up and do it'; 'Do it or I'll hit you!' This heavy form of discipline would bring out the worst in any of us. I would resent this confrontation and feel angry, drag my feet and wonder how I could get even.

As parents hammer their child into shape the young one thinks, 'Damn you, Dad! I'll make it harder for you next time.' Force and confrontation may get action, but often at a price.

Point 11: Confrontation and bullying lead to opposition and resentment.

Calm, not escalation

Let's imagine you are flying from Melbourne to Sydney when the engine falls off the plane. The confident pilot would transmit calm:

'This is Captain Smith speaking. I have to inform you that the port engine has just become disengaged. Don't worry, the crew will soon be through the cabin serving complimentary drinks followed by a hot meal, then we'll attempt a crash landing in Sydney.' The example has a bit of author's licence, but the message is clear: a calm attitude spreads calm.

Even the sweetest child can be intensely irritating, but successful parents don't escalate by adding heat to an already overheated situation. They communicate in a calm voice, repeat their request like a broken gramophone record and move away before they lose their cool.

Point 12: If parents can keep calm, children are easier to control.

Cool off and regain control

Your German shepherd guard dog has an attitude problem. In the park he starts a skirmish with a psychopathic sheepdog. As the hair flies, do you issue polite instructions such as 'Sit, Fritz', or 'Lassie, heel'?

When we are in the midst of a dogfight, the first priority is to separate and reduce the heat. Once calm is re-established, rules and discipline can return.

Point 13: When a child's behaviour has escalated over the top, this is not a time for rational reasoning. The first priority is to cool down the situation and regain control.

Forgive and move on

I do something really foolish. I know I have been silly and I apologise. But my words are not accepted. I apologise again and I ask what I can do to make up, but the door is slammed in my face. Now I feel intensely angry and am damned if I will say sorry again. Communication is now blocked and we have moved poles apart in our relationship.

Children don't want to be at war with their parents, but often they are left with no other option. Be a peace maker. If at first your efforts are not accepted, keep offering the olive branch. Children eventually grasp the leaves and come back in close.

Point 14: After anger or punishment, forgive fast and start afresh with a clean slate.

Don't stir up the animals

Life is full of frustrations, but we will go mad if we rise to every annoyance. When working in the lions' cage do you take a stick and poke them in the backside or do you tread gently and avoid trouble?

Some parents nitpick and escalate every trivial event. They are incapable of letting an unimportant behaviour pass. I spend hours every week trying to encourage parents to back off, but often I am wasting my breath. We don't want to let our children get away with murder, but it isn't clever to stir up the animals over every imperfection.

Point 15: Let the unimportant things pass.

Treating children the way you like to be treated

1. More than anything, children need parents to be available to admire, encourage and marvel.

2. Children behave best when they have a structured routine.

3. Children are at their most secure when they know the rules and how far they can push these limits.

4. Rules and consistency are important for children, but there must be room for flexibility and compromise.

5. School-age children respond best to choice.

6. To gain their attention, look a child directly in the eye, talk simply and speak as though you mean it.

7. Children switch off and go deaf when parents nag.

8. Encourage good behaviour by rewarding the good. Discourage bad behaviour by preventing any pay-off for the bad.

9. Soft, subtle encouragement is the most powerful way to boost behaviour.

10. Let children know when you are pleased. Change the focus from only seeing the bad. Catch them being good.

11. Confrontation and bullying lead to opposition and resentment.

12. If parents can keep calm, children are easier to control.

13. When a child's behaviour has escalated over the top, this is not a time for rational reasoning. The first priority is to cool down the situation and regain control.

14. After anger or punishment, forgive fast and start afresh with a clean slate.

15. Let the unimportant things pass.

Age five to twelve: how they think, feel and behave

You may be wondering why I didn't write this book years ago. The answer is simple: the way five-year-olds to twelve-year-olds think, feel and behave is far too complicated.

Writing about toddlers was easy. They only have one problem – a serious lack of sense. But school-age children are much more complex little humans, who regularly make parents wonder if they are the ones who lack the sense.

Luckily, you need not feel that you are losing your marbles permanently. Because school-age children are easier to understand once you realise that they go through not one but two very different stages of development during these years: the dependent and innocent stage between the years five and eight and the much more independent and grown-up stage between eight and twelve.

This chapter looks at how children of the two age groups think, feel and behave, so you can gain a better understanding of what makes your child tick.

The two stages: an overview

Five- to eight-year-olds

These little people still carry much of the unspoiled innocence of the preschool years. They remain close and immensely dependent on their mum and dad. They are cuddly, uncomplicated and usually keen to please. They skip, effervesce and believe in ghosts and monsters.

Eight- to twelve-year-olds

At eight years children stand on the first rung of the ladder that leads towards adulthood. Dependence on Mum and Dad starts to weaken. They are increasingly influenced by teachers, school friends, the media and their environment, and they start to question their parents' values and wisdom.

Children of this age compare their looks, school performance, social acceptance and sporting abilities, then become worried when they don't match up. Skipping and cuddles become rare, and now only babies believe in monsters.

Between eight years and twelve years they also lose that wonderful openness that young children have, and they start to be more secretive and to hold hidden agendas.

The five- to eight-year-old

Our story starts when they are five years of age. They seem so grown up as they stride off in their new school uniform. They can sit, concentrate, mix, communicate clearly and write and read some words. But don't be fooled by this superficial show of maturity, because the five-year-old is still a baby in many ways.

Total dependence

Little children can treat Mum and Dad like lesser beings, but behind the show they are still immensely influenced and dependent on us. The degree of dependence or independence varies greatly from child to child, but young children need us much more than we realise.

They may appear to ignore what we say, but behind this pretence they watch what we do and tune into our beliefs and values. If Dad believes that Elvis is alive and pumping gas on the Gold Coast, they believe the King still lives. If you think the greenhouse effect is caused by cattle passing wind, there's no debate, it's cows farting that does it. Other children and teachers may seed some ideas in their minds, but we parents are still the main source of wisdom.

Even your words get recycled. As you hear them talk to their friends, they might sound like you on a bad day: 'I'm tired of having to tell you'; 'I don't think I can play. I feel a headache coming on.'

At this age, children have few independent thoughts, and you are the main policy maker. For these few years you are seen as infallible. Enjoy this brief moment of power, because it passes all too quickly!

A magic mind

Six-year-olds are fitted with a technicolour imagination. They don't really believe in ghosts and monsters, but when the night is very dark, they worry that something might be out there. The idea of reindeer, chimneys and the North Pole may seem far-fetched, but as it gets close to Christmas, Santa becomes very real.

This blur between fact and fiction can add technicolour to the truth. So a passing car braking hard while the kindergarten class plays outside may become, over the course of the day, a multiple car accident involving the police rescue squad and a fleet of ambulances.

It's important to be aware of this imaginative exaggeration. Behind every exaggeration lies a seed of truth, but sometimes the story is bigger than the seed. If your six-year-old makes claims about his teacher, the story you hear may not be the complete truth. It is wise to first check the facts before you round up a posse of neighbours for a shoot-out with the principal.

Skipping and cuddling

This is a wonderfully unspoiled age of innocence. It is a time when children don't just walk: they skip, wave their arms and bounce with enthusiasm. They are like little lambs that frolic just for the joy of being alive.

It is a magic time when children sit on your knee and snuggle up close. If it's cuddles you are after, this is the age to get your share.

Also, young children are unfazed by nudity. A six-year-old will race around the house wearing nothing more than a whoop of joy. At this age they do what feels right and their minds are unpolluted by adult shame and modesty. Six-year-olds know nothing of apples, serpents and Original Sin.

Open and helpful

Seven-year-olds are remarkably up front, and if you listen you will hear most of what's on their minds. Such is their openness they can't keep a secret, so when they buy your birthday present they have to drop hints – they can't wait until the big day. Make the most of this forthrightness to establish clear lines of communication at this time because, as they get older, they will be less open.

Children of this age work well beside their parents and are usually happy to help. Obviously some requests are more attractive than others: 'Would you like to turn off the television and go to McDonalds?' gets more response than 'Would you like to turn off the television and tidy your bedroom?' This is hardly surprising – they're not stupid.

Too honest

Under-eights know nothing of political correctness. They call things as they see them, and have not yet mastered the almost-honesty of adults. So when a five-year-old spots a fat lady or a one-legged man, they will announce it to the world. They get confused when we tell Grandma her cooking was a cordon bleu extravaganza, because they know Dad thought it was boring mush. They are surprised when we tell Uncle Bill he looks good, because to them he's looking close to expiry. Even when they pass wind, they apologise politely rather than disown the noise.

Likes rules and tells tales

The six-year-old is a miniature bureaucrat who loves rules and regulations. Most six-year-olds enjoy the clear structure of school, where they work quietly and raise a hand before they speak. At this young age classroom regulations are like commandments delivered on tablets from the mount. Even at home they may quote these rules to brothers, sisters and babes in arms.

They are not only interested in rules, but also in their obeyance: 'Please Miss, Jack took Sarah's pencil'; 'Please Miss, Kate's talking again.' But this time of informing on others is short-lived, and by the age of seven or eight it's already uncool to tell on your mates.

Property is a fuzzy notion

The under-eight has little idea about money or value. They can quote the price of a lollipop, but that is the limit of their financial wizardry. If the ball they kick shatters a priceless vase, it is Mum's anger, not the monetary value, that catches their attention.

The idea of ownership is another fuzzy notion. Though most children are reasonably honest, the under eight-year-old is often fitted with remarkably light fingers. Some infant teachers joke that their pupils could do with a strip search at going-home time, as pencils, toys and trinkets seem to slip into pockets.

This immaturity with money and ownership is all part of growing up. Our response to petty pocketing at this age should be low key: just state what you believe happened, register your disapproval and watch out for repetitions.

Lives for the present

A five-year-old has no appreciation of the long-term future. The world they understand is happening now. Once I asked a little boy, 'What do you want to do when you grow up?'

'I don't want to grow up,' he said. 'I would have to drive a car and might not be able to stop it.'

This was a relevant answer for a five-year-old, but by eight years he will see beyond the present and by twelve he'll probably understand the advantage of four-wheel discs with an anti-locking option.

We might explain a complex idea to our under-eights but they won't really understand: 'Grandma got sick, developed pneumonia, went to hospital, died and is now in heaven.'

They can repeat this, but have no understanding of pneumonia, heaven or death and can't grasp the permanent nature of this event. To them Grandma is on a long holiday and may well come back.

Unspoken worries

As a young child, I was always warned about the dangers of germs. At that time we lived near a large hospital for infectious diseases that was bounded on its front by a high wall. Every time my parents drove along the road outside I crouched low in the back of the car and held my breath to protect myself from any germ that might vault over the wall and land on me. It was very real in my mind, and I believed my parents were negligent in subjecting me to such risk. But they never knew that this was troubling me: they just wondered why I was blue and breathless.

Psychiatrists are continually amazed at how five- to eight-year-olds can grasp the wrong end of the stick then worry themselves silly over unimportant things. If Mum and Dad have a major tiff their six-year-old may anticipate a break-up. If Dad is late to pick them up, they may fear abandonment. If Mum is admitted to hospital, they may worry she might die. If their sister develops leukemia, they might believe they are in some way to blame. It can be a confusing time for children, and little minds may worry more than we think.

Similarity of boys and girls

In the early school years, the size, strength and sporting ability of boys and girls are almost the same. While girls are generally more verbal and boys may have more behaviour and learning problems, at this age boys and girls are more similar than they ever will be again.

Both boys and girls wonder about their anatomical differences, but this is an innocent interest without any sexual overtones. At this age boys more often play with boys and girls with girls, but it's okay to mix any way you want.

However, after the age of eight years, growth, development and maturity race ahead, and with this comes a definite segregation of the sexes.

The eight- to twelve-year-old

It's now their eighth birthday and, as the last candle flickers out, they stand at a crossroads in life. Behind them are all the openness, innocence and unspoiled imagination of the young. Ahead lies a more serious world where they must compete and make the grade.

As parents, the years ahead will test both our patience and stamina.

Parents out of power

The under-eights know all about disobedience, but they still see our proclamations as the one and only truth. Sadly, all good things come to an end, and our divine power starts to ebb at seven years. By the time our child is eight, all our words and actions come into question.

Before, you could just lay down the law: 'Because I say so.' Now, you will get poor compliance without some explanation and good reason. In the past, you could tell them El Niño was caused by the French bombs in the Pacific. Now they laugh at your ignorance as they quote their teacher. Teachers are never wrong; mothers often are!

This shift of power takes many parents by surprise. It was never mentioned in the owner's manual: you had always believed that parents were in charge! Now you're not so sure.

The influence of others

The under-eights will spend the majority of their time at home. But after this age you may only see them at the pit stops, as they fuel up ready to hit the circuit again.

Parents lose their monopoly position as other people exert their influence. The soccer coach talks about the dangers of smoking, and now John confronts his puffing dad about fitness, heart attacks and toes dropping off. We have spent eight years teaching politeness, manners and healthy eating, and now the influence of their mates dismantles much of our hard work.

They are now affected by the attitudes of the herd. They watch the 'in' TV programmes, wear the right sort of clothes and buy certain brands.

This can be a strange time for parents, where we see less of our children and know they are being influenced by others.

A long-term view of life

The five- to eight-year-old's view of life is strictly in the here and now. But after eight they look into the distance and can see the permanent nature of events. If Grandma dies, they know she has gone forever and they now grieve like their parents. If a marriage breaks up they realise Mum and Dad have split for life. They can see how they will grow into an adult, and by twelve years some have started to develop major goals.

The silly worries of the younger child have disappeared, but they are replaced by the usual insecurities, fears and paranoia that trouble most people between the age of eight and eighty years.

Competes and compares

The young child will breeze along, not too concerned by their differences and difficulties. But at eight, they start to worry about how others see them. They develop an awareness of looks, learning abilities, body shape, strength, mixing skills and social acceptance.

We can tell our children they are bright, good-looking and wonderful, but they still match themselves against the group. They feel inadequate when they don't make the grade, and with this can come problems of esteem and even depression.

A loss of innocence

Before the age of eight they skipped, cuddled and believed in Santa. Now Santa is silly and skipping is for babies. The only time you will get a cuddle may be when they are almost asleep, ninety-eight per cent unconscious and unable to resist.

If you open the door on a naked nine-year-old they cover everything and protest. Now there is no talk of ghosts, monsters and pretend people: the imagination moved out along with the magic. The once uncomplicated mind has matured to a more adult plane, and with this, the age of innocence has gone.

The school-age smart arse

Beware! You are entering an age where children can verbally out-point you. From now on it's best to avoid arguments, as grown-ups will rarely win.

Children can make a nonsense out of our attempts to be serious:

'Don't bounce on the new lounge suite.'

'I'm not bouncing, just bobbing up and down.'

'Don't annoy your sister.'

'I'm not. She's annoying me.'

One friend opened her washing machine to find it white with tissues. 'Who left these in their pockets?' she asked.

Her nine-year-old looked her in the eyes and replied, 'It couldn't have been me. You know I only use my sleeve.'

They are also perfecting the art of put-downs. You make some earth-shattering observation to which they respond, with a yawn, 'Fascinating, Dad.' Soon you are told your jokes aren't funny, then your taste in music is geriatric – and that's just the start. It gets worse in adolescence.

School learning and language

There is a big difference between the mothering and spoon-feeding of the infants classes and what happens after the age of eight. From now on the successful students will need to self-motivate, organise and keep on task.

Learning takes a giant leap forward during the years between eight and twelve. The average six-year-old can read single words; by twelve, they can manage simple newspapers and almost this book. For eight- to twelve-year-olds, school is so important that those who have a learning weakness or who can't stick at a task are hurt by failure and suffer in esteem.

The use and understanding of language increases with age. At six years they can cope with a simple concept, for example, 'Why does the sign on the petrol pump say "No Smoking"?' By eight years they understand more complex questions and by twelve years they are fully versed in innuendo, double meaning and the subtle differences that come with a change in tone.

This is also the start of abstract thought, where they take pre-programmed information and use it to create something new outside the programme.

Segregation of the sexes

When little boys and little girls start school they enjoy one another's company and are pleased to play together. But after eight, boys tend to play with boys and girls with girls.

The boys often hunt in packs and don't welcome children who are different or out of step. Girls usually play two or three together and are generally more accepting of those who are shy or less popular.

The segregation that starts around eight remains an uneasy part of life until, in adolescence, boys and girls reunite in a more individual way.

Girls in general are easier-going and more mature. Boys have a higher incidence of learning difficulties and over-the-top behaviour. The pubertal growth spurt hits girls before boys, but once growth sets in, boys become physically stronger and more solid.

The five- to eight-year-old: the age of magic and innocence

1. Total dependence
   - totally dependent on parents
   - accepts parents' beliefs without question
   - parents remain the one source of true wisdom

2. A magic mind
   - believes in ghosts, monsters and Santa
   - has a technicolour imagination
   - truth and pretend get blurred

3. Skipping and cuddling
   - skips and frolics like a lamb
   - cuddles, sits on your knee
   - baths together, no worry about nudity

4. Open and helpful
   - communicates openly
   - can't keep a secret
   - likes to help and work with parents

5. Too honest
   - reports things as they see them

6. Likes rules and tell-tales
   - likes to have rules
   - likes to tell on rule breakers

7. Property is a fuzzy notion
   - has little idea about the value of property
   - has no idea about the value of money
   - some innocent petty theft

8. Lives for the present
   - their world is happening today
   - has no understanding of the long-term future
   - cannot understand the permanent nature of death

9. Unspoken worries
   - may get the wrong end of the stick
   - can worry greatly over non-worries
10. True equality of boys and girls
   - size, strength and sporting ability are equal
   - boys and girls play together

The eight- to twelve-year-old: life starts to get serious

1. Parents out of power
   - questions their parents' opinions and values
   - parents are no longer infallible
2. The influence of others
   - influenced by others outside the home
   - starts to follow the herd
3. A long-term view of life
   - starts to plan for the future
   - death and divorce are permanent
   - can now see their life as an adult
4. Competes and compares
   - starts to compare and worry over differences
   - worries over school work, abilities, looks, social skills
   - gets upset if don't match up
5. A loss of innocence
   - locks doors, covers up nudity
   - rations cuddles, stops sitting on your knee
   - stops skipping, stops believing in ghosts and Santa
6. The school-age smart arse
   - verbally too clever for their own good
   - verbally puts down parents
7. School learning and language
   - starts to self motivate and plan school work
   - language and reading become almost adult
8. Segregation of the sexes
   - boys play with boys and girls play with girls
   - girls hit puberty spurt before boys

THREE

Why children behave badly

In my early years of training I was taught that children were created equal and that bad behaviour came from bad parenting. This confused me, particularly when I came across some spaced-out punk couple who had been blessed with an angelic child, then the local vicar, who had an entire terrorist cell operating from his crypt. I finally realised that any parent who had more than one child would know what my teachers had missed: children are not created equal in their behaviour and temperament.

Once it was fashionable to regard differences between children as being a consequence of birth order: there was the dispossessed first child and the competitive middle child. But a child can be easy or difficult, regardless of birth position. I see first children who are so extreme, they set their parents on a life-long course of contraception. In this case no one is dispossessed or competing: the child is just plain impossible.

We have moved a long way from the guilt trips and parent blaming of the past. Instead, in this new millennium a child's behaviour is believed to be a mix of four influences:

1. temperament
2. parenting style
3. reaction to stress and uncertainty
4. the pursuit of attention and power.

Each child starts with a very individual genetic temperament, part of which arrives out of the blue and part of which comes from Mum and Dad. This unique package of temperament is then uplifted or depressed by the actions of us, their parents. It is further altered by security or stress in the child's living environment. Finally, behaviour is driven by the wish for attention and the pursuit of power.

Temperament

Variations in children's temperaments are immense. Children can be easy-going, intense, focused, fidgety, dreamy, distractable, demanding, oppositional, compliant, clingy, fearless, whingeing, dissatisfied, obsessive, disorganised, volatile. Often you get a mix of these qualities, which makes each parent's lot different.

The seeds of temperament are pre-programmed at birth. Look at a tiny infant of three months of age and, even at this early stage, you can start to see what joys lie ahead.

Temperament is the foundation on which we parents build our eighteen-year-long construction project. Some children have movable foundations while other children's foundations are dug so deep in the bedrock they are almost impossible to budge.

Difficult temperaments: the statistics

In the preschool years it is estimated that about 40 per cent of children have a relatively easy temperament, 35 per cent are on middle ground, 15 per cent are quite difficult and 10 per cent are going to be a challenge.

Follow-up studies suggest that the temperament of the preschool years carries through school age with reasonable consistency. If this is true we can expect that about one-third of children will be a breeze, one-third will be manageable and one-tenth will visibly age their parents.

Let's be honest here: there are some extremely challenging children out there. When I asked one mother, 'When did you first know you had a problem?' she answered, 'At birth. He was born by Caesarean section under epidural. When the obstetrician opened me up the little fellow was looking out wide-eyed at him. The obstetrician passed me the baby and said, "This one's going to be interesting." He was right.'

Another mum told me, 'We only once used a baby sitter. When we arrived home she was standing in the hall. "I don't want any money," she said. "I just want out of this house."'

This sounds bad, but it can get even more serious. I have had extreme children who crashed the family car, sold their parents' valuables at a street stall and accidentally burnt down the family home. And you thought you had problems!

Who creates temperament?

I often look at a child and wonder where they got their temperament from. The gentlest of parents can be devastated when they unexpectedly land an out-of-step child. But the difficult child does not always drop out of the blue: they may be very like their mum or dad. Temperament is God-given, but God often has a lot of help from us, the parents.

Mothers ask me with wide-eyed innocence, 'How did I get such an active, non-stop child?' As she talks I watch Dad rock, fidget, jiggle and become distracted by what's outside the window. Others complain their child is impulsive, explosive and has no patience. I ask, 'Is he like anybody you know?' Suddenly the penny drops as they realise he is a mini version of the person they chose to marry! An out-of-step child can arrive out of the blue, but often you don't need to look far to see where they came from.

Troublesome temperaments

There are three temperamental types of children that cause particular pain to parents:

1. oppositional
2. demanding
3. explosive.

When the **oppositional** child is asked to do something, they will look you in the eye and say, 'Make me.' You set a limit and they step over the line as if to say, 'Come on, make my day.' If you say hurry, they go slow. Chores may get done, but everything is an effort. For more information on oppositional behaviour see Chapter 8, page 91.

The **demander** interrogates, invades your space and is at you like a mosquito. 'Can we go now? . . . Is it time to go? . . . When will we go? . . . Let's go.' On a long car trip it's 'When will be get there? . . . Is it much further? . . . Are we there yet?' Demanders never realise how close they come to being put up for adoption or understand why their parents are getting so upset all the time.

The **explosive** child is fitted with a very short fuse. Their sister innocently sits on their Game Boy and the detonation is felt three blocks down the street. These children are like a stick of unstable gelignite: any sudden movement and you get your head blown off. They don't know when to back off or turn the other cheek.

I mention these difficult temperaments not to depress parents but to explain the differences. Even if you have scored an easy, compliant child, don't get too smug, because your luck may not hold out forever. If you have a child with a difficult temperament, don't take it personally: this is when the parenting techniques of this book will be put to the test.

Parenting style

Attention, temperament and environment are all part of the equation, but without a positive parent, nothing will work well. I don't tame children, I change parents, who then get the best out of their individual child.

As I get older, the toddlers I once treated are now adolescents or even adults. Most have done extremely well, but a few still live in the same war zone they occupied when we first met. Many of them started with a challenging temperament that their parents attacked head on. The parents' position was uncompromising: they were going to win this war and take no prisoners. As the battle got bogged down, both sides brought in ever-bigger artillery, until everyone was angry, resentful and oppositional. As I tried to move things along, the parents would say it was the child who had to change – not them. In cases like these, hostility feeds from both sides, and when no one will compromise, soon you are standing in a war-torn country where relationships are wrecked for a generation.

I can't overestimate the importance of getting attitudes right at the start. When children are treated nicely, they treat you nicely. When children know they are loved, they let you know they love you. When children set out on the rails, they generally stay on the rails.

As I observe parents and children interact, some seem so close, natural and in tune, while others are more angular and remote in their relationship. You can sense whether parents have a nurturing style or a negative style, but it's not so easy to put into words what the differences are. There are some things that stand out, though:

- Positive parents communicate warmly with and without words. Words are important but they make close communication with their eyes, tone of voice and body language.
- Positive parents listen, take time, and enjoy doing things with their children. Any human being knows when they are only afforded half of our attention. There is a difference between spending time as an act of penance and *savouring* time together.
- Positive parents use positive discipline. Discipline is not about waiting for a child to misbehave then dumping heavily on them. It is the moulding of behaviour through encouragement and reward. Positive parents establish good patterns, set limits, remain consistent, then catch their children being good.
- Positive parents forgive quickly and restart with a clean slate. It's easy to get angry and stay angry. A child may not openly apologise: they circle the perimeter, hoping we will extend an olive branch. Positive parents quickly pull their children back in close, end the issue and hold no grudges.
- Positive parents instruct with expectation. They transmit instructions with the expectation that things will happen.
- Positive parents see past the problem. Even the most angelic child will get into some pretty silly situations. It is important for parents to look past the end behaviour to see the preceding events and recognise innocence of intent.
- Positive parents watch with interest, pride and wonderment. This is what you see in the eyes of a besotted parent.
- Positive parents see the humour. One day later, you can look back on some of the things your children got up to and laugh. Positive parents keep their humour and their perspective.

On the other hand:

- Negative parents use hostile, critical communication. I would not like to be addressed the way some parents talk to their children. The tone is hostile and there is an expectation that instructions are not going to be obeyed. This confronting, trouble-seeking style creates opposition in a child.

- Negative parents can only see the worst in their children. Most of us see our children better than they are in reality. A negative parent sees nothing but fault and trouble.
- Negative parents show disappointment and resentment. Some parents transmit a feeling that parenting has not lived up to expectation. It's almost as if their children were sent to disturb and intrude upon their enjoyment of life.
- Negative parents focus overly on the bad. Even the worst-behaved child is good for ninety per cent of the time. Negative parents only see the bad ten per cent, which they reinforce with the full focus of their attention.
- Negative parents believe that the child has the problem. It takes two parties to fight and two parties to come to a resolution, but negative parents see the child as causing all the problems. They are reluctant to be part of the process of change themselves.

Reaction to stress and uncertainty

A child's behaviour is intimately entwined with the stress and difficulties of their living environment. The child may not always understand what is going on around them, but they are acutely aware of any tension.

However, parents are often blind to the link between problems at home and their child's poor behaviour. They tell me, 'Our relationship is a mess, but our children know nothing about it'; or 'My husband is about to be made redundant, but our children don't realise how stressed we are'; or 'I'm being treated for major depression, but I pretend I am happy when the kids are around'; or 'We moved across the country to a new job. We have a nice house with lots of space, but for some reason the children seem unsettled'; and 'Grandpa is dying from cancer, but we haven't told the children.'

I have two cocker spaniel pups. These dogs have never attended a university course in counselling but they are totally in tune with feelings. If I am about to leave on a lecture tour they act strangely, hiding behind curtains and becoming extremely unsettled. They are like little children: they don't know what is happening, but they *feel*. Never underestimate the effect of stress, change or parental unhappiness on a child.

How children react

Young children have super-sensitive antennae which pick up on upset and translate it back as a change in behaviour. Most commonly, a child will react to tension by becoming unsettled and ill at ease: they have a vague restlessness, seem unavailable, have upset sleep or their performance at school suffers.

Another reaction they have to stress is anger. Parents start by being upset with each other and the child tunes in to their feelings. The child doesn't know what is going on between Mum and Dad but they don't like what they feel. They react to this stress by digging in their heels, being difficult or dumping on Mum.

This reaction can easily escalate. The parents are struggling with their own emotions; the child picks up on their upset and gives them a blast. The stressed parent reacts to this with anger, and then the child becomes doubly confused. This problem is common where there is relationship stress, family illness, relocation or money worries.

The under-six-year-old may react with clinginess and regression. They pick up on the uncertainty in their environment and grasp tightly to that life belt, their mum. In a family break-up a child knows they have lost one parent and are quite determined they will not lose the other. So they may be reluctant to separate from Mum when she drops them off at school, or they may come to her bed at night.

A few children show their stress by withdrawal. The child feels ill at ease, becomes solitary and quiet and loses enthusiasm for their usual activities. This is most common in the over-eight-year-old. As they withdraw away from us, it is hard to know at which point a normal reaction to stress becomes serious depression. For more information on depression see Chapter 8, page 79.

Whatever the reaction, whether it is restlessness, anger, clinging or withdrawal, these children are shouting at the top of their voices, 'I don't know what you are doing but it hurts.'

What hurts children

For children under the age of eight years parent problems cause most pain. After this children react to troubles at school, problems mixing, learning difficulties and worries about the world. As parents, we can't protect our children from everything, but if we get our own emotional baggage in control we've won half the battle. Unfortunately, there are some hassles that we can't always avoid.

Break-ups

When I was seven I believed in happy-ever-after stories, but now I realise that Cinderella was a fairy tale. Many of today's children live in a war zone: there are no guns or bombs, because the hostilities are taking place within the home.

About one-third of today's relationships will have broken up by the time our children leave school. It's not the break-up that damages the child but the stress before, and the antics that can continue after, the event. These break-ups are going to happen no matter what I do. All I ask is that parents think of the children and handle the inevitable as amicably as is possible.

There is a story of two families who 'lose' a father. In one, a child loses a father to a bitter break-up, following which the parents are full of hate and hurt for years. In the other Dad is killed in a car accident. Psychiatrists looking at this scenario see that a child suffers much more emotional damage from the painful split than they do from the accident. As parents, we can cause much greater harm to our children through our deliberate actions than life's unavoidable accidents can cause. For more information on break-ups and sole parenting, see Chapter 20, page 208.

Employment, moves and money

These days employment is less certain, and for many families redundancy is a reality. A change of fortune caused by unemployment can alter the equilibrium in a family, affect everybody's esteem and stress children.

To improve opportunities many couples choose to cut the family ties and move away to a better area of employment. But, like animals, human beings can be destabilised by new surroundings. To make matters worse, in the new environment parents may be feeling emotionally vulnerable, support might be limited and children will feel uneasy.

Even without unemployment or moving, money problems are a major cause of stress for all the family, including children.

Learning and social difficulties

If life were fair all children would be created with equal learning and social abilities. But life is not fair, and not all children do well in or out of the classroom.

Children who aren't doing so well are often acutely aware of the fact. You can tell a child with reading difficulties that they don't have a problem, but they know otherwise. If this child were just slow, they might not feel so bad, but clever children who struggle feel pain and paranoia. No matter how positive we are, children with major learning weaknesses get stressed and may behave badly. For more information on learning difficulties see Chapter 11, page 125.

Attention Deficit Hyperactivity Disorder (ADHD) disadvantages about two per cent of our school-age population and upsets many good parents. These children underfunction for intellect and are out of step behaviourally. Their behaviour can be many times more difficult than any parent or teacher deserves. For more information on ADHD, see Chapter 12, page 138.

Some of the stroppiest young children I see have language problems. When children can't express or understand what is going on in their lives they can show immense frustration. Some stoics try twice as hard, others withdraw, some to the edge of autism, and some get angry and kick heads. It's not our fault, but it's often we who end up with the headache. For more information on language problems, see Chapter 11, page 130.

It is cool to be an out-of-step extrovert at school, but it's uncool to be shy, socially uncomfortable, obsessive, odd or clumsy. Shy children feel stressed, kids that appear odd are teased or treated like outcasts and clumsy children are excluded from games.

Some children with these difficulties keep going without complaint, while others act out their frustrations with bad behaviour. Stressed children clown in the classroom and take their upset home to dump on those they love. Such behaviour is not the fault of the parent but it still lands on them.

Attention and power

Whatever a child's temperament, the parenting style or the living environment, annoying behaviour is always to do with gaining attention and power. The main way parents and teachers mould behaviour is through the giving and withdrawing of attention. For some children, power is an important motivator, but not for all.

Attention

Every child loves to receive good attention, but when this is not on offer, they will try to attract any sort of attention that's going. Say Mum and Dad are having an important discussion. John feels excluded from their attention and tries to get in on the act. He asks a question but this is ignored. He interrupts and is pushed aside. Now he turns on the TV, torments the dog and imitates fart sounds. Mum and Dad close the conversation, become intensely irritated and John is rewarded with 100 per cent attention. This is poor-quality attention, but it's better than being ignored.

We shape our children's behaviour by boosting the good patterns with attention and reward while discouraging the bad by pulling back on our attention. This giving and taking of attention is the basic principle of effective discipline.

Every day we see how attention affects behaviour. A second-rate author wants to get their book mentioned in the media. They create a bogus beat-up, the media respond and sales increase. The behaviour is rewarded and more books will follow. Or a rock star dyes his hair orange, applies lipstick and wears fishnet stockings: with his new image he now fills the stadium. He gets so much attention, he keeps on cross-dressing. For rock stars, authors and children, attention is a powerful motivator.

In children it is the most powerful way to steer both good and bad behaviour.

Power

Some children are heavily into power politics, while others are much more easy going. Power play involves testing limits, dragging feet, arguing and opposition.

You draw the line; they see how far they can push you before you respond. You ask if they will do a simple chore; they respond with provisos and conditions. You say it's black; they say it's white. This power play involves having the last word, wanting more, acting the smart arse and just being difficult with non-compliance.

Attention and power are major factors in difficult behaviour. And that's what the next six chapters are all about.

A final word

The foundation of behaviour is in the genes, which is moulded by stress in a child's environment and the need for attention and power.

And then there is parenting. Since Spock's day it has been wrong to be a permissive parent, but research does not agree. Ideally, every child should have clear, consistent limits and discipline. But many times more important is the influence of warm, caring parents who enjoy being with their children. An upbringing which is warm, clear and consistent is the first choice but warm and permissive parents come a very close second.

Why children behave badly

1. Temperament
   - the volatile temperament – 'the stick of gelignite'
   - the demanding temperament – 'the KGB interrogator'
   - the oppositional temperament – 'Come on, make my day.'
   - the introvert temperament
   - the obsessive temperament
   - the disorganised temperament
   - the fearful temperament
   - the fearless temperament

2. Parenting style
   - nurturing, encouraging, positive
   - hostile, critical, negative

3. Reaction to stress and uncertainty
   - little children may not understand; they react to what they feel
   - older children understand and feel
   - common stresses:
     - marriage conflict and break-ups
     - employment, moves, money
     - illness, parent depression
     - school stress, bullying
     - learning and social difficulties
     - worries about the world

4. Attention and power
   - the giving of attention encourages a behaviour
   - the withholding of attention discourages a behaviour
   - power play involves limit testing, foot dragging, smart-arse behaviour, opposition

FOUR

The positive side of discipline

An eight-year-old has a rush of blood to the head and tidies her bedroom. We inspect her handiwork and reward her with enthusiasm and some extra privilege. With this pay-off, a clean bedroom will happen again tomorrow (and pigs might fly, I hear you say).

There is one important principle that steers our children's behaviour: *a behaviour that pays off for the child will usually be repeated; a behaviour that does not pay off will disappear*. This is the basic rule that allows parents to increase the good and decrease the bad. All it takes is a wise choice as to the behaviours that pay off.

The pay-offs we use are:

- soft rewards (enthusiasm, encouragement, noticing, words, body language)
- hard rewards (time, privileges, food or other treats, money)
- cumulative rewards (star charts, tokens, points).

Soft rewards

Recently I dined at a top Sydney restaurant. The food and service were so good I called the head waiter over to give specific praise to the chef and waiting staff. Later, with an expectant smile, the waiter approached and handed me the bill. My wife suggested I should leave a large tip, so at this point I took the opportunity to explain to her about soft and hard rewards. She listened graciously, then summed it up quite simply: 'An interesting theory, but you are still cheap and mean.'

On that occasion, my wife was probably right, but never underestimate the power of soft and subtle pay-offs, especially when it comes to children. Though these are of most importance to the under-fives, their influence is immense right through life.

Catch them being good

If humans are to continue doing good, their good needs to be noticed and reinforced. One of the greatest traps for parents is to become so negative that we see nothing but the bad: 'Don't annoy your sister'; 'Leave the dog alone'; 'You were such a pain at the shops'; 'What a mess'; 'You're so rude.'

Positive parents turn this around and use their words to boost the good: 'I like it when you both play so well'; 'Rover thinks that's fun'; 'Gosh, you were such a help at the supermarket'; 'Have the cleaners been here?'; 'I like it when we talk together like this.'

The power of body language

Every day I am asked 100 times, 'How are you?' Those who enquire have no interest in my health, happiness or emotional well-being; their greeting is as empty as a pre-programmed tape recording. Words can be meaningless but we sense genuine interest by attitude and body language.

Children know we are pleased by the tone of our voice, the way we look, the twinkle in our eye and the things we whisper. This subtle form of encouragement is one of the most powerful tools of discipline.

Be specific

School-age children are unmoved by unfocused, over-used encouragement. We blandly say, 'Good girl', 'Well done', 'Clever boy', which is about as genuine as the parrot who announces, 'Who's the pretty boy?' Older children may even react badly to these unfocused comments and turn our words back on us: we say, 'That's good' and they reply, 'No, it sucks'; 'You're looking great' – 'No, I'm not'; 'I like your story' – 'No, it's boring.'

I sympathise with this response. Often I bust myself to put on some special fundraising talk. I know it has gone well but a week later an impersonal letter arrives that might have been written by a computer before the talk. I know when people are genuinely appreciative – it's when the thank you is personal, specific and picks up on some part of my message. 'Dr Green, I like your ideas about refocusing on the good and being specific in what we say.'

Children also need our encouragement to be specific. 'Gosh, this room is not only tidy, you've even polished your desk'; 'In your story, I like the boy character who saved the ship'; 'I really like the way the sun lights up this side of your painting.'

Hard rewards

Now we are entering the real world where humans encourage action through gifts, favours, privileges, money and bribes. Hard rewards are particularly useful for the older child, adults and Olympic officials.

Some experts get their underwear in a knot debating the difference between rewards and bribes. A reward consolidates a good behaviour, coming almost as a bonus after the event. A bribe is arranged beforehand and if there is no performance there is no payout. We all prefer to use rewards rather than bribes, but sometimes the difference is academic. If what you are doing works, just call it a reward and we'll all be happy.

Choosing the right hard reward

This author might be motivated by money, a meal or some exotic, coronary-clogging ice cream. But I wouldn't move a muscle for the latest Spice Girl CD or a front-row seat at a boxing match. All humans are motivated by different means, and as parents we must find the magic motivator for our child.

When I set up a behaviour programme with parents, we first list the rewards that are likely to grab their child's interest. If we don't tailor our programme to that one child, what follows will always fall flat.

The most effective rewards for eight- to twelve-year-olds are

● time
● privileges
● little gifts
● food
● money.

Time

We often forget that time is one of our most valuable possessions and is also one of our most appreciated rewards. Your son has stuck at his homework and done it well: 'Would you like me to help fix your bike?'; 'Fancy going for a splash down in the pool?'; 'Would you like me to run you over to Steve's house?'

Privileges

These are great motivators for the six- to eighteen-year-old. When things have gone well, they are allowed some extra bit of the action. This may be time on the telephone, more television, a later bedtime, access to the computer, being excused from doing a usual chore, choosing dinner, having a friend to stay, picking where you go out for a meal.

Food

It may come as a disappointment to the animal admirers, but sea lions don't do tricks because they like to impress humans. They perform because each action is rewarded with a mouthful of raw fish. Purists dislike the idea of bribing children with stuff that rots teeth, but this technique has been popular since it was first invented by grandmothers. People may object, but if food works for all other animal trainers, it must be worth a try with children.

Of course, we can reward with the healthiest of health foods, but children tend to value these less than foods high in sugar, preservatives,

additives, colours and flavours, especially if they come with the latest in movie merchandise.

Food is mostly a motivator with the under eights, but it can focus interest at any age. I for one can always be bought by the offer of a good meal. With your children, don't go over the top but if some mouth-watering snack tunes in the obedience antennae, it can't be all that bad.

Money

This may be the root of all evil, but it sure grabs the attention of some children. Youngsters are created in two sorts: the emerging entrepreneurs who are heavily into the cash economy and the philanthropists who function on some higher plane.

Money becomes of increasing interest after the age of eight years, and if your child is a money lover, you may use the filthy stuff to reward compliance.

By ten years a small sum can be given for each completed task or you may add a productivity bonus to their pocket money. With the bonus, you give the base salary and this can be doubled in reward for extra effort without complaint. For a more immediate reward, a silver coin can be put in a jar to register completion.

There is one major drawback when you reward with money: it leaves you open to extortion. A task that was worth twenty pence this week may be worth thirty pence the next, and soon there is out-of-control inflation. So a productivity bonus should be capped at an appropriate level. Small cash payments can be varied and mixed with other rewards to prevent them becoming a God-given right.

Cumulative rewards

As children get older they can appreciate rewards that are more abstract and less immediate. Now they can visualise the payout from stars, points or tokens.

Star charts

Stars allow us to focus a child's attention on specific behaviours that need to be changed. The chart is a simple piece of paper, ruled into rows across the page and columns down. The column on the left-hand margin lists the days of the week and the row across the top the behaviours we wish to target.

Each time the behaviour is achieved we stick a star in the appropriate square. If there is compliance, soon a galaxy of stars illuminates the page and this is rewarded with some prearranged payout. The chart is put in a place of prominence, usually stuck to the fridge door. As fridges are opened continually, the average child can monitor their progress throughout the day.

Stars only work with children who are old enough to recognise what they represent. They have no meaning for the under-four-year-old.

You also need to remember that stars create maximum interest in the first week, less in the second and soon the star burns out, leaving a black hole.

Stars: the behaviours to target

The targets we star must be clear-cut and easily achievable. It's pointless expecting a child to 'be good all day', or to 'not annoy your sister'. A turnaround of this magnitude is reserved for faith healers, miracle workers and saints.

I use stars to highlight two or more simple behaviours; for example, brushes teeth, makes bed, does dishes, ready for school on time.

Stars can also be used when there are problems of bladder training. A dreamy five-year-old leaves things too late, which results in little leaks. Using the chart we focus all attention on short periods of dryness. If dry from the moment they wake until breakfast time, they get a star. From breakfast to mid morning break – a star. From break to lunch, to mid afternoon, to dinner, to bedtime – the stars continue.

Some use stars to motivate bed wetters, but this has little success. When children are asleep they are not thinking of stars.

We can also use the star system to treat children who still soil their pants (see Chapter 8, page 98). First you must ensure your child is not constipated, then use stars in a step-by-step way.

The first goal is to get them to sit for five minutes after breakfast, after school and after dinner. Each sit is recognised with a star. Once sitting is established the focus now moves to using the toilet. If on any occasion a poo pops out we give great praise and the appropriate square is coloured in. Finally, the focus moves to being clean from dawn to dusk with four gold stars for a soil-free day.

The token system

This is a popular technique that takes an impossibly big task and divides it into small manageable units. It is based on the same principle as my Frequent Flyer points. My favourite airline wishes to encourage a certain behaviour (loyalty to Qantas) so I receive 700 points each time I fly from Sydney to Brisbane. These points have no value but I know that if I keep producing the desired behaviour (flying Qantas) the individual points will eventually be rewarded with a free flight. After a year of this correct behaviour I get a special treat, like a holiday in Alice Springs.

Tokens in the classroom

A child with Attention Deficit Hyperactivity Disorder (ADHD) has great difficulty sustaining attention in the busy classroom. They can be motivated by a promise of time on the computer, for example, but even with this carrot they can't concentrate long enough to earn the reward. Our goal is to increase that child's time on task by focusing on small, achievable periods of good concentration.

The teacher breaks the day into ten-minute periods, and each period on task is acknowledged with a token. These are simply a bead, button or piece of chalk that is placed in a glass. When ten tokens have been earned, this is rewarded by time on the computer.

Tokens and car travel

Many parents dread the drama of long-distance car travel:

'He hit me.'

'She's looking out of my window.'

'He's taking all the space.'

'Are we there yet?'

You buy books and games and even place a large barricade of well-secured luggage between the combatants but the pain continues. Now try a token system. For every fifteen minutes of peace a token is dropped in a cup and this adds up to a payout of money or a special treat at the next fuel stop. Tokens won't turn a terrorist into an angel, but they are more appropriate than deep sedation or a straitjacket. See also Chapter 8, page 74.

Points and money

Good behaviour can be encouraged by a simple system of points or money. Feeding the dog gets one point or ten pence. Bedtime without complaint, two points or twenty pence. A tidy room at 6 pm gets three points or thirty pence.

When the points reach a certain number, this represents a special treat. When the money gets to a certain total it can be used to buy some much-wanted piece of junk.

Purists dislike the thought of buying good behaviour, but if it works and gets you off your Valium, I won't object.

Every child has their price

Parents often tell me that none of my suggestions will motivate their child. But I believe every human has their price. I expect if you placed a big enough sheaf of crisp new bank notes in the hand of a twelve-year-old, they might listen. I expect if a tip-truck were to dump 1000 Mars Bars in your front drive, most five-year-olds might show some interest.

It's up to us to work out what we can afford and sustain. Fortunately, for most children the major motivator is the subtle system of attention, noticing, time, interest and specific appreciation.

A final word

Start with the basic rule: a behaviour that pays off for the child will be repeated. Then it's up to us to find the pay-off that suits the individual. The secret of positive discipline is to tailor-make the reward to the individual child. But never underestimate the importance of soft, subtle encouragement. To put this into practice see Chapter 8.

This chapter was about the positive side of discipline. However, we can encourage all we like, but there are times we need to take a stand. Punishment also has its place, and that's what you will find in Chapter 5.

The positive side of discipline

1. Soft rewards
   - tone of voice
   - appropriate words
   - eye contact
   - touch
   - enthusiasm
   - noticing
   - genuine interest
   - be specific with praise

2. Hard rewards
   - time
     - working together
     - playing together
     - taking them somewhere
   - privileges
     - telephone
     - computer
     - television
     - later bedtime
     - excused a chore
     - a friend to stay over
   - food
     - a treat
     - dessert
     - choose from a menu
     - choose take away
     - choose a meal out
   - money
     - coins put in a jar
     - saving for a purchase
     - productivity bonus
     - costed system for chores

3. Cumulative rewards
   - star charts
     - for target behaviours
     - for daytime wetting
     - for school-age soiling
   - the token system
     - to increase attention
     - to soothe car travel
   - points and money
     - to focus on specific behaviour

Punishment without pain

By this point in the book it will be clear that discipline is based on encouragement and reward. There is, however, a small place for punishment, but it is punishment without pain. We don't hit or hurt children. Instead we punish using things like

- our tone of voice
- switching off attention
- active ignoring
- time out
- withdrawing privileges
- grounding.

You might also want to try setting up a system of penalties, but these can backfire.

The tone of disapproval

If your poodle piddles on the carpet or your basset barks all night, who are you going to call? Barkbusters! And these dog trainers will start by telling you, 'Use fewer words, but more tone.' You don't explain to your barking dog that your neighbour is on Prozac for a nervous disorder and it would be good if he kept quiet. You look him in the eye and sternly say, 'Bah!'

Now, I am not suggesting we get Barkbusters to sort out our children, but tone transmits more message than a chapter of carefully chosen words.

Switching off attention

Children thrive when they live in a home filled with interest and interaction, where they get plenty of positive attention. We know that giving attention is the greatest reward, so it follows that cutting attention is a potent punishment.

A six-year-old is being tickled and bounced on Mum's knee. In a burst of innocent enthusiasm he head-butts Mum in the mouth. As the pain rises you could explode or explain the dangers of horseplay. But it is more effective to briefly register your hurt then walk away. The child feels the cool change from full attention to total ignoring. This registers your disapproval and will encourage more care the next time.

A showing-off ten-year-old calls Mum an idiot. You could give a lecture full of biblical quotes about respect for one's parents. You could go psycho, or you could simply state, 'It upsets me when you talk like that', then walk away, cutting all attention for a short period.

Active ignoring

When a defiant child is hell-bent on confrontation, it's a hard call to ignore. Active ignoring allows us to take a step sideways yet remain in control. With this technique, you stay calm, make your point, disengage and then return.

The ten-year-old stands nose to nose, daring Mum to discipline. You quietly repeat your request, walk away, straighten the curtains, pour yourself a cup of coffee, then return to restate your position in a matter-of-fact way. Active ignoring sidesteps a stand-off, gives space and signals that we are not going to be manipulated.

Time out

This is one of the most useful weapons in our armoury. Time out has a double impact: first it punishes by withdrawing the child from positive attention, then it provides the space to cool off an overheated situation. Time out is effective from age one to eleven years. It allows us to put a lid on escalation and to sidestep a stand off.

The young child is moved calmly to a bedroom or a time-out chair. The older child is expected to take themselves. It is useful to have a trial run in a time of peace, to prepare for when the technique is used in earnest. The period of exclusion is calculated as approximately one minute for each year of age, but parents have to find the time that best suits their child.

Time out is signalled by a statement, a sign or taking the five-year-old by the hand. If they refuse we move to plan B and use techniques such as counting to three, active ignoring or giving a choice.

If they call out, this is ignored. If they ask whether the time is up, don't rise to the bait – set a cooking timer and let it be the adjudicator. If they come out early, the clock goes back to the start.

At the end of time out, briefly restate your case but don't heap guilt or demand an apology. Then forgive fully and start afresh with a clean slate.

Time out for toys

Another use of time out is to withhold toys, television and computers from feuding children who won't share.

Jack wants 'The Simpsons', Jill wants 'Home and Away', and as they squabble no one sees anything. Mum issues a warning, then the television is put in time out. Switch off the set, start the cooking timer and, when fifteen minutes is up, start again.

The boys Arnold and Sylvester both want GI Joe and they are prepared to go through a bloody military campaign to gain possession. Here Mum intervenes, puts the plastic marine in time out, and starts the timer. Ten minutes later the battlefield is quiet, GI returns to the front line and hopefully there is some compromise.

Withdrawing privileges

Good behaviour is rewarded with privileges and older children can be punished by the removal of privileges. Removing privileges can make children angry, so don't remove too much, and keep the sentence short.

Your eight-year-old annoys Grandma, and in the heat of the moment you say, 'No television for a month!' The child gasps at the harshness of the sentence and thinks, 'Let's find the old lady and get my money's worth.' Then over the next four weeks they nag, promise to be good and interrogate every day, leaving Mum the one who has been severely punished.

When removing privileges keep it fair and keep it short. They might miss the first half of a TV programme, have no television or telephone that night, no dessert or bedtime comes half an hour earlier.

Removing privileges is effective, but never issue a threat you are not prepared to carry through. It's pointless saying, 'I'll cancel your party', when the cake is bought, friends are being scrubbed up ready to attend and you have no intention of pulling the plug.

Grounding

In American sitcoms, parents often ground their troublesome teens. Hank is late home from the ball game and misses the Thanksgiving turkey; Dad looks perplexed and declares him grounded for a month.

This is mostly a discipline for older children, but at any age we can put on our American accents and ban sleepovers, keep them in at night, or prevent them from attending some entertainment.

A more flexible technique moves from the fixed period of punishment and ties the grounding to the completion of some work. They are still grounded but this will be lifted once the bedroom is cleaned, the weeds removed from the front flowerbed or reparations made to the one they have wronged. This gives children the option of paying their dues quickly or dragging their feet. If they refuse to deliver the goods they remain on the ground.

Penalties

Every day my life is a minefield of consequences and penalties. I don't put petrol in my car – I have to walk to work. I drive too fast – I get a speeding ticket. I annoy the butcher – I get tough meat. I don't pay the electricity bill – the lights go out.

By school age, children are members of this same world and need to feel the consequences and penalties that go with membership. You don't wear your bike helmet – the bike is locked up for two weeks. You don't brush your teeth – lollies are banned and water is your drink. You stick chewing gum on the dog – no gum in the house for one month.

Consequences are part of life, and school-age children need to understand them. Penalties are slightly different: they usually involve removing possessions or money. And here you can hit a lot of trouble – human beings get mighty stroppy when you start taking their stuff.

You set up a point or money system that rewards good behaviour. They have tried so hard they have almost enough to buy a much-wanted CD. Now, on the last day, the exuberant one bounces off the sofa and lands softly on the family cat. The cat and Mum scream, and then half the promised points are removed. Now you have a very angry child, mother and cat.

Most of our star, token and money systems should give for the good but don't subtract for the bad. Penalties are possible, but it's usually not worth the aftershock.

One penalty technique that encourages the positive is to start with ten points, then add two for the good and deduct one for the bad. With this it's hard to hit a negative balance.

Some parents discourage bad language by penalising with fines. When a colourful word slips out, twenty pence is docked from the next pocket money. This works well when the cash reserves are high, but when close to losing all, you may hear words that no amount of money could buy.

The three-strike system is used by some schools. A disruptive child starts each class with three lives. These can be shown as three cardboard stars sitting on the desk, a tally on the edge of the blackboard or three strokes on a sheet of paper. For each indiscretion, one life is quietly removed. If there are none at the end of the lesson, they must sit for five minutes before release.

Hitting, smacking, beating

These days, only outcasts would suggest a smack as suitable punishment for children. International organisations, local dignitaries and most professionals are united in making child care a hit-free zone.

While this is a worthy viewpoint, it has more credibility with library-bound academics than stressed parents at the battle front of child care. From my experience every parent has resorted to hitting at some time. But there is a great difference between the occasional limit-registering tap and the violence of a hostile, disturbed home.

Does smacking work anyway? In easy kids, smacking may get some response, but so do all the other techniques, so it is unnecessary. In difficult, defiant children, smacking doesn't work and it can be downright dangerous because it can lead to escalation. You smack, they defy you. You hit harder, they say, 'Damn you.' You wallop, and soon there is anger, resentment, hate and a wrecked relationship.

Besides, when do you stop smacking? Do you wait until they are bigger, quicker or more violent than you? And then what's the alternative?

I always ask parents why they smack, to which dads often say, 'It's the way my father brought me up and it did me no harm.'

I then ask, 'Is your dad still alive?'

'Yes,' they reply.

'Do you see much of him?'

'Well, not exactly.'

'Why not?'

To which they often answer, 'We have nothing in common.'

Wars start with a show of force that escalates into bloodshed. The United Nations may keep the peace but the force has resolved nothing. It takes generations for damaged relationships to repair.

I don't support the groups who wish to imprison parents and teachers who smack, but it does not mean I encourage violence. School-age children should not be smacked. There are much better ways to discipline and force leads to greater problems.

A final word

Punishment is not about smacking, locking in a bedroom or grounding for a month. We register our disapproval by the use of tone, switching off our attention, time out and withdrawing privileges. Our children may dislike punishment but they enjoy knowing where they stand and that we care enough to care what they do.

For advice on putting these punishments into practice see Chapter 8, page 92.

Punishment without pain

1. Tone
- few words, more tone

2. Switching off attention
- ignore
- walk away
- switch off

3. Active ignoring
- disengage, move away, then re-engage
- exerts control without escalation

4. Time out
- to punish
- to cool off
- for TV, or toys

5. Withdrawing privileges
- television
- early bedtime
- no dessert
- no friends to sleep over

6. Grounding
- for a fixed period
- until a chore is completed

7. Penalties
- point system
- money system
- three strikes

8. Hitting and smacking
- with easy children there are much better techniques
- with difficult children it doesn't work and is dangerous

The dos and don'ts of discipline

Now it's time to move on from general principles and get specific. This chapter will repeat much of the information already covered. The aim is to condense the techniques of the previous chapters into a useable form.

If you have had enough of basic theories, skip this and move straight to Chapter 8. There you will find how these ideas work with the common everyday behaviours of school age.

Children need routine, structure and consistency

Human beings are happiest with structure and when we know where we stand. Even in adulthood much of our behaviour is conditioned and quite automatic, a bit like Pavlov's technique of conditioning dogs to dribble at dinner time. Whether we call it conditioning, doggie discipline or the importance of routine, children behave best with consistent structure.

In the morning our children get two wake-up calls, they rise, wash, make their bed, dress, have breakfast, feed the canary, pack their bags and board the bus.

In the evening, after the meal is finished, they take the dishes to the sink, put the jam in the fridge, then think about homework. Then they shower, get into pyjamas, drink their cocoa, brush their teeth, choose a book and go to bed.

We are not promoting bureaucratic rigidity, but routine, structure and consistency are the first steps to successful discipline.

Children need rules

We don't want to run our homes like the army, with every action governed by 100 regulations, but we need a sensible framework of rules. These should be drawn up in advance when the situation is calm – not in the heat of battle.

Rules should be simple, fair, few in number and clearly understood: 'There will be no eating snacks just before your evening meal. You may bounce on the trampoline, not on our new lounge suite. You don't interrupt your sister while she is doing her homework.'

When a rule is challenged, it should be clearly restated and then enforced. Parents must allow some flexibility, but no amount of a child's nagging can change the referee's decision. A rule is made, a child is reminded, action follows.

Communication: get their attention

Whether you are training dolphins at Marine World, lions at the circus or children in your home, nothing will happen until you get their attention. Turn off the television, wait until the dog stops barking then transmit your message.

Look them in the eye and give instructions, clearly, simply and step by step. Mumbling, nagging, shouting and burying the message in words will get you nowhere. If your child is not one of the stubborn members of the species ask for feedback to ensure the message has been taken on board.

Try to make positive statements, not negative instructions. Instead of saying, 'Don't forget to wash your hands', say, 'Wash your hands so they will be clean for tea', Otherwise, life becomes a constant barrage of don'ts and negatives. The secret to communication is eye contact, simple positive words, enthusiasm and step-by-step instruction.

Ignore the unimportant

As parents we can't help ourselves – our child waves a fragment of red rag and we charge like a wounded bull. If the plan is to maintain your blood pressure at a life-preserving level, please try to ignore unimportant irritations. If they blow a raspberry, slurp their drink or a pea falls to the floor, ask yourself, 'Does this really matter?' Successful parents take a step back and only engage in the big battles.

Know what triggers behaviour

There are certain events that are dynamite to discipline: parties, tiredness, living with in-laws, visits from school friends, sickness, long car journeys and changes of routine. We can't always avoid these, but it is easier to cope when we are prepared for problems before they hit.

Make good behaviours pay off

The basic law of behaviour modification states, 'A behaviour that pays off for the child will be repeated; a behaviour that brings no advantage to the child will disappear.' If we reward the right behaviour it should happen more frequently, and by ignoring what's undesired, it should go away.

Unfortunately, it is just as easy to encourage the bad behaviour as the good. A five-year-old says, 'Bum.' We make a fuss and soon it's 'Bum, bum, bum, pooh!' Parents must take a step back and be sure it is the good we are encouraging, not the bad.

Use encouragement and rewards

Good behaviour is encouraged with soft rewards (praise, enthusiasm, interest, parental pride), hard rewards (money, food, special privileges) and cumulative rewards (stars, points, tokens). Though privileges, tokens (and even bribes) have a place, the most effective way to mould behaviour is through our voice, eyes and interest. Never underestimate the power of encouragement through these soft, subtle rewards.

Democracy without debate

When it comes to democracy, the under-fives can be told what they will do, the five- to eight-year-olds should be given some explanation and the eight to twelves need some say in their own destiny. Democracy is commendable but it can be abused by these over-verbal mini lawyers. Be respectful but don't be manipulated with arguments and debates. In these, parents never come out on top; it just shortens our lives. Make your point, state the limit, act – don't argue.

Avoid escalation

When we get irritated with our children it is easy to lose the plot and escalate every unimportant behaviour. Try to stay calm, use a matter-of-fact voice and repeat your instructions like a broken gramophone record. Children generate enough heat without us adding fuel to the fire.

Avoid last-straw explosions

It's a miserable, wet day, the children are stuck inside and they are at their most irritating. After a long series of annoying events, one final straw drops and snaps the camel's back. You blow a gasket and your child looks surprised.

I might ask them what happened, and they'd reply, 'Mum went ballistic and I was grounded for a week.'

Try to avoid last-straw explosions like this. Good mums and dads keep a check on behaviour throughout the day and give good warning before the straw hits the humpy bit.

Look at the start, not the end

Recently there was a crisis with one of my Attention Deficit Hyperactivity Disorder (ADHD) children who was referred with a request for an urgent brain scan. His school principal reported that the child had taken to beating his head against a wall, and in this man's twenty years of teaching, this suggested a psychiatric disturbance or brain damage.

On face value this was bizarre behaviour, but nobody had looked at the events that led to the incident. My patient was playing happily when he was deliberately taunted by the school bully. With the overreaction that is part of ADHD, he rose to the bait and soon was out of control. A teacher who came to the rescue threatened and blamed our innocent boy, which sent him over the top. The principal was summoned and further fanned the flames, the boy became hysterical and, in total exasperation, he hit his head against a wall.

This head banging was not a sign of severe disturbance or brain damage. It was the end point of an avoidable sequence of events. Those who needed treatment were the bully who started it, the teacher who blamed and the principal who lacked the insight to back off.

When analysing behaviour, always look at the beginning, not the end. A gentle puppy would never want to hurt its owner, but if frightened or teased, it may bite. The puppy is not to blame; it is those who upset and mishandle that deserve the punishment.

Use 'I' statements, not 'you' statements

It is possible to say the same thing in two ways, and each will get a different response. If I use an 'I' statement, it transmits how I feel. If I use a 'you' statement, it implies that you are being criticised.

51

When a child annoys us it is the behaviour we dislike, not the child. It may seem trivial but where possible change 'you' to 'I'.

'You are always hurting your sister' becomes 'I get upset when there's so much fighting.'

'You've ruined the outing for all of us' becomes 'I am upset when we have to come home early.'

'You are such a rude boy' becomes 'It makes me unhappy when I hear that talk.'

'I' statements are valuable when you wish to register upset but do not want to get into an argument. The aim is to make a brief statement of how you feel and quickly move away from the battle front.

Punishment has a place

Though the predominant part of discipline comes through boosting good behaviour, there is also a place for punishment. If you have laid down the rules, clearly stated the limits and given a warning, it's now time to act. The most effective punishments are described in Chapter 5 (see page 40).

When possible, warn before you punish and explain your action. Punishment should be of short duration, have a clear end and be followed by forgiveness.

The danger of confrontation

I sometimes see such hostility, hate and resentment in families that I can do little to help. Often a difficult, defiant child clashes with confronting, forceful parents and this starts a war where there are no winners.

Parents are strong, clever people and there is no doubt that we sail in a battleship with bigger guns than those of our children. If we choose to use all our fire power, we can blast them out of the water, but this settles nothing.

Parents are under pressure to be tough. When they have a difficult child they may feel they are being criticised due to the common attitude that firmer parenting is the only solution. In the street, people mumble under their breath, 'That child needs nothing more than a good boot up the backside.' Many families have given that boot, only to find themselves in a conflict of immense proportion.

The history of the world consists of wars, power struggles, wars and more wars. Someone fires a bullet, a hundred come back. They shoot off a shell and a thousand are returned. They drop a bomb and bigger bombs come back. Now you are standing in Bosnia and it will take generations before families can relate closely again. Parents do have the fire power, but for the sake of relationships I urge you to sidestep rather than to confront.

Sidestepping confrontation

When locked in a nose-to-nose confrontation our instinct is to increase the force. This produces a battle of wills, two angry parties, opposition, resentment and damage to relationships. All parents, particularly those with a defiant child, need to learn how to sidestep a stand-off. There are eight well-tried techniques:

1. keep calm
2. state the rule
3. count to three
4. active ignoring
5. time out
6. give a choice
7. use 'I' statements
8. use humour or diversion.

Keep calm

It is difficult to stay cool when a defiant school-ager is daring you to discipline. But if you increase the heat, things will escalate out of control.

One of the best methods to prevent a boil-over is called 'the broken gramophone record' approach. You tell the ten-year-old to get in their bath.

'No way.'

Normally you would respond with all guns blazing, but today you stay cool and be a calm, persistent gramophone record. 'It's bath time . . . Bath time now . . . It must be almost bath time . . . Time for a bath.'

Politicians, talk-show hosts and parents must all appear to be in control. We cease to have credibility when we lose control.

State the rule

Quoting a rule helps to depersonalise an argument. My local council places a large pole just outside my window. I am fuming with anger as I meet the chief surveyor. 'This is ridiculous,' I say.

'But Dr Green, under council by-law 21, subsection D . . .'

I explode, but all I hear is, 'Sorry, Dr Green, under council by-law 21, subsection D . . .'

With children rules must be fair and fully understood before the event.

'John, it's 8pm and 8pm is bath time.'

'But Mum!'

'Bath and bed are 8pm. You know the rule!'

Count to three

When you were a six-year-old your granny would ask you once, ask you again, then count slowly to three. Usually by two there was instant obedience. Counting may be an old technique, but it's a wonderful way to defuse a situation and allow time to back off.

'John, it's time for your bath.'

. . .

'It's eight o'clock. You know the rule.'

. . .

'One,' wait five seconds, 'Two,' wait five seconds, etc.

Counting can be used from about three years to twelve years. At eighteen it might look a bit out of place: 'John, bring in the keys of the Volvo . . . One, two, three!'

Active ignoring

This is one of the simplest ways to sidestep in a standoff. John still refuses to go to his bath. Mum has counted and stayed cool but he stands firm and dares her to make the next move. Active ignoring will stop you being beaten by deliberate defiance and challenge. Calmly disengage, go to the kitchen, pour yourself a drink, take some deep breaths and return as if nothing had happened.

'Now where are we – yes, it's time for your bath.'

This gives a moment for reflection and space. John sees that Mum is in the driving seat, able to steer, accelerate and brake as she wishes. It gives an opportunity to save face, start again and compromise.

Time out: separating the warring parties

You can be calm, have your rules and your counting techniques, but there comes a time when things are heading seriously out of control. Once behaviour gets past a certain point, there is no place for reason. This is where we need to back off and get some space. Now we use time out.

Time out allows a deteriorating situation to be defused by briefly removing the child from all audience. You can use a quiet corner, a time-out chair, sitting on a step or a period of isolation in the bedroom.

'Don't annoy your sister when she is doing her homework.'

'I'm not annoying her.'

'You know the rule.'

'One,' wait five seconds.

'Two,' wait five seconds.

'Three,' wait five seconds.

'John, go to time out now!'

Some parents don't put the child in time out, they take themselves to the back yard, or even lock themselves in their bedroom. Once time has been served, even though they are not openly repentant, the child restarts with a completely clean slate.

Give a choice

In theory calmness, rules, counting and time out give sure-fire success, but you may still be stuck in a stand-off. Remember that forcing is not the answer. You've aimed for calm, you've got space, it's now time to give a choice.

'I want you to go to time out.'

'No!'

'John, if you go now, you can come out and we will watch "The Simpsons" together. If you choose not to go, there is no television tonight.'

A choice allows some room to manoeuvre and lessens the risk of reflex refusal. Humans don't like being pushed into a corner. A choice will sidestep confrontation.

'I' statements

When you can take no more, make a statement and move away (see earlier this chapter). 'It makes me unhappy when we are at each other like this.' Then go.

Forgive: hold no grudges

If you listen to some families discuss their relatives, you hear of uncles and aunts who have fallen permanently from favour. It started years ago with some small incident, but no one has been prepared to back down and make an effort to heal the wounds. With time the rift has become impossibly deep and there is no chance of resolution. You would think that blood relatives would try to resolve the differences, but often no one is prepared to make the first move.

I see the same situation with many parents and children in my care.

They get angry and resentful with each other until they are poles apart. It's very easy to get a relationship into this situation; it's much more difficult to get it out again.

As peace-loving parents we must get rid of grudges, resolve differences and bring our children back to us. Your efforts at reconciliation will not always be accepted, but when the olive branch is genuinely offered, it is usually grasped.

Some time ago I was speaking on talk-back radio when one mother phoned with an interesting story. She and her six-year-old were constantly at war, to the point she despaired of what had happened to their relationship.

She said that one night her husband was away from home, the other kids had gone to bed, and she and the six-year-old were watching the telly, seated at opposite ends of a long settee. He moved up a little. She moved up a little. They moved more. He leant against her arm. She rubbed her hand over his back and held him close. With emotion in her voice she then said, 'Things changed that night.'

Children don't want to be at war with their parents. After they have annoyed us they may not make a formal apology but they circle the perimeter, hoping we will show them the olive branch. Be quick to put an end to hostility and pull them back in close.

The dos and don'ts of discipline

1. Most discipline comes from subtle feedback, where children sense when they are doing well or doing badly. They pick this up through the tone of our voice, the twinkle in our eyes and our level of interest.

2. If you want a child to respond, first gain their attention, look them in the eye, speak warmly and mean what you say.

3. Argument and anger inflame and we lose control. Let unimportant happenings pass, keep calm and repeat requests like a broken gramophone record.

4. Nagging causes irritation and deliberate deafness. Say what you want done, encourage action, monitor progress and get off their backs.

5. Wound-up humans are irrational and do foolish things. When a child is over the top, the priority is a cool-down period, not a lecture or discipline.

6. A hostile, heavy, confronting style of parenting leads to opposition and resentment. Children need to feel they are respected and have some choice.

7. Humans are happiest with structure and self-discipline in their lives. Children need rules and structure that lets them know where they stand.

8. Rules are important but they must be interpreted with sense and appropriate flexibility.

9. Children don't want to be at war with their parents, but often we hold grudges and refuse peace. After anger or punishment, forgive and pull them back in close.

10. Reward good intent and effort, even if the result falls flat. Change from seeing problems and bad behaviour, refocus and catch them being good.

11. A behaviour that is rewarded will usually be repeated. Make sure it is the good, not the bad, you are rewarding.

12. It's easy to squabble with children. Sensible parents take a step back and ask, 'Is this really worth it? Is this getting me anywhere?' Let the unimportant things pass.

SEVEN

Ways to approach a behaviour problem

When parents come to me many are in a state of numb confusion. They are quite clear that they don't like what is going on, but they can't see why it's happening. When I ask parents about the behaviour, they tend to become bogged down on some unimportant part, they over-interpret or they get entirely off-beam.

My first priority is to find the true nature of the problem. How much of the difficulty is in the child? How much of the difficulty is in the parenting? What stresses are stirring the environment? What brings calm and what triggers a blow-up? Then I need to know what techniques are being tried and which bring the best chance of success. There are a number of simple methods to cut through the confusion.

The magic wand

When parents are asked, 'What's the problem?' they often are so stressed they answer, 'Everything.' Only a miracle worker can sort out 'everything'. I can only deal in specifics.

To help narrow the focus I ask, 'If I had a magic wand and could only change one bit of behaviour, what would that be?' When I get that answer, I then ask, 'If you had a second wish, what is the next most troublesome behaviour?'

The magic wand helps parents think more clearly and shows me where I must target my treatment. Mums often see things differently to dads, but both know what is causing them pain. If you think your child has a behaviour problem first try the magic wand to pinpoint what's bothering you.

Describe a day

Children can be irritating and obnoxious at home, then act like angels in my office. Parents worry that I won't believe their story and secretly hope the child will be abusive and trash my room. Even the worst-behaved child can make you look a liar in a non-confronting interview situation. To get around this I get the parents to take me through the typical day.

What time does she wake? Is she usually in good form? What happens between getting up and breakfast time? I go through the day, getting a picture of every moment. I want to hear about the usual day, not the worst-case scenario. Armed with this information I know how to help.

Keep a behaviour diary

A good psychologist will usually start by asking parents to keep a behaviour diary. This measures the frequency, severity and duration of all behaviour, good and bad. From this baseline the psychologist documents the reality of what is happening and can then see when the techniques they suggest are creating change. It is useful to write down what is going on as our perception can be very unreliable.

Don't over-analyse

I meet some parents who are so analytical they would make Sigmund appear an amateur. Every action is interpreted as having some deep

significance. An ornament gets bumped by an exuberant child and this is analysed as a deliberate act of destruction. An impulsive outburst is seen as premeditated aggression. Even teasing their sister is labelled spiteful jealousy.

Parents who over-interpret may blame incorrectly, become paranoid and miss the point. The more I work with children the less I understand about their behaviour. My job is to help parents change to a happy relationship, not to over-analyse their children.

The ABC approach

ABC is a simple way to sort out behaviour. Each problem is looked at in three parts:

A. the antecedent (what triggered it off)
B. the behaviour (what the child did)
C. the consequence (how we reacted and what were the pay-offs).

Putting ABC into action

A mother complains that her daughter is obstinate, abusive and never does what she is told. I ask for a specific example.

'Last night was a disaster. I called Lisa to come for dinner, she refused, got angry and ruined the night for both of us.'

I now approach this with the ABC technique.

The antecedent
What was happening before the blow up?

'Lisa was in the lounge watching a TV soap. I told her to switch off the set, to tidy away her toys, wash her hands and come to the table immediately. She ignored me. I turned off the television, she shouted at me and I lost it.'

The behaviour
Lisa dragged her feet, came to the table, grumbled throughout the meal, fiddled with her food and provoked all the way until bedtime.

The consequence
Mum had a spoiled and an unhappy night. She felt resentful at what her daughter had done. Lisa felt angry with her mum, but secretly believed she had won the battle.

How the disaster could have been handled, using ABC

Now we have got the picture, let's see how things might have been handled differently.

The antecedent

Lisa's television programme had only eight minutes to run. Could she have waited until the next commercial or the end? Mum might have given a five-minute warning: 'Lisa, dinner is almost ready, can you start to tidy up please?' Was it important to tidy the toys before dinnertime, or could that have happened later? Was it helpful to turn off the television or was this an unnecessary act of provocation? Would Mum have treated one of her adult friends with such hostility? If Lisa didn't eat her dinner, who was going to miss out?

The behaviour

It takes two people to keep a battle on the boil. Was Mum committed to forgive or was she spoiling for a fight? Was this a time for a simple statement: 'I love you, but it makes me feel unhappy when we annoy each other?' Should Mum and her daughter have moved apart for a short time or even used time out?

The consequence

What was the pay-off for Mum? She showed she was tough, uncompromising and not going to give in to a child. What was the loss for Mum? Three hours of anger, a spoiled meal, disturbed sleep and damage to a relationship. What was the pay-off for Lisa? She proved she was a powerful person who could call the shots. She watched her mother lose control and credibility. She was given endless attention. What was the loss for Lisa? She missed five minutes of her favourite programme, she had a stressed mealtime and an uncomfortable evening. She upset the relationship with someone she loved.

Was it worth it? There were no winners, just losers. Things might have been different if there had been a warning, if Mum had waited until a commercial break, if Mum had resorted to less confrontation and had tried to stay calm, instead of stirring the conflict.

Finding the best behaviour technique

Life must be easy for those who write advice books but don't work with difficult children. By the time I meet parents, most have tried all the usual techniques and are still in trouble. I often look at the difficulties and wonder what more I can suggest. When faced with this I go back to basics. I review every possible method to see what brings some success, what is of little value and what is a total failure.

As a rule, shouting, smacking, nitpicking, confronting, arguing and escalating all make things worse. Rules, rewards, letting the unimportant pass, time out, keeping calm, 'I' statements and forgiveness give the best chance.

I ask parents to drop the techniques that don't work. But old habits die hard.

'Do you smack him?'

'Yes' they reply.

'Does it help?'

'No, it makes him angry and impossible.'

'Why do you keep doing it?'

'You don't suggest we let him get away with bad behaviour?'

'But is it working?'

'No'

'Then you should stop it.'

'But that's letting him get away with bad behaviour.'

'READ MY LIPS!'

A final word

Now you can clearly focus on the main problem behaviour. You know the triggers that set it off. You have listed the techniques that work and have discarded those that don't. In the next chapter we'll look at how this works with the everyday behaviour problems of school age.

Focusing in on a behaviour problem

1. Deal in specifics
   - 'If I had a magic wand . . .'
   - What is the most major behaviour?
   - What is the next major behaviour?

2. Describe a day
   - take an average day – not a disaster day
   - the extent of the problem

- the triggers
- see the pattern of behaviour
- the techniques that work
- the techniques that fail

3. Don't over-analyse
   - don't get bogged in academic theories
   - resolution is more useful than analysis

4. The ABC approach
   - A (antecedent) – the trigger
   - B (behaviour) – what happened
   - C (consequence) – the result

5. Find the best behaviour technique
   - What usually helps?
   - What occasionally helps?
   - What makes things worse?

EIGHT

An A to Z of children's behaviour

I have little patience with child care experts who have a quick fix for every behaviour problem. Quick fixes sound impressive, but life is not so simple in the real world.

When the late Benjamin Spock was asked to write his first child care book, he initially declined. Spock told the publisher he had too many failures in his day-to-day practice, and to write a book would imply he had all the answers. I can relate to Spock's honesty: I have a head full of clever theories, but I still struggle with children in my care.

As parents read through my suggestions some will think, 'This man is crazy. Some of his techniques are off the beam.' So a word of warning. What I present is a long list of ideas for every problem. Some are sure-fire, others are way down the pile. What you use will depend on the age and temperament of your child and, of course, the extent of the problem. The final decision will be based on only one thing – getting the right result.

Contents

Topics covered in other chapters

Accident prone

Insurance companies know all about how different people pose different risks. Sometimes, they will refuse cover for drivers under twenty-five, especially if they are male, aggressive and impulsive. Girls of this age are always a safer bet, but in both sexes there are a few high-risk individuals with an accident-prone temperament.

Research into accident proneness has often looked at bus drivers, comparing those who arrive safely with those who bump things along the way. As always it is the impulsive temperament that causes most trouble. The fast-moving drivers are useful when running late, but for safe arrival the calm, reflective temperament is the winner.

Meanwhile, away from the bus depot, an impulsive temperament leaves some children an accident waiting to happen. I see impulsive children with repeated fractures or following several near-death experiences. One mother wrote about her son: 'Our son has just had his seventeenth birthday. I never thought he would live this long. At two years he climbed to the top of a tall wardrobe and took his grandfather's heart tablets. He was rushed to hospital.

'At three years he released the handbrake on our car. This careered down our steep drive. The car overturned. Our son had one small bruise; the car was less lucky.

'At four years he hit our neighbour's beehive with a large stick. He thought they were blowflies. He only had two stings; the neighbour who went to his aid was not so fortunate.'

The list of disasters covered several more pages and it appeared that he had attained Gold Frequent Flyer status at the local casualty department. The letter ended on a note of panic: 'Today he is reading the Highway Code – he wants to learn to drive!'

So how can we help the impulsive child who shoots from the hip?

- An impulsive temperament is often inherited from an impulsive dad or mum (usually dad). Clever children should choose their parents with great care.
- Child safety must always be the first priority. Take special care with the crossing of roads, supervise closely and have strict rules about bike riding.
- Teach the traffic light technique of 'Stop. Think. Go.' (slow the pace, then encourage them to reflect for a moment, then act). It sounds very simple but it is a challenge when children are all go and no stop.
- Accident proneness is a classic symptom of Attention Deficit Hyperactivity Disorder (ADHD). If the child is found to be suffering from ADHD and is successfully treated, they will be much safer.

Arguing and backchat

Such is the talent of some children, they could start an argument in an empty room. In fact, one of my patients argues with his computer, complaining that it cheats when he is playing card games. Of course, you need two people to argue and talking to a computer is about as useful as squabbling with your mother-in-law. Life's too short for lost causes.

Children argue in order to hijack attention, look smart or push a power struggle. If attention is the goal, the arguing should be ignored. If it's to show off in front of visiting mates, give a warning then send the friends home.

A power struggle is much more complex, as the child is looking for a victim, and when this happens we must remain unruffled to avoid falling into that role (see also this chapter, Oppositional behaviour, page 91).

Here are some ways to handle a keen arguer:

- Improve communication. If a child is addressed with heavy, abrasive, sarcastic tones, these will bounce back at you in their reply.
- If possible, ask, don't tell.
- Be enthusiastic, show interest, be positive.
- Be matter-of-fact and use humour.
- Change tack with a different intonation or a whisper.
- When arguing and the child uses smart comments to wind you up, don't rise to their bait but let the water roll off the duck's back 'That's fine.' 'I hear you.' 'Now I'm just going outside for a moment.'
- Don't let protest change the referee's decision. If young McEnroe disputes a line call, don't bend to his bullying.
- Be a courteous listener, but at a certain point, state your position and close down that channel of reception.
- If they feel you are being unreasonable, give two minutes to put their case, after which 'It's finished.'
- Keep asking yourself, 'Is this getting me anywhere?' If the answer is no, it's time to start using your brain.
- When they show off in front of friends, give fair warning (preferably in private), then send their mates home. If their friends cannot go home, put the show-off in time out. Before the next visit give a quiet reminder of the rules.
- When stuck for ideas, use an 'I' statement: 'I feel embarrassed when addressed like that'; 'I feel sad when we argue'; 'I would feel happy if we got on together.'
- Give feedback for good times: 'Gosh, you are such good company'; 'I so much enjoyed being with you.'
- Arguing can be part of the power politics of the oppositional child. With these difficult young people the aim is to sidestep confrontation, give choices and let them feel they have a say in the outcome. (For more information on oppositional behaviour see this chapter, page 91).
- Most children do what they are told but there is a lot of argument and complaint along the way. They have to get ready for school, do homework, bathe, brush teeth and go to bed. All you are asking for is action without excuses. Use a star chart to encourage compliance without complaint or add a bonus to the pocket money for a grumble-free life.
- Some older children can be bought with a significant cash payment. One extremely difficult child in my care gets fifty pence for each hassle-free day. This sounds like extortion but nothing else worked and it was a small price to pay for his mum's sanity.

Bad language

Even royalty use rude words, but only in private. Our children get the same royal flush, but the words appear at inopportune moments. The reason for bad language is ignorance of the meaning, releasing tension, attention seeking and acting 'cool'.

In the early school years children use a lot of silly language where even the word 'bottom' is seen to be as entertaining as an entire season of 'Seinfeld'. This language has no malice; it's part of the fun and nonsense of being young. At this age children repeat words they have heard at school, but they have no knowledge of their meaning. Words may also be used to wind up Mum and Dad.

Silliness can be stopped with a simple comment, our tone of voice or the way we look. Handle innocent but inappropriate language with an explanation of its meaning. Where words are used to stir up parents, it is important to avoid rising to the bait.

By late primary school, bad language is normal behaviour for the herd. Some children use the f-word to register their position in the group, much like a dog might pee around a perimeter to stake his claim. At this age it is important to make it clear what we will and will not accept.

Primary-age children often have words and secret sayings that are part of the common language that bonds the group together. When my boys were at school, the in word was 'skills'. I don't know where it came from or what it meant, but it was like some special handshake of a secret group. The word lost favour when my older son bluffed the class: 'You shouldn't say "skills", it's a rude word.' The others looked surprised. 'It's a nasty disease of the bum. I know, because my father is a doctor.'

The words we use have a different significance in different cultures and countries. As I miss my serve at tennis it sounds so trendy to say, 'Merde!' but to a Frenchman it is still 'Shit!'

One ex-Australian prime minister was well known for his intolerance of groups that were all talk and no action. When working on a high-powered UN committee, he was forever baffling the interpreters. One day, exasperated by the lack of progress, he stood up and said, 'It's about time we stopped playing silly buggers.' With this, the interpreters flicked through their dictionaries and over the headphones came a confused statement about sport and feeble-minded homosexuals.

My list of suggestions gives a number of approaches, but what you use will depend on the age of the child, the extent of the problem and the reason for the bad language. In my experience, any young child with an extreme, abusive foul mouth, has acquired this from someone in their dysfunctional living environment. If language is a symptom of home disharmony or a rift in the parent–child relationship, the language is not the main priority for treatment.

- State clearly what you will not accept: 'John, that is not a word we use.'
- Use 'I' statements: 'I feel upset when I hear that sort of language.'
- In young children explain the meaning of rude words and show the silliness of describing reproductive anatomy in public.
- Notice and reinforce when they talk, and relate in an appropriate way.
- When language is used to bait parents, where possible, let it pass. When ignored, the baiting may initially increase then, with no pay-off, it will lessen.
- Older children enjoy shocking their parents. They think that their generation know words that we old timers can't use. We can capitalise on the surprise value of remaining completely unfazed and reply using their word. 'John, it's not very clever to say f——.' When response is laid-back it removes the shock from shock tactics.
- Some parents still wash out mouths with soap and water. This is old-fashioned, dangerous and creates children who resent their parents.
- Swearing helps release tension. Teach children how to let off steam in other ways: count to ten, punch a pillow or have a quick run around the block.
- Allow the use of almost rude words: 'Shoot!' or 'Fruit cake!'
- Put limits on swearing. 'You can use those words, but not here.'
- A lot of rude words involve religious figures and begatting, but they are not recommended in church.
- Give a warning and follow with removal of privileges: 'Bed fifteen minutes earlier.'
- Give a warning and follow with time out.
- Make good language pay off. Convert the weekly pocket money to twenty-pence coins and place these in a glass jar. For each blasphemy deduct one piece of silver.
- If they are acting smart to impress a friend, warn them that their mate will be sent home if they continue. After fair warning, act.
- Children parrot the speech, abusive attitudes and bad language of those they are close to. In the early years this comes from us, the parents.

- When parenting has been hostile, negative and verbally abusive since the early years, it is normal for children to treat their parents in the same way.

Bike riding

When I was young everyone either walked or rode their bike to school. The handful who were driven by car were seen as feeble, spoiled children. Today things have changed: it is the riders to school who are risk takers and the odd ones out.

Bikes can give children a great release for pent-up energy as well as freedom and mobility. We usually remove trainer wheels when the child is about five years old, but children continue to need close supervision until eight or nine years. It's important to have rules in place right from the start. Before purchasing a bike have a strict set of rules that everyone agrees on. 'No rules – no bike.'

- Have clear rules about helmets, stopping at intersections, crossing main roads and areas that are off limits.
- Have rules about care of the bike, locking and putting it away at night.
- Notice and reinforce safe riding.
- Teach about safe braking and keep brakes serviced.
- Teach about the dangers of bags carried on the handlebars that can catch in the front wheel.
- Supervise when children are challenging their friends on jumps, ramps and riding through the air.
- When rules are disregarded, lock up the bicycle for a week and don't debate or argue your actions.
- Bike ride as a family. This is good for children and helps unfit adults avoid heart attacks.
- If you worry about bicycles, wait until they start driving your car!

Birthday parties

Younger children are full of bubble and bounce. Parents tell me that sugar in the party food is the cause of this over-the-top behaviour. I'm not so sure: this age group would be airborne even if we fed them on the purest of sugar-free food and natural spring water.

When planning a party for the under-eights, make an invitation list then divide it by two-thirds, which is all you can manage.

The over-eights will want a more sophisticated party: a live performance from a famous pop group or the guest appearance of Manchester United would be popular but not essential.

- For timid partygoers, talk it through before they go. Role-play introductions and thank yous.
- With an over-rowdy raver, arrive a little late and pick up a little early.
- When organising your own child's party, ensure you have enough adult minders on hand.
- Consider inviting a favourite teacher from school. They can wander around and provide a form of police presence.
- Check all toilets are capable of quick throughput and full flush.
- Consider using an outside party centre. It may not be more expensive and it has the advantage that others tidy up.
- A trick candle (that won't blow out) never fails to impress.

Bragging and boasting

We recognise bragging as a suitable talent for the politician who wishes re-election. Yet despite the example of our leaders, we teach our children that it's vain and offensive to blow your own trumpet.

The under-seven-year-olds live in a world where everything is larger and more spectacular than life. Listen at bath time as five-year-olds discuss their most private parts:

'My dad's is bigger than your dad's.'

'No, my dad's is huge! It's like this!'

Maybe it isn't an exaggeration but it's still part of their quaint, uncomplicated world.

After eight years of age, boasting is either an adult-type behaviour or a sign of emotional insecurity. When my boys were at school, the taller stories came from friends with the most convoluted, much-married backgrounds. Certainly I couldn't work out how all the relatives fitted together, and the children must have been equally confused where they belonged.

How you handle a boast depends on the child's age, the extent of the problem and the state of their esteem.

- For minor bragging, ignore it altogether.
- Explain how boasting can make you look stupid. Illustrate with a play

on your own brilliance: 'My spaghetti bolognaise is the best in this street. It's better than anyone's in this city, in fact, aliens from far off planets may land on our lawn, knock at the door and ask for the recipe.'

- Put the brakes on bragging. 'You have talked all morning about your goal. We know you are a top player, but this is bragging.'
- With tall stories, listen and then state, 'I hear what you are saying but this is not quite true.'
- Ask the ten-year-old how they feel when others brag. Does it impress them or not?
- Notice non-bragging days or weeks. 'Today you played a blinder of a game, you were brilliant, yet not a brag or a boast!'
- Don't be too tough. Life would be pretty boring if we didn't stretch the realms of credibility. Every successful author knows that you can't let truth get in the way of a good story.

Breaking things in unthinking rage

When children have a short fuse they may overreact and even destroy their own treasures. After the event they see the stupidity of their behaviour, which makes them twice as stroppy.

- The angriest human beings are those who are angry at their own silliness.
- Don't nag or say, 'Told you so', as this adds insult to injury.
- If they break something important to them, for example, an almost-completed model aeroplane, support, don't criticise.
- Don't rub salt in the wound. Even if they say they don't care, they hurt deeply.

Breaking their sibling's property

Some children have fiddly fingers. They have to touch and things get broken. Here's what you can do:

- Have a small number of rules about what can and what cannot be touched.
- Notice when care and respect is shown for other people's property.
- Distinguish between the occasional unthinking act and damage that follows the deliberate disregard of a warning.
- Instruct siblings to keep their treasures secure and make their personal space a no-go area.

- Breakages can be replaced via a small levy on the pocket money.
- Don't set up an impossibly harsh repayment system, as this causes resentment and hostility.

Car travel

One mother with three extreme ADHD boys told me of her trips to and from school. 'Car seating is run on a strict roster. On week one John sits in the front seat, Tom in the back right, and Jack in the back left. Week two, Jack moves to the front, John moves to back right, and Tom to back left. On leaving school the occupant of the front seat can talk for five minutes, then the back right, then the left.' Finally, the mother said, 'And we never allow the car to stop. Even if the fuel needle is on empty, we speed past service stations.'

It doesn't need to be this bad but some children make cars a moving hell:

'It's not fair, she's looking out my window.'

'Mum, he's making that noise again.'

'Are we there yet?'

Just because adults like long-distance driving, it doesn't necessarily follow that this suits their children. If your child fights, squabbles and protests on the trip to the corner store, a 200-mile car trip could be a challenge. When long-distance travel ages parents and is a hazard to mental health, consider a quick air flight, a seat on a train or a holiday at home.

In case you have to take that trip, though, here are some ideas:

- Before you start, set down the ground rules about teasing, poking and annoying.
- Plan regular breaks and keep the passengers informed of the time to touchdown.
- If the car tape player is to be used for everybody, allocate tape time in advance.
- Borrow some talking books from your local library.
- A Walkman may help.
- Construct a token system where short periods of peaceful travel are rewarded with a small token (a tick, star, bead, etc). These all add up to a worthwhile reward (such as spending money) at the next fuel stop.
- Secure a large piece of luggage between the occupants of the back seat.

Chores

Child care experts are divided into two groups: the philosophers who expect children to work for the common good of the family; and the pragmatists who buy and bribe. I would like all children to help, just for love, but I can accept anything that keeps the peace and achieves results.

Children are genetically created with different attitudes to helping. Some have an unquestioning wish to tidy, wash, clean and cook, while others expect room service from the age of five to fifty years. Of course, example is important. I see teenage boys who treat Mum like an inferior-intellect housemaid. Often their father is equally arrogant and insensitive.

With my own family, I always hoped that our adult sharing and working together would rub off on the children. But with both boys now in their twenties, the jury is still out on the verdict.

It is important to introduce chores at a young age, as this capitalises on the under-fives' wish to be helpful. Give a few responsibilities, then build on this with age. Start with a small number of important tasks that should be completed with minimal reminding and zero complaint. Here's what to do:

- Start young and give a few basic chores.
- Clearly communicate what you expect from your children.

- Draw up a list of duties together.
- Set a time for completion and inspection.
- Work together where possible, as this gets jobs done and helps relationships.
- Give one reminder, but don't nag.
- Divide chores equally between boys and girls.
- Don't be a nitpicker, but don't pay for substandard work.
- Appreciate effort, and notice when tasks are done without asking.
- Stand back and share the satisfaction of the completed job.
- Use a star chart to highlight specific tasks, for example, making their bed, washing dishes, tidying their room.
- Pay a basic level of pocket money then add a bonus for work completed without complaint.
- Use an immediate reward system where coins are placed in a jar.
- With older children, consider suspending payment for all those incidentals, for example, cinema tickets, drinks and treats. Cost out each chore then pay real money for a real week's work.
- Set an example. Parents who work together have children who we hope will become helpful husbands and wives.
- The ultimate aim is to encourage children to see what needs to be done and get on with it without being asked.

Clinginess

One- and two-year-old children are clingy by nature but this eases with age, and most will separate confidently by three or four.

However, there are a few who still cling right into the early school years. If friends visit or when addressed by a stranger they hide their face and hold onto Mum. Relatives become the expert psychiatrist:

'That child has an emotional problem. It's about time you toughened them up.' But the child's fears are real to them and forcing makes things worse.

A few children cling because they are stressed. This is common following a marriage split where the child knows they have lost fifty per cent of those they trust, and they are determined to stay close to the remaining half.

- If the environment is in equilibrium I encourage parents to steer gently and go with the flow. Little people vary in their ability to separate and they have another seventy-five years to sort things out.

- Let them know about visitors before they arrive. Role-play eye contact, greetings and small talk.
- Notice, praise and reinforce appropriate behaviour.
- Encourage small group friendships, then build to bigger numbers at more distant venues.
- Don't push. They know how they feel and don't need railroading by some insensitive adult.
- When reacting to family change, tread softly. They need all their supports at this time.

Conflict cycle

This negative spiral is one of the most damaging situations I see. The parent gets angry, the child returns fire, no one backs down and the relationship turns to resentment. Soon parents see every action as a deliberate attempt to provoke them. Now they address their child with a negative, antagonistic tone that presumes non-compliance. The child responds with anger and foot dragging, insolence and opposition.

I encourage parents to get off their high horse but I am often told that the child has the problem and must change, not the parent. They return again and again over the years but nothing changes and I am powerless to help.

Some of this conflict starts with an irritable infant who is impossible to settle, or with a relationship damaged by post-natal depression. Many of these children are born with an oppositional temperament. Whatever the cause, the only remedy is to get in early, then teach parents to use an olive branch rather than a stick.

This is not a holy war. Forget about who is right or wrong. Without compromise and change everyone will end up in the wrong.

- Avoid cold, condescending tones, quiet anger and passive aggression.
- Be positive and transmit the message that you expect action.
- Avoid 'you' statements like 'You expect everything'; 'You give nothing'; 'You are never satisfied'.
- Use 'I' statements: 'I feel sad that we annoy each other this way.'
- Notice and appreciate any small gesture of compliance and closeness.
- Have a round-table conference. Discuss how you annoy them and they annoy you. Each side can then try to change two of their specific irritating behaviours. Review progress one week later.
- Use the techniques suggested for oppositional behaviour (see also this chapter, page 91).

Dawdling and won't get dressed

I am told there are children who jump with enthusiasm out of bed, get dressed and are ready for school hours ahead of time. But this endangered species is outnumbered by whole divisions of dawdlers.

Dawdlers come in two sorts: those created with a dreamy, slow-moving brain, and the ones who go slow to damage their parents' health. You send the dreamer off to get dressed; half an hour later they're stuck in a catatonic trance, blankly staring at a sock. This is different to the wind-up child who is deaf to all warnings until Mum is close to seizure. Then they grab their belongings and jump on the bus.

Dreamers need to be woken early and reminded many times. Their clothes should be laid out and ready the night before. They get rewarded for the little steps they make: 'He's got his pants on! . . . Wow, now he's got his vest on too!'

The secret is to nudge gently yet be immensely patient. In reality nothing short of a faith healer will transform this temperament. Often their dreamy style is quite like someone you chose to marry.

The deliberate dawdler also needs an early start, but after this, only allow a limited number of reminders. After two or three prompts, set the kitchen timer to announce ten minutes before departure. If the child is running late, that's their problem and they must sort this out with the school.

It takes an exceptional parent to watch as their child leaves home hungry and partly dressed. But change can only come when a child takes responsibility and is allowed to feel the repercussions of their actions.

Daydreaming

Some children are created with a dreamy temperament. Teachers despair as the child glazes over and their thoughts slip out the window. Schools may dramatise daydreaming, diagnosing this spaced-out boredom as 'petit mal epilepsy' (see Chapter 21, page 228).

A few of these dreamers have the predominantly inattentive form of ADHD. Here they lose attention and drift off target and this is often associated with moments of unreliable impulse control.

Some children switch off to escape from the difficulties in their life. We often see this with family breakdowns and other unhappiness. If a previously sparky, alert child becomes detached and disinterested, suspect an emotional trigger or even depression (see below).

After the age of eleven years children develop the ability to use abstract thinking. Some of these older children become dreamers as the potential Einstein tries to think through a new theory of relativity.

Here are some tips for dealing with dreamers:

- Dreamers need structure, encouragement and reminders of time.
- Work beside the child to keep the focus on the task at hand. Use a kitchen timer to add some urgency to homework completion or eating dinner.
- Consider the possibility of predominantly inattentive ADHD (inattentive, slightly impulsive, disorganised, poor short-term memory).
- Exclude specific learning disabilities (such as dyslexia) where attention drifts as they lose interest in that one area of difficulty.
- Daydreaming may be in the genes. The child may be just like Mum or Dad!
- Sometimes we can't change the daydreamer; we can only change our expectations.

Depression

Though our greatest worry is the depressed teenager, children of all ages can be depressed. Depression is more than the kind of short-term sadness we all experience. True depression immobilises, dulls interest and turns out the light at the end of the tunnel.

The depressed five-year-old becomes unhappy, quiet and less animated, usually in response to an upsetting life event. Depression in a ten-year-old may be less obvious, with the main symptom a change from their usual outgoing state. School grades slip, attention fades, they retreat inward and lose friends and interests.

Depression tends to draw adults and children into their own claustrophobic company. Now everything is an effort, and with this can come open or hidden feelings of hopelessness.

Though I am supposed to be skilled in my understanding of children, I rarely diagnose depression in this age and know I must be missing some. The main warning signal is a change in behaviour, particularly when related to some disruption or loss in life.

- Be alert to a change where the child withdraws from friends and interests.
- The child's feelings are real. It's pointless to suggest they pull themselves together. They would do this if they could.
- Try to keep the child busy. Encourage them to get up at weekends, get out and look neat.
- Encourage them to talk about, write down or draw how they feel.
- Try to distinguish the common martyr statements like 'I'm ugly' or 'No one would care if I died' from a true call for help. There are a thousand martyrs for each crisis call but it's this one cry we can't afford to miss. Words alone are probably unimportant; words accompanied by isolation and a change in behaviour are of greater concern.
- Opposition and anger often accompany depression. This makes the child extremely difficult and it is our instinct to retaliate with hostility. Tread gently as it is easy to deepen the depression.
- Depression has some hereditary link. If you have personal experience of this problem, be more alert to the possibility in those around you.
- When a child has severe learning problems this causes stress at school and blocks many avenues of success in life. These children are more vulnerable to depression and it is hard to show them the achievement they so much need.
- Encourage outside interests and looking forward to something.
- Professional psychological or psychiatric help is recommended for all depressed children and is a matter of urgency when self-harm is a possibility.

● The old-fashioned anti-depressants like Tofranil (imipramine) have little effect in depressed children, though there is some evidence that the newer selective seratonin re-uptake inhibitor (SSRI) drugs like Zoloft and Prozac may bring some gains.

Diet and behaviour

A horse trainer knows that the right diet gives speed on the final furlong, but it doesn't make a horse behave badly. A good diet prepares our children for the long run of life but, for most youngsters, it has no effect on behaviour.

In about five per cent of all children diet affects their behaviour, and their most common symptom is irritability or restlessness. There is a myth that diet only affects ADHD children but any child, whether ADHD or not, can show a behavioural change. A second myth suggests that the only food offenders are artificial colourings, preservatives and additives, but the evidence shows that organically grown oranges, tomatoes and pure honey can sometimes be just as troublesome.

There are four common groups of chemicals that cause food intolerance: salicylates, amines, monosodium glutamate and food additives.

The salicylates are natural chemicals found in many fruits, vegetables, nuts, herbs, spices and jams. Salicylates are highest in unripe fruits and there is more near the skin than inside.

The amines occur in high levels in cheese, chocolate, yeast extract and fruits such as bananas (especially when overripe).

Monosodium glutamate (MSG) occurs naturally in strong-flavoured foods like tomatoes and cheeses and is also sometimes used as an additive in stock cubes, yeast extracts and some styles of cooking.

Food additives are either preservatives used to keep foods fresh or colourings to make them look more attractive. Hundreds of these are used but only a few are likely to cause trouble. A code number on the product label indicates which chemicals have been added, for example, sulphites are numbered between 220 and 228, while antioxidants are numbered 310 to 321.

In my experience, when there is a sensitivity, parents are usually aware of the offending drink, food or fruit and give this a miss. But the situation can be much more complex where the effects of food chemicals are cumulative. For example, the natural preservative salicylate can come from a variety of sources. A child who is sensitive to it may eat first tomato paste, then some raisins, then peppermint and finally a glass of orange juice. In the cumulative child any two or three of these would have been no problem, but the total intake creates an overload. Parents are now confused as orange juice previously caused no reaction but today it has tipped the balance.

It takes a clever dietitian to untangle all this. If they suspect a natural or artificial product is affecting behaviour they will withdraw it and then reintroduce it at a later time to see what happens.

Diet has a lesser effect on behaviour than popular belief might suggest. Sugar is the target of much criticism but this has not been shown to cause behavioural problems. I rarely suggest the diet approach to behaviour, but I support parents who want to give it a fair go. For them I recommend that the diet be supervised by a knowledgeable dietician.

Fears

We all have secret fears, which may seem silly to others but are very real to us. The adult who fears flying can be shown safety statistics, but at 30 000 feet they remain terrified by the slightest change in engine sound. Everyone is allowed their fears – it's only when they become major phobias that damage our day-to-day lives that we need help.

Children have different worries at different ages. A three-year-old might be terrified of loud noises, electric hand dryers, ambulance sirens and dogs. By six years they may fear the dark, falling, losing their mum, wind, thunder, ghosts and monsters. At ten years they worry about school failure, speaking in front of the class, looking foolish, how they appear and possible friction in their parents' marriage.

Most school-age fears are fed into our children by what they see in the world or hear from their parents. Our necessary warnings about road safety, stranger danger and home security may cause our children to fear injury, abduction and burglars.

Miscommunication also raises fears. When Grandma is rushed to hospital it is often easier to say she has a severe cold than explain heart failure. But if Grandma dies in hospital, the child's next cold may be seen as a serious event.

I remember family gatherings when adult relatives talked in whispers about the sadness of senile decay. It seemed an entire generation of my blood relatives were suffering from this incurable illness. It must have been very serious or people wouldn't whisper and pray about it.

To make things worse, 'senile' sounded like an important male personal part. The thought that this might decay or drop off filled me with fear. If the adults in my life had said straight, 'Your relatives are getting old', I would have understood.

I often see school-age children who have a fear of walking around the house alone at night. We can support them through this fear by holding their hand as they walk through a dark room then standing near the door as they go alone. If dark is the problem, keep lights on dim and reduce the power until confidence starts to grow.

It seems crazy that a nine-year-old can't go from the family room to the toilet without an escort, but for some reason it's important to them. They gradually get better with help from an accepting, reassuring parent. I do not psychoanalyse these children; I aim to support and use gradual desensitisation.

Forgetfulness

In the brain, the bit that imparts intelligence is not always attached to the centre of organisation and reliable memory. This causes some children to leave their belongings on the bus, have the wrong books for homework and forget the tutor after school. Parents look on in disbelief. You are not asking much: they have to deliver a note to their teacher, not the Gettysburg address.

With the disorganised and forgetful you can't work miracles, but memory jogs help reliability. For more information on teaching children to be organised see Chapter 10, page 120.

Teach children to stop for a minute before they leave home, to think through the day's programme and check they are carrying the right gear. They can stop again on leaving the swimming pool and when they finish school for the day.

- Write notes and 'To do' lists.
- Write a reminder word on their hand.
- Tie a knot in their handkerchief.
- Put a rubber band on one wrist to remind them.
- Set a watch alarm.
- Put their watch on the wrong wrist to jog their memory.
- Have a chart on the fridge door that lists all important activities throughout the week, and encourage them to refer to it regularly.

Gratitude

'It's not fair,' Dad unloads to me. 'I took him to the zoo, we had a fantastic day of father–son togetherness then, on leaving, he saw a Mr Whippy van, created a scene and grizzled all the way home. I bust myself for him – so where's the gratitude?'

I have news for you. Don't expect gratitude in this world. Your reward will come in the hereafter! You are in this parenting because you love them, not for thanks and reward.

Many children are full of thanks and appreciation, but for others it's all take and no give. If it makes you feel better, deliver them a lecture about the injustice of it all, but it won't change anything. Enjoy it when you receive it – even if it's a once-a-year event.

Grazing

There are some children who nibble all day like sheep. Grazing is not unhealthy as long as the pasture is of reasonable quality.

For some, grazing is their favourite way to feed. Others graze out of restless boredom. In school holidays these are the children who pace around, opening and closing doors until the fridge is unable to keep food cool.

The solution to boredom is to steer children towards more structured activity. When scavengers are on the prowl lock away the goodies and avoid buying treat snacks.

Bored or not, grazers need easy access to healthy affordable snacks. A chilled jug of tap water, unflavoured milk, bread, fruit and plain biscuits are a start.

Hair and eyebrow plucking

I don't know what pleasure children get from pulling out and nibbling their hair, but it's probably similar to the pleasure they get out of nail biting and finger picking. I have seen school-age children with no eyebrows or eyelashes and others with thin hair or even a patch of baldness.

If there is some obvious cause of tension this must be addressed, otherwise adopt the gentle redirection, minimum-fuss approach. Children usually pull and chew when they are bored, falling asleep or watching television. At these times consider getting something more appropriate to twiddle, like a worry ball. Give a gentle nudge but don't ridicule them as this increases the tension and they will become an underground plucker.

Have fancy hairstyles and focus on attractive eyebrows and lashes. Be quick to notice any improvement or any area of regeneration.

Occasionally a patch of hair drops out for no good reason (alopecia areata). This may be associated with stress but more often it just falls out for no good reason. Time will tidy up the alopecia, but you may want to pay a visit to the paediatrician or skin specialist for reassurance.

Interrupting

Children who are impulsive or forgetful may interrupt. The impulsive have no patience and can't wait. The forgetful will lose their words if they don't get them out immediately. We want to keep the lines of communication open and also encourage them to wait.

- Give a gentle reminder: 'Your turn in a minute, John.'
- Keep repeating the rules of conversation, without becoming a nag.
- Allow the forgetful child to interrupt with a cue word that you pick up later. As you are talking they say 'New teacher', and when appropriate you ask, 'What's this about a new teacher?'
- Teach through role-play how to interpret body language. Show when you are receptive and when your eyes are telling them to back off.

Lying and bending the truth

When the children of this impeachment generation hear of young George Washington they think, 'What a dork.' Fancy standing in front of your dad and saying, 'I cannot tell a lie.' George's father was probably more worried about annoying the environmentalists than his horizontal tree.

Every adult knows that lying is a sin, while bending the truth is a talent much cherished by lawyers. Children under the age of eight years tend to be open with their parents and are quite transparent in their dishonesty. But by ten years their deceit is much more subtle and some events in their lives are guarded with secrecy. The aim is to establish honesty in the early years and to ensure that openness gets more reward than hiding the truth.

- With the four- to six-year-old, don't overreact. Calmly say, 'I don't think this is true.'
- Don't debate; quietly state your opinion.
- Make sure that honesty pays off. There must be less punishment for owning up than denying fault.
- Notice their honesty and appreciate their openness.
- Before the age of eight children are immensely open. If we encourage this when they are young, they will confide more in their tempestuous teens.
- It is unfair to expect our children to be more truthful than the adults they live with. See also Chapter 10, page 115, and this chapter, Shoplifting, page 94).

Martyrdom

Through the ages, martyrs have shown great talent at grabbing attention. It may seem a bit extreme to be stoned or burned but it sure puts you on centre stage. Martyrdom is still alive and well and being practised by many six- to twelve-year-olds. They approach their mum, look pathetic and state, 'I'm dumb. I'm ugly. You don't love me. I've got no friends.' Occasionally some of this may be true, but for most, martyrdom is used to get an avalanche of attention.

We don't want to be insensitive to genuine concerns but when playing for attention, remember that martyrs get nowhere without an audience. Avoid getting dragged into debates about intellect, good looks and their number of friends. Make a brief statement: 'You are clever and brilliant at swimming'; 'I think you are a real good looker'; 'I love you all'; 'You have good mates.' Then give a reassuring cuddle and move on.

Meal-time behaviour

When a foreign dignitary lands in our country they are welcomed with a state banquet. Leaders since prehistoric times have known that sharing a meal boosts relationships and increases communication.

As the president chats, his emphasis is on communication, not manners. There is no chief of protocol saying, 'Sit up straight, sir . . . Stop slurping . . . Don't talk with your mouth full . . . You can't leave until you eat your broccoli.'

Every night the evening meal provides time when families can sit, listen and relate. It is essential that the television is switched off and we turn a relatively blind eye to mess and imperfect manners. Initially there may not be deep conversation, but with time the guttural grunts may become words.

- Food is about nutrition and meal times are for families to get together and communicate.
- Don't let squabbles and nitpicking cause stress. We want peace, not perfection.
- Establish basic rules about leaving the table, rushing and dawdling.
- Rushers must stay for a certain time and when they depart, they should leave the room.
- Dawdlers are given time, then left to sit by themselves.
- If dawdling is extreme set a cooking timer and when it rings, clear the table.
- Have some non-negotiable rules: 'You can touch or kick anything you want, as long as that "thing" is not your sister!'
- Give feedback for good manners and fun times.
- Clear the table together and establish good habits through example.

Nail biting and finger picking

There is a very simple reason why children bite and pick their nails – they enjoy it. When parents see the raw sores they wonder about pleasure, but humans do many things we don't understand. Grown-ups light their first morning cigarette, convulse with coughing and say, 'Gosh, that was good.' Though I can't understand this, it must give pleasure or they wouldn't do it.

Nail biting is probably an extension of the preschooler's thumb sucking or twiddling the tag on a security blanket. It is unusual under the age of five years. It occurs in about one in three eight-year-olds, one in two fifteen-year-olds and one in four at the age of twenty.

Biting is worse when tense, bored or watching television. There are many recommended remedies, though none are very successful. Whatever happens, don't nag, nitpick and create a battle. The best results come with gentle reminders and noting the good.

- Find the peak times for biting and picking. Keep your child better occupied during these times.
- Let them hold a little toy, a smooth comfort stone or a stress ball.

- When tempted to bite, they could try clenching both hands super tight for fifteen seconds, then relax and move on.
- Give a simple sign or gentle touch to alert them to biting.
- Compare their nails against other unbitten nails.
- Let them bite their fingers while in front of the mirror. This is not a pretty sight.
- When enough nail appears, manicure and make this special.
- With girls, use nail polish to draw attention to intact nails.
- With the older child encourage them to preserve one nail, then build on this quota.
- Use skin softeners and encourage hand care.
- Prepare a star chart to focus on each two hours without a pick or bite.
- Consider your chemist's best anti-bite nail paint. This may tip the balance but only when there is motivation.

Nightmares

All children have dreams, but not all of these have happy endings. A nightmare is an unsettling dream that leaves a child upset and semi-awake. They respond to our comfort, drift back to sleep and are aware of what happened the next day. Children have their most disturbed dreams when sick and almost hallucinating with fever.

Dreams were once seen as the window to our inner emotional state, but nowadays dreams are seen as nothing more than a normal part of sleep. Though daytime stress, heavy television and scary stories will upset children, there is uncertainty that these cause a child's nightmares.

What we do know is that children sleep best when we put them to bed calm and relaxed. There is no place for stress, arguments and heavy exercise before their head hits the pillow.

Distressed children need cuddles and comfort, but there is one trap for parents. Young children may pretend they are frightened just to attract an audience. Bad dreams occur occasionally, while regular call outs are probably an attention-seeking hoax.

- Come to the child, hold, stroke, comfort, soothe.
- Emphasise that this was a dream and the bad people won't come back.
- Turn over the pillow. The cool side has special properties that prevent bad dreams!
- Place a dim light in the room.

- When ghosts and monsters cause fear, explain they have gone; even do a joint search behind the curtains and under the bed.
- One boy said he couldn't sleep as his bed was full of insects. His mother got the dust buster and after a whirr of vacuuming he was assured they were all gone.
- Creative parents use ghost repellent spray. This is a simple water spray with glitter particles in the bottom. Spray around doors and windows for guaranteed security.
- Talk about dreams by day to emphasise what is real and what is pretend.
- When they are distressed with fever give them paracetamol.
- Allow frightened children to come to your bed.
- Beware the child who repeatedly cries wolf, using fear as a way to attract attention. When attention seeking is the aim, gradually lengthen the response time until the reward is not worth the effort.

Night terrors

Night terrors are different from nightmares. They are not a dream, just an uncomfortable move through the deepest part of sleep. The child cries out apparently frightened, yet totally switched off, open-eyed and unaware. Nothing seems to soothe; all we can do is to stay close, talk gently and wait until they settle. In the morning they have no recollection of any disturbance.

Night terrors are more common in the preschool and younger school ages. They occur in the early part of the night and, if regular, can be avoided by waking the child half an hour before the usual time of terror.

Obsessive behaviour

It is cute when your child hops down the footpath, avoids the lines and steps only in the squares. It's impressive when they can name and draw every dinosaur. But there comes an extreme point when this is neither cute nor impressive – it is obsessive and odd.

There are thousands of children out there who are normal yet very unusual. Most are boys and most have a preoccupation with order, routine and an area of over-interest.

One eight-year-old I work with has an obsessive bath routine. Only he can insert the plug and the bath water can only rise to a certain level. The bath cannot end until he has lifted out his toys and placed them in an exact spot. Then he removes the plug and some normality returns.

Another seven-year-old insists that only he turn off the television set. If others interfere, it must be turned on, run for a minute, and then only he can switch it off. On leaving for school he must close the front door and can only enter the car through the back left-hand door.

We see others who will only eat at a certain spot at the dining table, insist on wearing specific clothes despite the temperature or hold tight to a favourite object.

Some parents who read this will think, 'Stop pandering to the brat. Just knock him into shape.' But those who have tried this find the explosive aftershock is not worth the effort. We often try to desensitise and remove the obsessions, only to find they are replaced by a new area of over-interest.

Many of these children are fixated on some part of learning. They may have an immense knowledge of animals, cars, planes, football, video titles or events in history. Their conversation is often inappropriate, turning into a lecture on their special topic. At school some are branded 'weird', while others are accepted as an eccentric professor.

Sometimes there is a worrying over-interest in wars, guns and death. Though this is no more sinister than an over-interest in football or dinosaurs, it usually results in psychiatric referral.

As I work with these children I must decide when this is a normal odd temperament and when it is a pathological problem like Asperger syndrome, autism spectrum disorder, semantic pragmatic language disorder (see Chapter 11, page 125) or obsessive compulsive disorder.

My decision is based on the depth of the fixation, how it interferes with life, the child's social skills and the quality of both verbal and non-verbal communication. When in any doubt, children who may have obsessive behaviour should be referred to a paediatrician, child psychiatrist or specialist in child development.

Only children

The only child is often said to be lonely, spoiled and over-influenced by adults. There is a seed of truth in this, but there is more to the story. On average, the only child gets more stimulation, education and individual attention at home. This shows as a slight increase in academic ability, and they are more in tune with adult thinking.

The downside for the child is the lack of company and absence of a playmate. They may be weaker in the skills they need to mix with other children. Their attitudes may be too adult and their talk can be inappropriate for a child.

There are more only children born to older or sole parents. One of these groups is disadvantaged by lack of energy, the other by lack of cash. But when you add it all up it's a case of swings and roundabouts. If we use a good preschool and arrange for extra mixing with other children, everyone is a winner.

I believe that an extended family upbringing is of more importance than having a brother or sister. This lets children see their roots and gives them experience with babies and family relationships and a respect for the elders of the tribe. There is a saying, 'It takes a village to raise a child.' I think a village full of people is more important than a brother or sister in an empty city.

Oppositional behaviour

One of the most common and difficult problems I see is the child with entrenched opposition. When this problem is in its most minor form the child is reluctant to comply with any request. When it is major, home life becomes deadlocked and parents feel they have lost control.

You ask politely, 'Would you please do this?'

They reply, 'Try and make me!'

You draw a line in the sand, they jump over the limit and ask, 'What are you going to make of it?'

Parents with compliant children have no understanding of how difficult this can be. Opposition generates immense hostility, which ruins relationships.

When I am told, 'My eleven-year-old refuses to do anything she is asked,' I know this is not a new behaviour. Opposition usually starts at about the age of three years and gets deeper as parent and child become more entrenched. Opposition hits its peak in teenage, by which time it is almost impossible to move.

The amount of opposition in a child depends on their individual style of temperament and how this has been managed. Many children are created with an obliging temperament, and whatever we do they generally remain compliant. But most children have the potential to some opposition. If they are nurtured and encouraged, this rarely poses much problem, but if they are parented with force, confrontation and hostility, this seed may sprout into considerable trouble.

A few children are created with a large potential for opposition. Even with the best parents, behaviour will be a battle, and when pushed heavily these children become defiant, angry and totally immovable. Some of this extreme group are spiteful and paranoid, blaming all the other ratbags for their problems.

There is good and bad news about opposition. The bad is the damage it does to families where mums and dads may get no pleasure from parenting. The good news is that most turn into well-adjusted, normal adults. Many will later feel remorse and wish they had done things differently, but this is often at their parent's funeral, and by then it's too late.

Opposition is extremely hard to treat. Be realistic in your expectations. A twenty per cent change in six months is an appropriate goal.

- Go gently with the difficult three- and four-year-old. This is the best age to nip opposition in the bud. At three and four years be positive, encourage the good, let the unimportant pass and steer around confrontation.
- With the oppositional school-age child avoid debate as this escalates and places parents on the back foot.
- Don't rely on reason. This does not impress the oppositional child.
- Avoid hostile, cold, passive-aggressive or sarcastic comments.
- Avoid ultimatums and rigid limits. These provide a clear line to challenge.
- Avoid backing the child into a corner. Allow them to feel they have some choice and power over the outcome: 'You can choose not to do your homework now but you will be choosing not to watch "The Simpsons" – it's your choice.'
- Communicate in a way that transmits an expectation of compliance.
- Talk in a calm, matter-of-fact way. Use the broken gramophone technique, quietly repeating the message.
- Use the technique of active ignoring. Briefly move to another room, or water the garden, then return and re-engage.
- Use an 'I' statement. 'I feel sad when we are angry with each other.'
- Make your statement and move on. Don't hang around waiting for retaliation.
- Immediately grasp any good behaviour and appreciate the positives.

- Work as a team: 'We managed that well together.'
- Calmly give a choice: 'You can do this now or I can wake you early and you can do it before school.'
- With older children consider a trade-off: 'You can choose not to do your chores and I can choose whether to drive you to soccer training.'
- Withdrawal of privileges may be of benefit, though it can backfire. 'No television tonight'; 'To bed half an hour early'; 'No telephone'; 'No friend to stay over'; 'It's your choice'.

Pocket money

Little children have no need for pocket money before they start school. A six-year-old gets a small allowance that is usually squandered or lent to their sister, the con-artist. But by the age of eight years the potential Bonds and Bransons have realised that money talks. These short-pants entrepreneurs can be motivated by the sight of a silver coin, but by teenage it takes crisp notes, gold bars or share-option certificates to have the same effect.

The amount of pocket money depends on how much you can afford, what extras the child must buy and your neighbourhood norm. After this you have three choices:

1) Pay a fixed weekly sum that is reviewed each year, with adjustments based on inflation, the world economy and how you are feeling on that day.
2) Provide a base salary, then pay double for each day that work is completed without reminders or complaint.
3) With older children you can draw up a carefully costed contract. List what purchases will come from consolidated revenue and those they must fund themselves. Agree on a fee-for-service scheme where you are charged a small levy for every chore. This provides a basic wage with extra pay for productivity.

Pretend friends

At my age, if I start talking to imaginary people you would probably call for an ambulance. But normal young children are allowed to talk and play with pretend people.

This occurs in about one in ten children, usually starting at about the age of three years, an age of technicolour imagination. The friend is usually of the same sex as the child and always has a name. To the outsider there is an air of reality, but the child is actually quite aware of what is fact and fiction. Imaginary friends are not a sign of disturbance, loneliness or emotional stress. They are more common in girls and may signify a more creative style of temperament.

If your child prattles on to some pretend person, just relax and enjoy this brief window of undisturbed innocence. These friends have usually evaporated by the age of six years. Some children befriend an animal. One little boy used to bring a dinosaur on a rope when he visited me in my office.

Some families chat to objects as a bit of fun. One well-known Australian told how his daughter loved the Sydney Harbour Bridge. Every time they drove across she talked to the bridge and her dad joined in to keep her company. 'Recently,' he said, 'my daughter and I were driving across with my mother-in-law. I talked to the bridge as usual, at which point Grandma asked, ''What's your father up to?" My daughter looked blank and replied, "Beats me if I know."'

Shoplifting

Petty shoplifting is probably more common than any parent wishes to acknowledge. It is more likely when children are allowed to loiter around shops or they associate with friends who set the wrong example.

With shoplifting, it is easier to pretend it never happened, but parents and child must front up to the shop. It's tough, but unless the child faces up to their actions no lesson is learnt. Goods must be returned and if this is not possible, repayment comes from future pocket money. Don't set impossible reparation demands: this is how the Second World War started.

In my experience, children from functional families will usually respond to a firm, friendly, non-critical approach. Some parents introduce the offending child to the local constable who gives some fatherly advice, but this is further than most need to go.

If stealing ever becomes a major problem, you may need to seek help from a psychologist or community clinic.

Short fuse

There are a lot of sparky children, some with the stability of out-of-date gelignite. Parents handle these with the greatest of care, knowing that the slightest bump may blow their head off. Poor impulse control is predominantly a boy problem, though girls, including mothers, are not exempt. This style of temperament has a strong hereditary link, and many of these children are like a parent or grandparent.

This is often part of the spectrum of ADHD, a condition caused by inadequate function of the frontal parts of the brain. These parts affect the self-monitoring of learning and behaviour. The biggest problem of ADHD comes from the child's unthinking actions and impulsive behaviour. For more information on ADHD see Chapter 12, page 138.

Short-fuse ADHD behaviours are more common in sole-parent situations. This may be because ADHD can be inherited from a parent, and in these cases conception may have been somewhat impulsive and ongoing impulsivity has destabilised the relationship. I work with many mums who are left with the difficult child of a difficult man.

Explosiveness is at its most extreme in the three- and four-year-old. With age, the fuse gradually lengthens. One of the most memorable children of recent times was a boy aged three years. After a consultation punctuated by tantrums and flying toys, I asked the mum, 'Is it always as bad as this?'

She calmly replied, 'Yes. I can't cope, my husband can't cope, the grandparents can't cope, even our German shepherd guard dog is terrified of him.'

This story did have a happy ending. Tim had extreme ADHD, which responded well to treatment. Three months later I asked his mum, 'How are things?'

'The difference?' she said. 'Now I love him.'

The main problem at school age is volatility and unpredictability. The smallest unimportant event can trigger the most unexpected explosion. Parents gasp in disbelief: 'How so little can result in so much!' Outside the home other parents look over as if to say, 'Is that child mentally all right?' At school the sparky child is sought out by bullies who know they are easy to stir. When upset they may go berserk and hit out, and many may be suspended from school.

A parent who has not experienced this short-fuse type of temperament has no idea how it affects discipline. Mums and dads are in a dilemma about whether to stand firm and treat the child the same way they treat their other children or to back off and preserve the peace. The more I work with these children, the more often I promote the path of peace.

- With young children anticipate, avoid triggers, divert, keep calm. With older children get them to think how the behaviour appears to others and teach self-control techniques.
- Avoid debate and argument; this inflames and escalates.
- Try to maintain a calm, matter-of-fact appearance.
- Avoid actions and words that inflame. One mum said, 'We get on much better if I avoid the word "no".' There are better ways to say it without using that word.
- Move yourself away from the scene.
- Put the child in time out. This is a good idea but often it's impossible.
- Do not interpret the hysterical actions of a child as premeditated or malicious. The gentlest, most good-natured puppy may bite when stressed and frightened.
- With older children talk about the behaviour when they are calm. Get them to realise how stupid they appear in front of their friends.
- Try the stress-control techniques of taking deep breaths, counting to five, punching a pillow, getting outside.
- Notice and encourage when they turn the other cheek and let irritation pass.
- Try the 'traffic light' technique, where they stop, think and then go.
- When impulsivity is part of ADHD, its treatment will dramatically improve this behaviour.

Sleep problems

By school age most children sleep through the night. The main sleep problem they have is a difficulty getting off to sleep. This comes from one of three reasons:

1. a poorly disciplined sleep routine
2. a temperament that needs less sleep or
3. a busy mind.

A disciplined sleep routine is essential for all children and adults. Every night we should go through the same sequence of preparation at the same time. Don't accept procrastination in six- and seven-year-olds; get them horizontal and hope the eyes glaze and shut. Only allow slight modification of routine at weekends, as late nights and long sleep-ins disrupt the week-day pattern.

The need for sleep is similar in most children at a given age. But there are extremes, where some children need much more sleep and others run happily on less. If a child settles late, yet is fresh and well-rested in the morning, they may be designed for a later bedtime. Often the child with low sleep needs will have a late-to-bed, early-riser parent.

A busy mind stops some children from settling at night. They go to bed with their brains racing and they can't let go. We see this in busy or anxious children as well as some with ADHD.

With these circling minds we need to help them unwind and establish a routine that prepares for bed. Stories seem to relax, particularly when a child is old enough to read to themselves. Video games and television in the bedroom tend to stir. Relaxation tapes and gentle music are said to be of benefit, but despite all this I still have great difficulty helping this group.

In recent years I have reluctantly sedated some extreme four- to six-year-olds who had never been able to settle before 11pm.

A few five-year-olds still come to their parents' bed each night. If everyone is happy with this situation there is no need to act. Children soon get fed up sleeping with their parents in the same way that we get fed up sleeping with them. If you have had enough of this intrusion, give advance warning and then evict. You can accommodate the occasional visit by placing a mattress on your floor, but they must lie down low and not rise to a higher altitude.

Sleep walking

This is not a rare condition – about ten per cent of all children have an occasional walk and two per cent are quite regular. It's more common in boys and usually occurs in the early part of the night.

Sleep walking is not a dream state – these children are in the deepest part of sleep. They sit up and start to move in a stiff, robotic manner. Their eyes are glazed, yet they can navigate around obstacles, open doors and perform simple tasks. If addressed, they respond but the words are like computer speech or unintelligible. If woken, they are unaware, and in the morning they remember nothing. Each walk lasts a few minutes, though some can continue for up to an hour.

There is no need to wake the sleepwalker. This can be extremely diffi-cult and causes nothing but confusion. Instead, bring them back to bed and protect them from danger. One of my earliest experiences as a junior in paediatric emergency was treating a seriously injured girl who had walked through an upstairs window. Parents can't stop sleep walking but they must keep their children safe. This is done with security locks, alarm bells or saucepans balanced on door handles. Sleep walking lessens with age, though some are still on the move as adolescents or adults.

Socially out of tune

Most children are out and out charmers, but a few are socially clumsy. They play poorly, mix with difficulty and don't see how their behaviour irritates others. If you feel that your child may be socially out of tune there are some things you can do to help:

- Reinforce when they play well and interact appropriately.
- Give a brief reminder when their actions are upsetting others.
- Don't become negative or constantly criticise.
- Discreetly ask them how it would feel if they were in the other person's place.
- Social skills training programs are sometimes suggested but these are often more successful in the therapy room than the outside world.
- The development of social skills comes gradually with age and maturity.

See also Chapter 14, page 157.

Soiling, or encopresis

Almost two out of every 100 children at the age of seven years will still poo in their pants. Over half of these have never been bowel trained, while the others have slipped from the straight and narrow. There are more boy soilers than girls. The literature suggests that most of these are chronically constipated, but this is not my experience.

Soiling rarely occurs during the night, is unusual in the morning session of school and is most common between 2pm and bedtime. Analytically minded psychiatrists interpret this timing as a symbolic landing of manure on your mum.

But I believe these children are created with a soil-prone gut, which is tipped over the edge by some known or unknown trigger. This may result from the pain of constipation, the birth of a sibling, admission to hospital or stress in the family. But most commonly there is no obvious triggering event.

Some parents believe the child has control and the problem is deliberate. But this is not true: the children I see would like nothing better than to stop soiling. I see parallels with adults who smoke – the majority would love to quit, if only they had the strength. The adult only changes when one night they attend an inspirational session with the Dalai Lama. They leave the hall uplifted and never smoke again.

Often it takes an outside force like this to change entrenched human behaviour. When soiling has gone on for years parents are defeated, and children can't do it alone. Often the change comes with the enthusiasm and inspiration of a talented psychologist or paediatrician (the outside force).

The first step in treatment is to exclude constipation. This is not always straightforward as some children are badly blocked yet present with the confusing symptom of diarrhoea. This happens when a large ball of constipation grossly distends the gut and allows looseness to seep around the edges. This block can be excluded if the child is able to regularly pass sausage-shaped motions. When in doubt we trial a laxative such as liquid paraffin in its more palatable form of Parachoc.

Behavioural change comes with an encouraging attitude and a simple star chart (see Chapter 4, page 35). We initially put all the focus on sitting three times a day: before school, following school and following dinner. After this we direct the attention from sitting to encourage one moment of success. Then we concentrate on regular usage and clean days. About one-third respond to this rapidly, one-third take six months or more and the remainder are extremely hard to shift.

Suicide talk

Youth suicide is a great concern and any child who talks of self-harm must be taken seriously. Though teens and young adults are at greatest risk, the child of ten years or younger can occasionally commit suicide.

In the five- to twelve-year age group talk of self-harm is a common means of hijacking attention. Children will often say, 'I'm dumb. I'm bad. I've got no friends. What's the point in living? What would you do if I killed myself?' The dilemma for parents is to separate these martyr statements from a genuine cry for help.

Though cautious, I generally underplay such comments in these younger ages, but only if all else is on track. The alarm bells ring when there is a change in personality, loss of interest, withdrawal from friends, major sadness or an over-focus on the means of self-injury. Children are also at greater risk following the suicide of some major public figure or someone in their close community.

At this young age most of the talk of self-harm has the sole purpose of stirring up mums and dads. But nothing in this world is completely certain, so when in the slightest doubt be quick to ask for help. See also this chapter, Depression, page 79.

Suspension from school

Most suspensions follow unthinking outbursts where a child hits, hurts, insults or gets so angry they refuse to comply. This is usually associated with the short-fuse temperament described in this chapter on page 94.

In my experience most of these children are kind, sensitive kids with no malice in their make-up. They simply have a vulnerable Achilles heel in their volatile temperament. When pushed too far they snap and hit trouble.

With many school suspensions the wrong person has been blamed. One child in my care was suspended for abusing a teacher and kicking the principal. It all started when he was peacefully eating his lunch. A well-known bully pushed over his drink and called him a retard. This ignited the fuse and he went wild. A passing teacher misread the situation and abused him further. The principal intervened clumsily and got a kick for his ineptitude. The boy was banished for a week, the parents, who worked, were disadvantaged and the thug who started it all was never cautioned.

Recently, a seven-year-old was suspended and referred to me for psychiatric assessment. He was seen as severely disturbed as he had tried to hang himself in the school yard. Everyone was so busy psychoanalysing the child they failed to think back to the previous day's teaching on the outlaw Ned Kelly and his death by hanging. This ADHD boy, with mild intellectual disability, was playing out a story. His problem was imagination and lack of sense, not a death wish.

When a child is suspended from school, always look past the reported crime to see why it happened. It may not change the decision, but the true culprits should be brought to justice. When suspension results from the impulsivity of ADHD, this is the priority for treatment.

Parents will be annoyed but they must not get too heavy and bully the school. Even in suspension the parent–teacher relationship must be guarded at all costs (see Chapter 9, page 109).

Thumb sucking

This is an innocent habit, not a sign of emotional insecurity. It gives pleasure to one-third of young children; the other two-thirds never suck their thumbs. The average age that children stop is three and a half years, though many continue until they're five and two per cent are still sucking at thirteen years.

The main reason that parents discourage thumb sucking is the criticism they get from passers by and well-meaning relatives: 'That child has an emotional problem. He's behaving like a baby.' Dentists become worried once the second teeth are about to appear, because heavy sucking increases the risk of protruding front teeth, which may need wiring to realign. Bank managers are not unhappy with thumb sucking and are quick to provide a large loan to fund the wires.

At school age most thumb sucking is in times of boredom, tiredness and especially when settling to sleep. A little gentle comfort is never a problem, but hours of heavy tooth bending could prove expensive.

The old-fashioned psychoanalysts had no interest in tooth alignment. To them this was full of the sexual symbolism of large upstanding lighthouses, trains and tunnels. Treatments used to involve elbow splints, sleeping in gloves and covering thumbs in foul-tasting paint. Nowadays there is no such interpretation: we just let the child know we worry what other people think and we explain the risks of sticking-out teeth.

It's okay to allow gentle sucking while settling to sleep, but on other occasions distract or give a low-key reminder. Never nag or become too heavy as this causes stress, which increases sucking and then drives it underground. When in doubt, talk to your dentist. They will advise and tell you if damage is occurring.

Tics and twitches

A tic is caused by an involuntary twitch of a small muscle. Usually this involves the head and neck, the most common being a blink or twitch of the eyelid. Tics may show as movement of the lip, nose, neck or shoulder or a clearing of the throat.

When a child twitches they have no direct control of this movement. Stress makes things worse, while the tic totally disappears in sleep. Tics can be there most of the time, but they are usually intermittent. They tend to wax and wane and many, if not most, resolve spontaneously. The peak starting age is around seven years, but tics can appear at any time from four years to twelve years.

Tics cause frustration to parents and teachers, but are usually of less concern to the child. By themselves they are benign, though they are often not alone, being associated with ADHD difficulties with learning and behaviour. In this combination it is ADHD that causes most of the problem and is the main priority for treatment.

The best management is to remain calm and make a minimum of fuss. Give gentle reminders but don't over-focus, as this makes things worse. Counselling to reduce tension, relaxation and reward techniques are sometimes recommended, but the results are fairly unimpressive. Very occasionally we treat children with tic-reducing medication but this is only in extreme cases. A severe case may be termed Tourette syndrome, which involves major movements of the neck and shoulder and noises in the throat.

Tidying the bedroom

I often wonder if there is a tidiness gene. If there is, some children are born with this vital bit missing. With untidy children we must accept there will be some shambles and hope a good spouse will fix them in the future.

There are other children who have reasonable tidiness, but their over-tidy parents have the problem. I know one family where the son is average-messy, but his mother has an overdose of organisation. On her return from the fruit market she can't relax until the apples are polished and the carrots lined accurately in the veggie drawer.

Everything at home is in its place and it is no surprise that she fights with her son over his untidiness. For most of us parenthood brings new meaning to the word 'mess', but it's a concept this mother has not grasped. Her ordered brain is better suited to the obsessive administration of the contraceptive pill than children.

The secret of tidiness is to start early. Children between the age of one and four years like to be helpful, so build on this while it is there. After the age of five there are a number of strategies you can try:

- Provide easy access to storage and hanging space.
- Get stackable plastic boxes and label what goes where.
- Regularly cull all junk and outgrown clothes.
- Sort through toys, removing stuff that doesn't work and small items that constipate the vacuum cleaner.
- Remove glass marbles from the toy box. When they hit the Hoover the beaters go berserk.
- With a young child, tidy together.
- Before complaining, make sure your children know what you expect of them.
- Ask them to tidy, and make it clear that you will follow up with an inspection.
- Use a kitchen timer to count down to inspection.
- Use the 'carrot' incentive: 'You tidy this, I'll get your drink ready.'
- Have a preset inspection time each day.
- A star chart can help focus attention on the clean room at inspection time.
- For each day of relative tidiness add a small productivity bonus to the pocket money.
- Be quick to notice effort and tidiness: 'Gosh, have the cleaners been here?'
- After giving adequate warning, place all untidied items in a large polythene bag. Lock this away for several days.
- Go one step further and gather all you see at a fixed time each evening. Lock away for one week. At an agreed time, empty the week's collection in a pile and reimpound anything that is not put away.
- Don't expect children to be more organised and tidy than their parents. Children who live with pigs learn to grunt.
- If you don't have this sorted out by teenage, take a step back and ask, 'Is it worth driving my children from home for the sake of a clean bedroom?'

Tooth grinding

When teeth are noisily ground by day, this is usually associated with severe intellectual disability. But tooth grinding at night is extremely common in normal, well-adjusted children.

Dentists worry that the repeated grinding can cause long-term tooth damage, while parents are more concerned by the noise. Some people believe that tooth grinding can cause malocclusion of the jaw, while others suggest that malocclusion can be the reason why they grind. Whatever is going on, discuss it with your dentist. If your child's teeth are becoming worn your dentist will provide a small night splint to give protection.

In your great-grandmother's day tooth grinding was thought a sure sign of worm infestation. But she got her ends mixed up: any worm that is out and about at night is at the bottom, not the top end.

Whingeing

Some children are born with an amazing talent for whingeing. When smacked by the midwife at birth, they don't cry, they just start whingeing. The grumbles go on through childhood, and presumably, as adults they complain about everything then join a protest group.

At the other end of the spectrum there is a remarkable breed of children who are totally whinge-free. They take life as it comes and never complain. As adults they can cope with all the major disasters such as flood, fire, earthquake, even bad hair cuts, wet Saturdays and parking tickets.

Finally, there are those children who don't start out as complainers but learn to whinge because it gets them what they want.

If you have a whinge-free child, light candles and give thanks for your good fortune. If whingeing is a learned habit used to change our decision, we must stand by our guns and prevent paying off.

- Give maximum attention for no whinge and, when possible, withhold attention for whingeing.
- When addressed, recognise the child is speaking, even if you can't answer their question immediately.
- If you ignore a child's attempts to talk politely they may replace this with whingeing.
- If you can't address their problem now, state clearly when you will answer their question. Say, 'I hear you – I will be with you in thirty seconds.'
- When you make an unwise decision, be quick to say, 'I got it wrong.' A quick turnaround removes the need to whinge.
- When you have got it right, don't let whingeing change the referee's decision.

- Label whingeing for what it is: 'That's whingeing. I don't answer whingeing.'
- Set some rules: 'If you are quiet for two minutes and ask again properly.'
- With a child who is a born whinger, anticipate, divert, ignore, occupy, put in another room, go outside, play music, use time out.

NINE

Starting school: the first weeks

School has an immense impact on our children. It's their seat of learning, their place of employment, their office and their social hub. Here they compete with others and develop the skills they need to achieve in the world.

School is supposed to be the happiest time of our lives, and this will be true for those who are academically and socially strong. There are some children, however, who tolerate but don't enjoy school, and others who hate it with a passion.

We feel the ups and downs of school as children bring their stresses home and dump on their mums and dads. Parents of star students walk with confidence and are prominent on school committees. Those with children who struggle or disrupt keep their heads down and react with an adult form of school refusal.

In the years between five and twelve there is a massive explosion of knowledge. At the start a child can barely hold a pen, write their name, count past twenty or read a word. By their thirteenth birthday most write with style, perform complex calculation and read like an adult. All this comes from hours of effort by teachers, parents and children.

Modern parents suffer from a speedy condition called hurry sickness. Life is lived at such a pace there is no time to savour the present. From the moment of birth they are pushing their children on the fast track to independence.

There is no need for such a rush: school enrolment is not compulsory until the age of five years.

The first day

The start of school for a child is like arriving to take up a new job for an adult. There are strange faces, names to learn and uncertain expectations, and unease hides behind every smile. This out-of-depth feeling is different from the tears and clinginess of the first day in preschool, which had all the dampness of a Kleenex advert. It takes two months for an adult to feel comfortable in a new situation, so do allow equal time for a child to settle.

Preparation is important. Talk about the school, let them try on the uniform, visit the class and participate in the orientation program. Be positive but be realistic – school is for education, not entertainment. School may cater for a lot of children but it's not Santa's cave or Disneyland.

Find out whether a child from preschool or the neighbourhood will be in your child's class and, if possible, ask them over during the holidays. Plan the food to take for lunch, but don't overcompensate with treats that rot their teeth and clog the coronaries.

On the first day allow yourself plenty of time to avoid the pressure of a rush. Ensure there are no clashing appointments so that you can have as much time as it takes. Walk in with a positive stride, introduce yourself to the class teacher, locate the toilets, put down the school bag and help your child find a friend. Let them know what is going to happen, when you are going to leave and the time you will be back. If there are any problems the teacher will tell you what to do. When they are settled, depart decisively.

Home behaviour: up and down

As learning and playing consume so much energy, excessive tiredness is almost universal among children starting school. Whether they want to discuss their day with you is much more variable. Some children arrive home with their heads full of adventures and a wish to talk non-stop. Others would divulge nothing, even if the KGB were providing a prompt.

For many, school becomes so important they talk, think and play it all the time. Infant sisters, dogs, cats and anything that can sit will be commandeered to become part of their teacher–pupil games.

Some children behave well at school but bring home their stresses and dump these on Mum. A few become nasty and spiteful to younger siblings, for a reason unclear to anyone but themselves. Occasionally they call on the sympathy vote and become the martyr: 'I'm dumb. No one likes me. I have no friends.'

Starting school is a major disruption to the stability of life, and behaviour that is normally good can slip off the straight and narrow. It's quite common for children just starting school to suddenly have unreliable bladders, unexpected clinginess, be defiant, or experience disturbed sleep and start coming to their parents' bed.

Some children start off well but after the second or third weekend they think, 'Home isn't all that bad after all.' This can produce temporary school refusal which resolves quickly if we are supportive but completely firm about attendance.

School behaviour: up and down

Teachers never have it easy, but the main problems for teachers of infant classes are holding attention, curbing call-outs and keeping bottoms on seats.

Sometimes I see a child who is emotionally or intellectually unsuited to start school. They may opt out, won't comply, crawl under desks or run off. These children may need a school counsellors to pinpoint their general or specific area of weakness.

At the start of school, children who suffer from Attention Deficit Hyperactivity Disorder (ADHD – which affects two per cent of school-age children) may be disruptive, distractable and out of step with others. A few of these children are immensely volatile, with explosive outbursts that occasionally put other children at risk. For more information about ADHD see Chapter 12, page 138.

Teachers in general are tolerant people who allow time for all but the most extreme behaviours to come good. For this reason it is unusual for parents to hear much negative feedback in the first month.

However, occasionally it is almost instantaneous that the muck hits the fan. With major problems I always ask the parents when they got that call. For a long time the record stood at twenty minutes on day one, but another mum trumped this: 'My son was suspended on orientation day.'

Good parent–teacher communication

At the start of school make a commitment to keep in touch with the class teacher. It's unfair to ambush a tired teacher every day and expect an in-depth consultation, but a lack of involvement may be interpreted as a lack of interest. It's best to take a mid-position: not too pushy but make sure you know what's happening. Aim to touch base every two weeks. Just ask, 'Is everything okay? Is there anything I can do to help?'

If you hear rumours, worry about any part of learning or are just concerned, be quick to talk to the class teacher. If there is a major problem, make an appointment to meet, so that the school can be prepared and allocate ample time to address your questions.

Over the years I have dealt with a lot of unreasonable, aggressive parents who have more interest in kicking heads than supporting their child's education. Don't begin with anger, accusations and heavy confrontation. Teachers are human and, like anyone else, they will become defensive, official and distant when aggressively challenged. So if you

intend to keep your child at the school, establish close and respectful parent-teacher communication from the start.

Worries about learning

At least one child in ten has some weakness in learning (see Chapter 11, page 125). The most common problems include specific learning problems with reading and spelling (dyslexia), problems with attention, memory and work output (ADHD), problems with expression and understanding (language delay disorder), or a general slowness in learning (borderline or mild intellectual disability). The specific learning weaknesses are strongly hereditary, which means that a parent who struggled at school may have a child with the same difficulty. If your child seems to be following in your footsteps, be quick to ask for help.

Most early concerns are just a lag in maturity that will come good with short-term help. For others, the difficulties will cause pain throughout the school years and into adulthood. Be aware that learning problems can pass unnoticed and may only be looked into when a child opts out or expresses their frustration via bad behaviour.

As schools tend to give children the benefit of the doubt and allow time to settle, it is often the parents who will make the first move in asking for help. If you have the slightest concern talk to the class teacher. Ask direct questions about your child's abilities in general learning, reading, maths, independent work output, mixing and playground behaviour. Ask if they are middle of the class, above average or below average in each one of these specifics.

Ask if these concerns should be taken further. The help is out there, but it's often you, the parent, who needs to make the first move.

Starting school

1. Preparation
   - attend orientation day
   - talk about school
   - find a friend who is starting
   - prepare for independent feeding and toiletting

2. The first day
- allow plenty of time
- let them know what's going to happen
- let them know when they are going to be picked up
- if there is any trouble, talk to the teacher

3. Home behaviour
- tiredness is universal
- some dump on Mum or a sibling
- some become unreliable in sleep or night wetting
- some refuse to go to school after two weeks (this is temporary)

4. School behaviour
- attention drifts
- call-outs
- walkabout
- behaviour may be a sign of a learning problem

5. Good parent–teacher communication
- make this a priority
- show interest but don't be too pushy
- ask how you can help
- don't overreact or get too heavy
- when parents are aggressive, teachers become defensive and communication stops

6. Worries about learning
- one in ten have some learning difficulty
- specific difficulties, especially reading, language and attention, can run in families
- talk to the teacher

The early school years: behaviours and concerns

Each morning parents face an uphill challenge: how to steer that slow-moving body towards school. Mission accomplished, the child's day is filled with periods of listening, learning, mixing, acting smart and getting annoyed. In the afternoon they return home to do homework and to unload on their parents. Let's look at the behavioural hurdles that concern parents as they try to make a success of school.

Wriggling and walkabouts

At the start of school most little children sit, listen intently and marvel at the words of their teacher. A few are much more noisy, wriggly and disruptive. They are not naughty, it's just that they haven't located the switch to control impulse. Every infant teacher will regularly restate the rules of the class: 'Stay in your seat. Keep hands and feet to yourself. Speak only when you're asked. Hand up if you need help or need to go to the toilet.'

Compliance is reinforced with positive statements: 'Good sitting'; 'Good attending'; 'Good work'; 'Good manners'. When the rules are broken the teacher registers this with a sign, a single word or the shortest of short statements.

As children get older, the most inattentive can be refocused using a token system. For every ten minutes they stay on task, a bead is popped in a container. When the total reaches ten, there is a payout with a privilege such as a special book, delivering a message, or possibly computer time. Privileges motivate but are tough on the silent majority, who wonder why the 'bad boys' get all the good stuff.

Teasing and taunts

When my children started school I taught them to sidestep taunts. My wife, who is more practical, suggested they turn the other cheek then aim carefully and hit hard.

The child who is most teased is usually the one who overreacts to the smallest annoyance. Bullies target the impulsive, short-fuse child because they provide a jackpot every time. The teased child is usually innocent, but because they throw the last punch they are labelled aggressive.

I see children suspended from school following their justified overreaction to an annoying bully. They are put out for a week while the aggressor who caused the problem gets off scot-free.

When a five- or six-year-old is victimised at school parents should discuss the problem with the teacher or principal. Don't get too heavy: just state the facts as you see them and ask for advice. Teachers can deal with the problem by extra supervision or through a general instruction to the class about the treatment of fellow humans. In some schools a buddy is attached to those who are vulnerable for extra support.

When children are eight years or older parents can discreetly discuss the problem with the teacher, then use role-play to show how to sidestep conflict. Act things out in the calm of your home: get them to count quietly to five, walk away or respond with a set piece – 'That's interesting'; 'You seem to be having a bad day.' You would probably like to teach them a cleverer response like 'Did someone talk or did a dog pass wind?' but this might get them flattened.

Our aim is to teach children to fight with their brains rather than their bodies. But it is much easier to talk about turning the other cheek than it is to put it into practice. Ignoring annoyance is hard enough for an adult – it's almost impossible for a young child.

Bullies

We teach our children that bullying is bad, but bullies are often the ones that make it big in our adult world. Children may bully because they have low self-esteem and feel uplifted by dragging others down. Some have poor social skills and are slow to realise they have overstepped the mark. A lot bully because that's what they see at home.

Bullying takes many forms: intimidation, physical force, standover tactics and the emotional cruelty of isolation and exclusion.

As parents, our first aim is to protect our children; the next is to promote assertiveness. Giving in to bullying all the time can bring peace, but it has its own dangers. Children who always give in may never develop assertiveness, or may begin to enjoy being the victim because it attracts adult attention: 'Why does everybody treat me so badly?' (see also Chapter 8, Martyrdom, page 86).

With a five- or six-year-old, take your worries straight to the class teacher. With older children help them to develop assertiveness. Teach them to use words instead of retaliating physically or just surrendering: 'I don't like you pushing me'; 'I don't want to be held or touched'; 'I'm not going to chase you'; 'That's my property'.

A good school accepts that bullying does happen but makes it clear that it will not be accepted at any level. The class teacher can intervene directly or talk to the class about the feelings of others. If the school develops a herd resistance to teasing and bullying, the problem will diminish.

School refusal

It is quite common for a child to start school with great enthusiasm then, after several weeks, have a change of heart. Absence makes them see home as a pretty special place and they decide to opt for early graduation. The child has a point: if we make home life so good, why should they want to go to school? This temporary reluctance can be easily overcome if parents are gentle but firm and work closely with the teacher.

At older ages school refusal is a more serious problem. Sometimes it is

due to learning difficulty or the child is socially uncomfortable. If you see it from their point of view, why should they go to a place that causes such pain? The remedy is to address the primary problem and try to create areas of success that will make school worthwhile.

School refusal can be a psychological symptom where a child is frightened to leave their mum or dad. Sometimes these worries are without foundation, but often, where there is smoke there is a fire. I recently saw a ten-year-old boy who refused to go to school. Two months previously his mother had been diagnosed with early breast cancer. Though no one had said much in words, he picked up on his parents' fears and upset. This boy didn't want to let his mum out of sight as he was frightened he might lose her.

Sometimes it is a parent who secretly clings to their child and generates separation anxiety. This can be hard to unravel and solve because the parent's manipulation is often subtle or subconscious. Here we need to address the parent's unresolved problems of emotion with psychiatric intervention.

The first step in managing school refusal is to return the child to the classroom. Missing school is like falling off a horse: if you don't get in the saddle now it becomes much more difficult in the future. If decisive returns and quick exits have not worked, the parents and class teacher need to meet and work out a joint plan.

There can be concessions but also firm limits. Dad will drive the child to school and walk in the gate with them, but then they are in the hands of the class teacher and they must stay. When the situation is stuck in deadlock a school counsellor will provide more specialised support. Where a child or parent's emotional baggage is causing the block, it's time for expert psychological or psychiatric intervention.

Tall stories

The mind of a six-year-old still bubbles with magic and innocence. They have the ability of a Fleet Street editor to blur truth and fiction. If your little one still believes in Santa and the Easter Bunny, their account of what happened at school may be pretty unreliable. If they come home to report that they are being beaten because they can't read, this may not be fact. Start by finding the truth – 'The truth is out there.'

When stories are over-colourful or untrue, it's best to listen, then simply state, 'I hear what you say, but I don't think it's quite like that.' Don't get too heavy; this magic age ends all too quickly. After eight we have a more secretive little person with many of the hang-ups and strange ideas of an adult.

Telling tales

A five-year-old is not only fascinated by rules, they believe they have a duty to inform on their mates. 'Miss, Jenny isn't listening'; 'Jack made a rude noise'; 'He can't go to the toilet without asking.' Though no one has published the research, it is possible that the fairer the sex, the more frequent the telling of tales.

This is a quaint behaviour that only lasts for a very short time. It's best to be deaf to tales or to make a brief comment: 'That's telling tales. I don't want to hear that.' Telling tales hits a peak between five years and six years, but by the age of seven it's on the fade. After eight there is a code of silence where it becomes uncool to tell on your friends.

Petty theft

Young children are not adults: they don't understand our attitude towards possessions, ownership, money and the finer print of contractual law. At infant school, if a piece of property is left within reach, it may end up in a pocket. This small-time stealing is quite common and relatively innocent.

Unfortunately, however, there are always other parents who think the worst: 'That child has home problems'; 'He's a deprived child who is stealing love'; 'It's a throwback to her convict or bushranger relatives'.

I often see parents create a major drama. A child lifts another's pencil or some piece of valueless plastic junk. The parents feel their child has been violated, and they almost dial 999 to summon a team of detectives to interrogate the kindergarten kleptomaniac.

In the early school years children should be discouraged from bringing small stealable items to school. When an offence happens, make the minimum fuss, just state that the property is not theirs and return it to the owner.

With age we need to be far firmer. A few, apparently well-adjusted children continue to steal belongings or money from their mates. In general it is overcome by a firm but low-key response, followed by close supervision (see also Chapter 8, Shoplifting, page 94).

Acting smart

After the age of eight years every class has its prize smart arse. These children are masters of the art of taunting teachers. They clown, answer back and generate strange bodily sounds. Boys cause the greatest bother and the problem gets worse right through to the end of high school. Many of those who clown are weak in some area of education and their performance allows a few moments of recognition.

The skilled teacher has a nose for stirrers and will seat them apart while keeping them well in view. They anticipate times of trouble, hold attention and keep minds occupied. But it is hard to handle these intrusions. To turn a blind eye gives a message of acceptance; to make a fuss takes the bait and keeps them fishing.

With a class clown, it is essential to lay down some ground rules in a time of peace, after which the teacher will give a pre-discussed sign and follow through. Some use a three-strike system. The child starts each lesson with three 'lives', and for each intrusion, one life is lost. Zero at the end results in a five-minute wait before release.

Acting smart is often a sign that the child's ability to learn or the teacher's method is inadequate. Unfortunately for teachers, some children are unsuited to school. They think of it as worse than a prison sentence, except that at least when you're sent to prison you usually score less than thirteen years.

Hard-working, achieving class mates sense the injustice when the worst-behaved child gets the most attention, earns extra rewards and receives merit certificates. At this early age children are discovering a well-known fact of life: 'He who makes the greatest fuss gets the most.'

Homework

Most children see homework as a necessary evil that has to be done, but for some it's about procrastination, foot dragging and excuses. In the early years homework plays a small part in learning but by teenage the ability to organise, stick at a task and study independently is vital for tertiary success.

The foundation for good study is to start early and for parents to be actively involved. Parents can provide structure, encouragement and a means of quality control, but it's not about spoon feeding or doing it yourself (one father recently complained that his highly researched project on the environment had scored a worse mark than the multi-page thesis written by another class parent). The ways to encourage homework are:

- Establish the importance of home study right from the start.
- Have knowledge and interest in the syllabus, check that work is completed and be enthusiastic about marks for effort.
- Have a regular homework time and keep strictly to this every day.
- After school give twenty minutes to change, snack and prepare.
- Give a ten-minute, five-minute and one-minute warning – then start.
- Let them work in a special place that is always associated with homework.
- Get them started, go through the instructions, give structure and set time limits.
- If attention span is weak, expect twenty minutes full output, a ten-minute break, then twenty minutes more. Use a timer to act as a referee.
- When the work is completed, check but don't dishearten or snoop. Sign it off if necessary.
- Some children manage better when homework is done before arrival home. The school may have a homework class or they might use a room at Auntie's office.
- Some children are morning people. An hour before breakfast may be worth two hours in the afternoon.
- Don't let homework destroy your parent–child relationship. If it gets too heated, discuss the options with the class teacher. Sometimes we have to let the school police their own problems.

To hot-house or not?

Recent research suggests that preschoolers carry a large number of unused brain cells just waiting to learn new skills. Then between two years and twelve years of age they shed the unused neurones, leaving a more trim, focused brain.

These cells may have nothing to do with important learning. For all we know, at twelve, children may discard the throwbacks from our ape ancestry, perhaps the pathways needed to swing from trees and scratch our bottoms. But it is possible that our children are losing a reservoir of untapped talent that is only available at this young age.

Certainly little children show great abilities to learn. I see new migrant children, without a word of English, yet six months of preschool has them chatting like native Australians. I am also impressed by the fact that many sports people, singers, movie stars and musicians have children with similar talent to their parents. Part of this may be in the genes, but early teaching must also make a difference.

We live in times when academic attainment seems all-important and an early education must have a value. But life education may be of more importance in the long run. In life, a child learns as an apprentice to their parents as they watch and work together.

The question on every parent's lips is, 'How much pushing is enough pushing?' The answer from this expert is, 'I don't know.' My heart favours the path of apprenticeship, example and time together, but I can't escape the evidence for teaching new skills early. Until we under-stand more clearly, there must be some sort of compromise. Not hot-housing; just a warm, nourishing home environment with some extra stimulation.

Tutors

When your children are learning to drive, you employ an outside instruc-tor because, not only are they willing to risk their life, but they are usually more patient and effective than a parent. Tutors are in the same league: they can impart more knowledge than Mum or Dad and with a lot less stress.

Tutoring can lift a child who is weak and maintain their enthusiasm to learn. The down side is that any remedial work naturally focuses atten-tion on the child's areas of difficulty and failure. Parents misunderstand the pain children feel and will tell me, 'He's lazy, he won't do his extra reading.' Of course, the child is not lazy; they are telling you it is hard and, in fact, it sucks!

Think of it from an adult point of view. If my wife had me tutored in line dancing and synchronised swimming, you'd see one mighty stroppy Christopher Green. For me, root canal therapy would be preferable – at least that's done under anaesthetic.

When arranging a tutor, try to get a personal recommendation and don't continue if the individual does not suit your child.

Never replace all play, sport or even television, with tutoring. There must be a balance: if school is stressful a child doesn't need to be further traumatised in their relaxation time.

Time and 'quality time'

I am a sailor who loves to escape to the blue sparkle off Sydney. If I have a few hours and the wind is fair, that is the time to get out there. I have various friends who crew, but not all are prepared to sail at the moment when the weather is just right. Some make so many conditions before they give of their time, it seems that Venus must be in line with Mars and the moon in its first quarter. Then there are the flexible enthusiasts who enjoy life and seize the moment. And they're the ones who get the benefit.

Parents can be like my sailing friends: they can either seize the moment and enjoy their children now, or forever put it off. And I'm not talking 'quality time', a trendy term that I hate with a passion. 'Quality time' implies small allocations from a parent's busy diary that is almost like a weekly appointment with a therapist. In fact, there is no such thing as quality time unless it is time that tunes in to a child's needs.

As I look back on the time I have spent with my own children, I have some regrets. I gave quality time but, as a busy paediatrician, it was usually on my terms. My youngest son had a fabulous stunt kite, which we loved to fly together. He often asked, but usually on occasions when I was too busy. When I had time, there was no wind. The kite has long since disintegrated; an opportunity was lost that will not return.

Organisation: teaching children to lower the wheels before landing

I have had some memorable landings in Sydney, watching from the flight deck of an in-bound Jumbo. The bridge and the harbour are spectacular but more impressive is the organised attitude of the pilots. They have landed thousands of times before but they still check, double check and talk through every step.

I don't know when a person first has that ability to stop, think ahead and move on. I doubt if there is much planning before the age of eight years, and in some humans, organisation is never a strong suit.

When I was at school I blocked valuable brain space learning Latin, algebra and a smattering of Greek. I might have been a genius if they had taught me instead the art of setting priorities, managing time, thinking ahead, jogging memory and giving the impression that I was in control.

As a child leaves the swimming pool we want them to stop for a second and ask, 'Have I got my towel? My cossie? My goggles? My bus pass?' At the end of the school day: 'What is my homework? Do I have the right books? Are there any notes for Mum? Is there anything else?' (see also Chapter 8, Forgetfulness, page 83).

Organisation starts with the tiniest baby who establishes a routine where they sleep, interact, feed, play and sleep. The toddler has a routine that leads to their bedtime, a bath, dinner, a story and then sleep.

At school age our goal is to get children to stop, think and plan. We can help this by asking at bedtime, 'What day is tomorrow? What's your first lesson? What do you need to bring to school? Any forms, money or messages for the teacher? Any sport or swimming?' Before leaving for school ask them to stop for a minute and run through the pre take-off checklist. Some parents act like the entertainment officer on a cruise ship: each morning they post the day's programme on the fridge door.

As children get older we should encourage notes and 'To do' lists, and we direct the focus onto priorities. We might attach written reminders to important objects like the bus pass, the lunch box or to prevent early entry to the mid-morning drink.

When a child rambles when they are talking we can give some structure: 'You saw a dog – which dog? . . . What did the dog do? . . . What happened after Jack was bitten? . . . What then?' With written work we introduce order: 'You went on a school excursion – where did you go? . . . What did you do? . . . What did you learn? . . . How did it end?'

As exam success is so essential we need to teach children to be organised in tests: 'Read the question carefully. Stick to the instructions. There are six questions and there's one hour. That's ten minutes for each question.'

At home we can teach forgetful children to do things at once or to use a memory jog. They can write on a hand, tie a knot in a handkerchief or move their watch to the wrong wrist. Help them remember things with simple rhymes: 'Thirty days hath September, April, June and November'; 'i before e, except after c'; 'It's your **pal**, the school princi**pal**'; 'The **car** is station**ar**y.' When children have a poor memory for names they can learn the technique of association. When they are introduced to Francis, Elizabeth and Monica, they think, 'Francis – he's the saint'; 'Elizabeth – she's the queen'; 'Monica **was** the president's friend.'

All this sounds so unnecessary when a child has an organised brain.

But many children have been created with all the forgetfulness of an absent-minded professor and need all the memory jogs we can give.

Maintaining the magic

As I was writing this chapter I received an unusual letter. The first two pages described a five-year-old boy who was pure perfection. Then the letter continued: 'You can see that Matthew is a well-adjusted, happy little person. So what's the reason for writing to you? I'd like to keep him that way!'

Most mums can relate to this. You spend five years getting close and supporting, nurturing and immersing your child in the values of your family. Then, at the start of school, the innocent Christian is cast to the lions.

There is no doubt that they will meet teasing, spite, drag-downs and bad language, but the home foundation will always remain the strongest influence. Even the twelve-year-old who treats their mum as if she's mentally impaired is far more influenced by the family circle than those outside.

It would be cosy to maintain this age of trust. These eternal Peter Pans could fight pirates, believe in fairies and know they will always come out on top. But living is about leaving the past and moving on. If we prepare our children properly and keep the family foundations strong, no Darth Vader will turn them to the dark side.

The early school years: behaviours

1. Wriggling and walkabouts
   - remind of rules
   - reinforce good sitting
   - wriggling may be caused by ADHD

2. Teasing and taunts
   - the short-fuse child is the one most teased
   - with five- and six-year-olds tell the teacher
   - with older children, role-play a better response
   - teach to fight with the brain, not the body

3. Bullying
   - can be physical or emotional
   - use assertiveness techniques
   - consider the buddy system

4. School refusal
   - often happens in week two but is temporary
   - may be due to a learning or social problem
   - may be due to worry about the family
   - may be due to a parent's problem
   - don't let refusal get entrenched
   - talk to teacher and school psychologist

5. Tall stories
   - part of the magic mind of the under-eight-year-old
   - get the facts straight before you overreact

6. Telling tales
   - a common behaviour of five- and six-year-olds
   - label this as telling tales
   - discourage tale-telling

7. Petty theft
   - under-eights have little idea of ownership
   - maintain a low-key response
   - with children older than eight years supervise closely and seek help if needed

8. Acting smart
   - often a symptom of learning problems
   - lay down ground rules and give a sign
   - use the three strikes technique

9. Homework
   - start early and be involved
   - set aside a time each day
   - don't spoon feed
   - don't let it spoil your relationship: refer the problem to the school if necessary

10. Hot-housing
    - we need to compromise between keeping children stimulated and over-pushing them

11. Tutors
- tutors can be more effective than a parent
- tutoring can maintain a child's enthusiasm to learn
- don't overly focus on the child's weakness
- make sure the tutor suits your child
- don't replace all relaxation and leisure time with tutoring

12. Time and 'quality time'
- children need you to be available to tune in to their needs

13. Organisation
- help your child to stop, think and plan
- when they are talking help them avoid rambling by giving structure
- help them to be organised and prepared for tests
- help them to remember things using rhymes and sayings

14. Maintaining the magic
- children are influenced by others as they get older, but they remain most influenced by their family

Help for learning difficulties

For some children, school is a time of stress and struggle. At least one in ten in each classroom will have a weakness in some area of learning. If a parent had a problem at school, such as weak reading or attention deficit, the risks that their child will have difficulties are many times higher. With major learning difficulties we cannot move mountains, but smaller hills can be levelled off a little.

Dyslexia, or developmental reading disorder

Dyslexia refers to a specific weakness in the area of reading and spelling. Purists prefer the term developmental reading disorder, but I like dyslexia.

This old label comes from the Greek (dys–bad + lexis–speech), and indicates a difficulty with language. This is more appropriate than ever, because modern research sees dyslexia as a problem of decoding words into language. This emphasis on language has attracted the interest of speech pathologists, who are now some of the leaders in the treatment of reading difficulties.

Strongly hereditary

When I diagnose a child with major dyslexia, I usually find a father or mother (or a close relative) with the same problem. The parents often deny any problem but when you ask them specifically about their spelling and their enjoyment of more solid literature, it often becomes apparent that the residue of childhood dyslexia is still there. This is an extremely common condition that disadvantages at least five per cent of the population. Figures as high as fifteen per cent are often quoted.

It is often said that parents who read to their children will prevent dyslexia. Certainly, parents who love books and read avidly are likely to be strong readers who will probably pass on strong reading genes to their children. On the other hand, parents who find reading stressful and read less to their children may tend to have more children with dyslexia. (I talk of the reading gene as though it were identified and sitting in a jar. Such a gene has not yet been located but I guarantee we will have it within the next decade.)

Dyslexia, learning disabilities and ADHD are much more common in children who are adopted or in foster care. When you think about it, there are sensible reasons why this might be the case. These conditions have the potential to affect adversely a child's education and their esteem. If we're right that problems like ADHD and dyslexia can be inherited, then the poor planning and impulsivity of ADHD may increase an adult's risk of ill-considered conception, and the child may inherit their parent's problem. Or, learning problems may increase an adult's risk of bottoming out and being unable to cope, so their children may end up in care.

Temperament, learning, language and behaviour are intimately entwined in our genes. It comes as a surprise to parents when I point to the origin of their children's problems. If the parent was a racehorse breeder, they would research more carefully before conception, but with humans it's done in the name of love.

Identifying a reading weakness

Reading requires a number of skills. We must scan and quickly recognise the shape of a known word, or break down the parts of one we have not met before. Then there are all the rules and exceptions. After this we learn to anticipate through groups of words that go together and by the flow of meaning. Finally we must take the decoded words and turn them into meaning.

The simplest way to assess reading is to look at a child's skill in recognising known words (sight word reading) and their ability to break unknown words into their various sounds (phonemic awareness). We can test sight words by asking a child to read irregularly spelt words that are not able to be sounded out, for example, yacht or duchess. We can test a child's ability to sound out using non words, for example, oripandom, which is easy to break down, but as we haven't met it before, it cannot be recognised by its shape.

A weak reader may initially use their visual recognition ability and may seem quite talented at reading. But problems appear when they have to break down the words and learn the rules, or some children seem to read quite well but such is the effort it involves, they miss the meaning.

The slow starter

All children develop at different rates. John may be slow to ride a bike or learn to swim, but he may eventually star in the Tour de France or get a medal in Olympic freestyle. A late start at reading does not necessarily mean a long-term problem. Many children fully recover with maturity and tutoring. However, despite the good outlook, it is important to call for help when worried.

Encouraging reading

Before rushing to get outside help, remember that there is much you can do yourself. Whether you have a child who is a strong or weak reader, read to them as much as possible. When they are slow and struggling, you read a bit, they read a bit, and this keeps the story moving. Choose books that are interesting yet written in a simple style. Before turning the page, stop for a moment and ask what is about to happen next. Read, read again, and then read some more.

Older children with a major reading problem are eligible to borrow the talking books from the local library.

Dyslexia, or developmental reading disorder

1. General facts
   - the most common specific learning weakness
   - more common in males
   - often hereditary
   - often associated with ADHD or language delay
   - severe dyslexia is present for life
   - some children are late starters, but eventually read well

2. Problem areas
   - sight word recognition
   - ability to sound out a word (phonemic awareness)
   - a mix of both
   - difficulty with reading comprehension
   - difficulty with reading speed

3. Testing the weakness
   - sight word ability: whether they can recognise an irregular word such as 'yacht'
   - sounding out ability: whether they can sound out a non-word such as 'oripandom'

4. Other indications of a weakness
   - avoids reading
   - weak spelling (often continues through life)
   - does not read for pleasure
   - loses attention, daydreams
   - poor writing abilities
   - difficulties with looking up information

5. Helping weak readers
   - parents read to, and read with, all children
   - schools can provide reading help by using a special teacher or speech therapist
   - major dyslexia is painfully slow to help
   - reward creativity ahead of punctuation, spelling and setting out

Our aim is for all children to develop an interest in what's written, rather than what is spoon-fed through television and videos. A good book allows a child's mind to create colours, tones and characters, which is much more exciting than the work of any film director.

Help for the weak reader

If you are worried about any part of your child's learning ability, be quick to discuss this with the class teacher. If they are also unhappy they will call on the services of the school counsellor. The basic assessment will check general learning, measure the degree of reading delay, then pinpoint the area of maximum weakness, for example, whether it is phonemic awareness, visual recognition, comprehension or speed. Then your child can receive remedial teaching through the path of learning that is strongest. As most dyslexia comes from a difficulty with turning visual symbols into language, some of the most effective remediators are speech therapists.

Whatever therapy is used, don't go overboard. Remember you are focusing on the child's area of weakness and that can cause stress and unhappiness. Don't expect that the problem will be resolved in a matter of months. In reality, there is no quick fix for a major weakness in reading. Unrealistic expectations lead to immense frustration.

Also, when traditional methods seem so slow, it's easy to become seduced by alternative claims. Eye exercises, tinted lenses, stimulation of the balance centres, sensory motor integration, Vitamin B6, primrose and fish oils. Most of these sound quite spectacular as presented on the Internet, but there are few scientific studies to support their claims. A minor sub-group of children may be helped by tinted lenses, but they are very small in number. The best treatment for a language-based learning problem is a language-based approach. This is usually provided by a remedial teacher or a speech pathologist.

Mathematics: a mystery

There are clever children with a specific learning weakness in reading (dyslexia); there are also children with a specific deficit in mathematics (dyscalculia). Some never get a grip of the basics, others can't cope with tables, and many drown with complex calculations. Dyscalculia is less common than dyslexia and is often associated with problems of coordination and writing. These children are probably helped more by a special teacher than is a child with the same degree of dyslexia. Extra help gives children confidence and enables them to catch up.

Problems of speech and language

Language is the vital link that lets us communicate and enjoy the company of each other. It's no surprise, then, that language delays and disorders are a common cause of stress in children and concern in parents.

Speech is made up of what you say (expressive language) and what you understand (receptive language). Children may be slow to develop language (language delay) or children may develop the right words but they may be oddly expressed or only partly understood (language disorder). Or the words may be there but the child's pronunciation is poor (an articulation problem).

Expressive delay

Einstein did not talk until he was four years of age, yet he was quite smart. Einstein must have had a pure expressive language delay that often appears in isolation. This is sometimes a hereditary problem and I often find brothers and sisters are similarly delayed.

However, as a specialist in child development, I am always on my guard for the sinister side of expressive delay: deafness, global intellectual disability or autism spectrum disorder. But if a child has normal hearing, understanding, awareness, interaction and general development I will then diagnose pure specific expressive language delay.

Parents can encourage early language skills by talking, listening and enrolling their children in a good preschool. Speech therapy is helpful, though often hard to gain access to or afford. But it is always possible for a speech therapist to assess a child then give them a programme that can be followed at home.

Receptive delay

Receptive delay is when a child continues to have difficulty understanding language. It is usually associated with expressive language delay and often with global developmental delay or autism spectrum disorder. However, some children can suffer from receptive delay alone and this puts them at great disadvantage. For these children it is as if they are living in a foreign country where they don't understand the language. They may smile and seem to comprehend, but they are out of their depth. If you are worried that your child is having difficulty understanding what is said, speak to your doctor. He can arrange to have them assessed by a paediatrician, a community health team or a speech pathologist.

Language disorder

Some of the most puzzled parents I see have children with lots of words but they don't quite make sense. These language-disordered children may sound like a tape recorder, and use smart-sounding phrases that aren't quite appropriate. They find it hard to describe their day's activities or to have a rich, two-way conversation. Questions are answered off tangent. I might ask, 'Where do you go to school?'

They respond, 'I'm in First Class. Mrs Smith is my teacher.'

Some children get stuck and either repeat one word (echoing) or keep on at one topic (perseveration). Echoing is strongly associated with, but is not exclusive to, autism spectrum disorder (see this chapter, page 134).

I see other children who mix meaningful speech with unintelligible nonsense (jargon). Sometimes there are new migrants who are thought to be speaking a mix of English and, say, Russian, but when we get a Russian interpreter they don't understand either.

Language disorder is often hereditary. I regularly find myself struggling to communicate with apparently normal parents who have immense difficulty giving a clear history of their child's problem. That's because they have the same problem as their child: they can't quite answer the question that has been asked.

Articulation problem

Some children continue to pronounce words in a way that is immature and like a child who is much younger. They miss ends or mispronounce bits of words, so 'dooce' means juice, for example. This sounds cute, and usually it will resolve with time.

But other children have a more serious pronunciation problem that makes speech quite unintelligible. I sometimes see children whose mums understand eighty per cent of what they say, while I pick up only about forty per cent. This is often (but not always) associated with problems of swallowing, tongue movement and dribbling. This combination is called oral dyspraxia, and it can be quite disabling and slow to remediate.

Stuttering

An under-four-year-old may stutter when they are excited and tired. But by school age, stuttering is not usual and must be taken seriously, especially when there is a family history. Children are allowed the occasional jumble in their expression but if they have an impediment that continues whether they are tense or calm they need to be referred to a speech therapist.

Problems with concepts, subtleties, semantics and pragmatics

Some children hit great difficulties when they move from concrete language to concepts. I might ask, 'If you had a can of Coke, a box of tissues and a Mars Bar, which would you drink?'

The child with difficulties might answer, 'The water.'

They don't understand the full question; they just react to the one word 'drink'.

A child who is weak in concepts will tend to be literal rather than lateral in their thought processes. They might repeat the rhyme about three blind mice, yet not know the number of tails that were axed. If asked, 'Why does it say "No Smoking" on the petrol pump?' they answer in a concrete way, 'Smoking is bad for your health.'

Some of these children can't generalise. They look blank when I ask, 'Where do you live?' or 'Where is your home?' They can only understand if I ask in the specific way they have been taught: 'What is your address?'

Semantics involve the subtleties of understanding, and children who have problems with subtleties and semantics may have difficulty understanding humour, for example, which plays on double meanings. Many of these children can't tell the difference between a joke and a wind-up, making them a target for teasing.

This literal language amazes parents. One mother told her son, 'Run off to the toilet before we go home.'

He looked at her seriously and replied, 'Mum, we are not allowed to run in the school yard.'

Another child was told, 'Put a sock in it,' and he wondered what to do with his sock.

With problems of pragmatics the child is unable to play the tennis match of good, two-way communication. You open, I respond, you return, and I answer in tune. Pragmatics refers to the appropriate focus, picking up on cues, intonation, eye contact and body language.

Children with this language disorder may feel the stress of not being able to fully express and understand. Some try hard, but others withdraw and become detached and almost autistic. This subtle area of language disorder has a grey edge of overlap with autism spectrum disorder and the current fashionable diagnosis of Asperger syndrome. I'm a specialist in this area and it confuses me. No wonder parents get totally bewildered!

Language problems

1. Problems involve:
   - expressive language (what we say)
   - receptive language (what we understand)
   - language delay (slow to develop)
   - language disorder (the words are not spoken or understood in a normal way)
   - articulation (words are not pronounced in the normal way)
   - stuttering
   - concepts, subtleties, semantics and pragmatics

2. Expressive language problems
   - language delay
   - slow to develop expressive language
   - usually an isolated problem
   - often runs in families
   - can be associated with receptive delay
   - occasionally caused by deafness, intellectual disability or autism
   - check hearing, understanding, relating to the environment and general development

3. Receptive language problems
   - language delay
   - slow to develop receptive language
   - usually associated with expressive delay
   - when expressive and receptive are both delayed, there may be other problems
   - can be a sign of global delay (intellectual disability)
   - can be due to autism spectrum disorder
   - check hearing, expressive language, general development and the relationship with the environment

4. Language disorder
   - echoes what has been said
   - perseverates – goes on and on
   - uses jargon – talks in 'Russian'
   - responds in a rote, preprogrammed way
   - has difficulty describing a new experience
   - has difficulty with two-way conversation
   - response is almost appropriate

5. Articulation problem
   - young children often mispronounce (immature articulation)
   - immaturity usually resolves with time, school and possibly speech therapy
   - major articulation problems can cause speech to be unintelligible
   - oral dyspraxia is a major problem often associated with feeding difficulties, unusual tongue movement and dribbling
   - major problems can be very slow to resolve
   - rhythm problem (dysfluency)

6. Stuttering
   - a family history of stuttering is of concern
   - persistent stuttering in a school-age child needs immediate speech therapy referral

7. Problems with concepts, subtleties, semantics and pragmatics
   - misses concepts
   - responds to one word, not the group meaning
   - misses a sequence of instructions
   - has difficulty generalising
   - has problems with double meaning, innuendo, humour; takes things literally
   - teased as can't see past the words
   - may withdraw and appear autistic
   - a grey area between pure language disorder and the language disorder that is part of autism

Autism spectrum disorder and Asperger syndrome

Autism spectrum disorder varies greatly in its severity and presentation. It covers the widest spectrum from the totally detached institutionalised child to the university professor who is brilliant at maths but quite disabled in social skills. It refers to a child who communicates poorly in both verbal and body language. One who is inflexible, somewhat obsessive and repetitive and works to their own agenda. These children may be distant and detached and may relate inappropriately. Most autism spectrum children have areas of relative brilliance, particularly in visual memory (for example, sight reading) and rote learning (for example, knowing every dinosaur). The majority of children with autism (seventy per cent) have associated intellectual disability.

The high-functioning edge of autism is sometimes called Asperger syndrome. This has a great overlap with some of the more withdrawn temperaments we see in children with the pure language delay disorder just described.

Children with a major degree of autism are aloof and most unusual. Those with less severe autism are slightly detached, socially unaware language-disorder children. This milder group cause great confusion as they may simply present as square pegs in round holes. Many of these children show the obsessive behaviour described in Chapter 8.

If you are concerned that your child may suffer from autism spectrum disorder, Asperger syndrome or a language disorder, speak to your doctor who can arrange expert assessment from a paediatrician or speech pathologist.

Autism spectrum disorder and Asperger syndrome

1. A biological condition – in the child's make-up

2. Not related to environment or poor parenting

3. About seventy per cent have associated intellectual disability

4. A much more common problem than ten years ago

5. A wide spectrum that ranges from the severely disabled person to a socially inept professor

6. The milder, high-functioning edge of the spectrum is termed Asperger syndrome

7. There is a grey area where Asperger syndrome joins language disorder

8. Autism and language problems are both more common in boys

9. The mildly affected child presents as a square peg in a round hole

10. The autistic child has a problem with communication
    - language
      - delay or disorder
      - literal not lateral
      - echoes

- rote replies
- speaks like a tape recorder
- not a flowing two-way conversation
- body language
  - lack of facial expression
  - poor eye contact
  - doesn't talk with their eyes

11. The autistic child is inflexible
- obsessive, over-interest
- likes routines and sameness
- over-focuses, repetitive play
- overreacts when obsession is disturbed
- fixed and works to own agenda
- plays for hours with one interest

12. The autistic child is hard to steer; like a train running on tracks

13. The autistic child is detached and distant
- unusual relationship with their environment
- aloof, looks past you
- more interested in objects than people

14. The autistic child has areas of talent, such as
- strong visual recognition (photographic memory)
- reads
- recognises change
- knows the layout of places
- remembers street names after one look
- strong rote memory
- repeats detailed information
- repeats stories, rhymes, advertisements

15. The autistic child has areas of weakness, such as
- communication
- picking up on unspoken messages
- picking up on emotion
- the ability to generalise
- reading comprehension weaker than their expressive reading
- working out problems that have not been directly taught before

Fine motor and gross motor problems

Some children are created with the fine motor coordination of a world-class watchmaker. Some have the gross motor skills of a gold medal gymnast. But for many, their fingers fumble and they have two left feet.

Some children are truly clumsy and others appear clumsy due to their bull-in-a-china-shop temperament. Others move well but have problems planning.

Gross motor clumsiness affects a child's self-esteem. When their mates are choosing the sports team they always select the potential Olympian ahead of the stumbler.

Motor planning is a more subtle problem where a child appears in tune until they try to coordinate three actions at the one time. These children have difficulty tying shoelaces, swimming with style and following the flow in aerobics. Fortunately Velcro laces have replaced knots, swimming does not need style and aerobic exercise can be left to the high-stepping hyperactives.

However, many of these children may underachieve in written work because their handwriting is illegible. While some have a difficulty with letter formation, others have problems planning work, or may rush without checking. The clumsies, motor planners, awkward movers and poor writers need help from an occupational therapist (or see Appendices IV and V, pages 264–7). The rushers may need treatment for ADHD (see Chapter 12, page 138).

Understanding ADHD

Attention deficit hyperactivity disorder (ADHD) refers to a cluster of learning and behaviour problems that cause a child to underfunction for intellect and underbehave for the quality of parenting they receive. These behaviour and learning problems are caused by a subtle difference in the fine-tuning of the normal brain. This difference seems to be related to a slight imbalance in the brain's message-transmitting chemicals, the neurotransmitters. This mostly affects those parts of the brain that self-monitor learning and put the brakes on ill-considered behaviour (the frontal lobes and their close connections).

ADHD affects at least two per cent of the school-age population, and some quote figures as high as five per cent. Boys are more affected than girls. The first signs of ADHD are usually apparent before three years of age, but few children require treatment before they start school.

ADHD is a chronic condition and it is now believed that approximately sixty per cent of children who suffer from it will take some of their symptoms with them into adulthood. Happily, adults with ADHD can now be successfully treated.

A modern view of ADHD

When parents describe their ADHD child they talk about four separate parts, but only two of them correctly fit the ADHD diagnosis. The two parts of true ADHD are

- ADHD hyperactive impulsive behaviours
- ADHD attention deficit learning weakness.

Most ADHD children have a mix of both the first behaviour part and the second inattention learning part. But some have one of these in isolation (when they are termed ADHD predominantly inattentive). This is probably more common than we realise and is often not picked up because these children underachieve but do not underbehave. A small group have an even purer presentation of ADHD inattentive only, which makes them like dreamy, drifty 'space cadets'.

These two ADHD parts are then affected by the presence or absence of a third part, the comorbid conditions. Comorbid conditions are associated problems that are not caused by ADHD but coexist in over half of the children who have true ADHD. They may be problems like dyslexia, oppositional defiant disorder or conduct disorder.

And finally, this mix of ADHD and comorbid conditions is greatly influenced by a fourth element – parenting and the child's living environment.

ADHD: the four parts

1. ADHD hyperactive impulsive behaviour: poor self-control of behaviour
   - Impulsiveness: speaks and acts without thinking, interrupts, calls out in class, has low frustration tolerance, can't walk away from trouble, may appear aggressive, has difficulty putting the brakes on behaviour, rushes carelessly through work, accident prone, volatile

- Demanding: unaware of when to let a matter drop, intrudes, generates tension, has difficulty backing off
- Social clumsiness: misreads social cues, overpowers, bosses, wants to do things their way, acts silly in a crowd, makes inappropriate comments, intrudes into others' space
- Overactivity: restless, fidgety, taps, fiddles, has to touch, overcharged, has an overwound spring

2. ADHD attention deficit and learning weakness: problems of output
   - Inattention: works poorly without one-on-one supervision, has difficulty regrouping after distraction, has a busy, circling brain, self-distracts, daydreams, flits from task to task, has inconsistent work output, gets over-focused on one part and misses the big picture
   - Poor short-term memory: forgets instructions, loses focus, reads but does not remember, has difficulty with mental arithmetic, learns a spelling list but has forgotten it by test time
   - Disorganisation: forgets homework books, misjudges time, procrastinates, has poor prioritisation, variable performance, poor planning, loses things like uniform items, lunch boxes, swimming costumes, bus passes, has difficulty starting, sustaining and completing work

3. Comorbid conditions
   - Over half of those with ADHD have at least one associated comorbid condition.
   - Between forty and sixty per cent have oppositional defiant disorder where they say no on principle.
   - Approximately fifty per cent have a specific learning disability such as dyslexia, language delay disorder, weakness in mathematics, etc.
   - Other comorbidities are conduct disorder, tic disorder, poor coordination, motor planning problems, depression, anxiety, obsessive compulsive disorder and bipolar disorder.

4. The child's living environment
   - Supportive, nurturing parenting versus hostile, critical parenting
   - Supportive schooling versus unaccepting, punitive schooling
   - An extended stable family versus an isolated, unstable, rejecting family

Typical symptoms of ADHD

When a child with ADHD has predominantly hyperactive-impulsive behaviours they may be out of step with brothers, sisters and other children. Often these children were easy babies, but once they started to walk many were active and into everything. At preschool some were more restless and found it hard to sit at story time, while others had low frustration tolerance and caused great trouble through their unthinking aggression to other children. Despite some difficulties, most manage reasonably well until the start of school.

At home, the hyperactive-impulsive child is demanding, intrudes into others' space and generates tension. These children stir, wind up their siblings and don't know when to let a matter drop. Many have a short fuse, act without thinking, interrupt and are accident prone. Some are messy, disorganised, forgetful, restless and constantly fiddling. They may unintentionally break things: 'It just fell apart in my hands.'

In the playground some are socially out of tune, come on too strong, annoy other children and may not get asked to birthday parties.

Many children are taken for treatment at the start of school, when they have been said to be distractable (due to attention deficit) and disruptive (due to hyperactive-impulsive behaviours).

Children with ADHD do best when stood over or encouraged enthusiastically. Otherwise they don't complete work. Teachers are confused that such an apparently intelligent child is so erratic and underachieving. Some may have been tested by the school psychologist, who often finds a surprisingly good concentration in the one on one of the quiet test room.

Children who have the predominantly inattentive type of ADHD may experience problems of learning, memory and underachievement at school.

When is a child normal and when do they have ADHD?

There is no clear cut-off between those children who have a normally active, impulsive and inattentive temperament and those who suffer ADHD. If these behaviours are not causing anyone any trouble, they can be ignored. If these behaviours are causing a child to significantly underfunction at school and underbehave at home, they must be taken seriously.

If we use the American Psychiatric Association's criteria for the diagnosis of ADHD (called the DSM-IV guidelines), six out of a list of nine difficult behaviours must be present. But life isn't as simple as this. If one child has these six behaviours yet has a saint for a mother and the best teacher in the country, we may not consider diagnosing or treating them. If they have only five behaviours but home and school are hanging by a thread, the child may be diagnosed and treated for ADHD. If a child has only four of the listed behaviours, they are not said to suffer from ADHD, but they will still be difficult for parents and teachers. Academics deal in pure black and white situations; but when you're operating in the real world you see life in much more flexible terms.

The cause of ADHD

Until relatively recently, professionals blamed parents' attachment or relationships for causing ADHD in children. Others said that ADHD was due to additives in the food. Now we know that neither of these is the cause of ADHD, though, of course, the standard of parenting and some food substances may influence already existing ADHD.

Two things are for certain: first, ADHD is strongly hereditary, and second, it is a biological condition.

Heredity is obvious, as so many families have a parent or close relative who has similar problems. If one identical twin has ADHD, there is about a ninety per cent chance the other will also have the condition. If one sibling has ADHD there is about a thirty per cent chance another child will also be affected. The majority of children in my care have a parent or close relative who has experienced many of the same difficulties.

And now it has been shown that ADHD is a biological condition. For years it was presumed, but not proven, that ADHD was caused by a minor difference in brain function. Now this can be shown by the most modern research scans (PET, SPECT and special MRI). In ADHD these scans show a slight difference of function and anatomy in the behaviour-inhibition areas of the brain (the frontal lobes and their close connections). This underfunction seems due to an imbalance of the brain chemicals that transmit impulses between certain nerves (the neurotransmitters – noradrenaline and dopamine). So the stimulant medications that are used to treat ADHD work to normalise the imbalance of these natural chemicals. One researcher has shown a normalisation of the SPECT scan of an ADHD sufferer after such stimulant medication had been administered.

Diagnosing ADHD

Many professionals claim that their method is the only way to diagnose ADHD, and this can be confusing for parents. In fact, there is no one conclusive test, and such is the greyness of the cut-off point no two professionals will have exactly the same limits regarding diagnosis.

In fact, there is no clear and simple dividing line we can pinpoint that separates the two per cent of children that we believe have a major degree of ADHD from children with an active, inattentive temperament. The cut-off is blurred by other factors such as the calmness and consistency of home, the tolerance of the parents and the skills of the class teacher. Diagnosis sometimes remains a matter of trial and error. I believe that if a child responds well to medication treatment it confirms the diagnosis, but many see the suggestion that diagnosis should be made by means of treatment as politically incorrect.

In general, though, diagnosis can be approached in four steps:

1. Be alert to the alarm signals

Alarm bells ring when a child underfunctions at school for intellect and underbehaves at home for the quality of parenting. In other words, they are significantly out of step with brothers, sisters and peers who have the same background and level of development.

2. Exclude ADHD lookalikes

Exclude major developmental delay, the normal spiritedness of a preschooler, or parenting or family problems.

3. Use pointers to help with diagnosis

There may be some other pointers that could help with diagnosis, like parent and teacher questionnaires, test profiles, brain tests or a continuous performance test (CPT). The CPT, such as the Conners or TOVA CPT, is of particular help when a child has predominantly a learning problem or the picture is clouded by comorbid conditions.

4. Take a careful history and observe the child

'When she walked she was into everything'; 'He would never hold my hand but was always running ten steps ahead of me'; 'At the start of school he was disruptive and distractable'; 'She only works well when stood over'; 'He goes on and on, intrudes and causes tension'; 'He's impulsive, short fused, and socially out of tune'; 'He breaks nearly every-thing he plays with'; 'Discipline and management are many times more difficult'; 'She's disorganised and has a poor short-term memory'; 'School reports say he could do better if only he could focus'.

Treatment

Managing ADHD involves:

- helping school and the classroom teacher
- structuring home for peace
- boosting self-esteem and developing outside interests
- medication
- considering other therapies.

At school

At school teachers need to accept that an ADHD child's behaviour isn't simply naughtiness – it is part of their make-up and they can't help it. As well, ADHD children at school need:

- a structured class run by a teacher who will be there every school day, all year
- a firm but encouraging teacher who knows when it is best to back off
- seating near the front, away from distracting influences
- clear step-by-step instructions and constant feedback
- special supervision at times of change, such as coming in from a break or when they are on a school excursion
- trying methods like token reward systems to help increase time on task.

At home

At home all members of the family need to accept that this is the way your child has been made and no amount of force will beat it out of them. Be patient and have realistic expectations.

But remember that while poor parenting can cause bad behaviour, with ADHD, the child's bad behaviour causes good parents to appear poor. Normal techniques for coping with behaviour work poorly with an ADHD child, because they have a biological difference in their ability to inhibit behaviour (they act before they have thought of the conse-quences). For this reason, disregard anyone who believes that a standard behavioural program or parent effectiveness course will easily change your ADHD child. But it is possible to change behaviours using small, well-planned steps and there are things you can do to help your ADHD child:

- Routine is essential.
- Rewards should be frequent and constantly repeated.
- Think before you act and learn to ignore all but the important misbehaviours.
- Don't lock horns with an ADHD child then increase the pressure. This produces a battle of wills, two angry parties, opposition, resentment and damage to relationships.
- Don't argue. Don't get heated. Don't escalate. Use a matter-of-fact, unemotional, controlled voice.
- Give yourself room to manoeuvre:
  - state the rule
  - count to three
  - use time out
  - give choices
  - don't force the situation into a cul-de-sac.
- When it's all over, be quick to forgive. Don't hold grudges.

Remember, even the worst-behaved child is good ninety per cent of the time. Reward this positive side – catch them being good!

Esteem

Try to avoid being too negative or always using negative words, because this can affect a child's self-esteem. Listen, value what they say and give them a reasonable amount of responsibility.

Encourage them to try out a variety of sports, hobbies and interests, in the hope they may savour success at something. Swimming, bike riding, walking, fishing, cooking, judo or computers may all be useful. Team sports and scouts suit some ADHD children but not all. ADHD children may have poor coordination making some sports difficult to master. For ways to help with coordination, see Appendix IV, page 264. When they are successful at sport, ADHD children get an immense boost.

To help with school work, out-of-school tutoring may be useful, but don't overdo it. Tutoring puts all the focus on your child's areas of failure. Some ADHD children have poor handwriting. For ways to help with handwriting see Appendix V, page 266.

ADHD children often have trouble building friendships. Encourage them in this area by inviting school mates over or taking one of your child's friends on outings.

Medication

Stimulants

The main medications used to treat ADHD are the stimulants dexamphetamine and Ritalin (methylphenidate). These have been shown to be effective in over eighty per cent of ADHD children in the short to medium term, but there is still a lack of data on the long-term benefits.

Ritalin is similar but not identical to dexamphetamine. I would recommend that both preparations be trialed to ensure that a child receives the most effective medicine with the fewest side effects.

Stimulant medication has now been extremely well researched and proven and was first used to treat ADHD in 1937. The drug Ritalin has been used since 1958. See full details and research references in Green and Chee, *Understanding ADHD*, Vermilion, 1997.

However, there are still people who say that stimulants are new, controversial, addictive, dangerous and unproven. Be extremely suspicious of anyone who voices such out-of-date ideas, as the rest of what they say may be equally unreliable.

Stimulants act by normalising the imbalance in the brain's natural neurotransmitter chemicals, that is, they increase noradrenaline and dopamine. Stimulants are not sedatives. Instead, they enhance normal brain function. While stimulants may work to a minute degree in a child without ADHD, when they are effective in treating a child with ADHD the benefits are usually quite miraculous in both behaviour and learning.

Stimulants help focus attention, keep the mind on task and allow a child to consider the possible repercussions before they act. Successfully medicated children become more organised, less impulsive and are easier to reach.

Stimulants are short acting, starting about half an hour after the child takes them, and the effect has largely passed three to five hours later. But while their effect is short lived, about half of the medicine is still in the blood after four hours and one quarter after eight hours. For this reason we tend to give children larger doses early in the day, which are then topped up by subsequent smaller doses, for example, one and a half tablets at 8am, one tablet at 12 noon, and three-quarters of a tablet at 3:30pm.

Usually children take the medication in three doses during the day (although this may vary for different children from two doses to five doses). But not all ADHD children take the medication every day. When there are only problems with schoolwork, medication may only be given to the child on school days. While when there are problems with behaviour, socialisation, and stress to parent–child relationships, medication may be given every day, including weekends and holidays.

There is no evidence to suggest that a correctly diagnosed ADHD child will become addicted to their medication. Stimulants help a child focus and bring them into reality. You don't get addicted to reality.

Side effects are remarkably rare and can usually be avoided if your doctor trials both preparations and fine tunes carefully. The most common side effect when starting medication is for a child to become withdrawn, teary and irritable. This usually only happens at the time of commencing the medication or raising the dose. If it does happen it can be solved by introducing medication gradually or by trying the other medication.

Also, many children report that they have less appetite and a few find it is more difficult to settle to sleep. These and most other problems can be avoided by careful fine tuning of the dosage.

Non-stimulants
ADHD is also treated using other, non-stimulant drugs like Catapres (clonidine) and Tofranil (imipramine), either alone or in combination. Catapres is particularly useful when stimulants alone are unable to adequately control a child's impulsivity and overactivity. It is also used when they have trouble settling to sleep. Tofranil is the second-line drug that helps behaviour and attention when stimulants are shown to be ineffective.

But these non-stimulants are not without their risks, and they must be used cautiously. In particular, there is the danger of accidental overdose, so tablets must be given correctly and stored securely.

Other therapies

Be sensible when it comes to finding treatments for your ADHD child. Use the well-researched therapies that are known to be safe and successful ahead of those that are controversial and unlikely to bring big benefits.

However, there are a range of therapies that parents try. When you are looking for alternatives, the things you need to know are:

● Diet does not cause ADHD and too much or too little sugar doesn't influence ADHD behaviour. Most current research suggests that less than ten per cent of ADHD children are affected by natural or artificial preservatives, additives and colourings. Where diet is incriminated, most parents have pinpointed one or two foods, which they now avoid. Irritability and overactivity seem to be the most diet-sensitive behaviours, but these are not the main problems of the true ADHD child.

- Occupational therapy can help ADHD children to improve their handwriting if it is poor (see Appendix V, page 266 for ways to help with handwriting).
- Speech therapy, with emphasis on phonics, may help when a child has spelling and reading difficulties.
- Many researchers view brainwave-modifying techniques of biofeedback as controversial.
- Multivitamins and natural products are unproven treatments (even those promoted on top-rating television shows).
- Eye exercises, tinted lenses and sensory integration are all of questionable benefit in the treatment of learning and attentional difficulties.

Long-term effects of treatment

While the long-term side effects of medication are not a concern, the benefits of long-term therapy are still to be conclusively proven. One study has shown that ADHD children who are treated with stimulants are less likely to drop out of high school or engage in substance abuse than those left untreated.

In my experience, ADHD children become closer and relate better to their friends and families when given medication. And relationships are of vital importance for long-term happiness and esteem.

Medication can continue for as long as a child's parents and teachers see significant benefits. But if you are ever in doubt, stop for a week and see what happens.

Remember, parents, not doctors, are in charge. Doctors can recommend these medications, but it is always the parents who have ultimate control. Stop the medication if you think it is not working or is causing any unwanted side effect. If you are worried, call for help.

The hazards of not treating ADHD

Many untreated children are at war with their parents and get to adolescence with destroyed family relationships and a second-rate education.

Some are accident prone, and a number may be seriously injured or even killed. While there is no completely safe drug, the dangers of medication are much less than the emotional and physical dangers of untreated ADHD.

A final word

ADHD is a real condition which has only recently started to be understood. When misdiagnosed and mistreated, it can cause amazing stress and long-term damage to esteem and family relationships. At school, these clever children underfunction and start to believe they are stupid.

We cannot cure ADHD with medication and other treatments. But we can keep a child's enthusiasm to learn, keep families at peace and help a child maintain self-esteem until, hopefully, adolescence brings some academic acceleration and a more reflective style of behaviour.

In the past most ADHD children remained undiagnosed, and arrived at adulthood with a belief that they were inferior and dumb. This may have been acceptable in the past, but we are not going to let it happen today (see Appendix V, page 266).

ADHD: the essentials

1. Attention Deficit Hyperactivity Disorder (ADHD) is the same as ADD.

2. ADHD disadvantages at least two per cent of our school-age population.

3. ADHD is related to an underfunction in the frontal areas of the brain (the parts that self-regulate behaviour and learning).

4. The ADHD child has behaviour that is out of step with the quality of parenting they receive and learning problems that are out of step with their intellectual abilities.

5. ADHD children have behaviour problems of poor self-monitoring and inhibition (impulsive, unthinking behaviour, difficulty putting the brakes on behaviour, unaware when to back off, misreading social situations, restless and fidgety).

6. The learning problems involve an underfunctioning for intellect (self-distracts, difficulty working without one-on-one super-

vision, problems starting, sustaining and finishing work, poor short-term memory, disorganisation).

7. Most ADHD children have a mix of behaviour and learning problems. In addition, many have associated comorbid conditions (specific learning difficulties, oppositional defiant disorder, conduct disorder, coordination difficulties, tics, etc).

8. Family doctors find it hard to access quality care for their ADHD children. Help comes from paediatricians, psychiatrists, community health centres, private psychologists and the specialised ADHD clinics.

9. A number of diagnostic techniques are promoted but no one method is essential or completely reliable in making the diagnosis.

10. Some of the most difficult ADHD children will behave relatively well in the quiet of the doctor's or psychologist's office. But ten minutes of good behaviour does not rule out the diagnosis of ADHD.

11. Treatment involves accepting the reality of the diagnosis, then using behaviour programmes, school support and increasing the child's ability to self-monitor with stimulant medication.

12. Behaviour techniques work poorly in a child who acts before they think. Parents have most success with routine, avoiding the unimportant and using rewards. Many ADHD children are oppositional and defy on principle. Meeting opposition with force leads to battles of Bosnian proportion. This wrecks relationships.

13. Parents need to learn how to sidestep escalation by keeping calm, active ignoring, counting techniques, time out and giving choices.

14. The stimulant medications Ritalin and dexamphetamine help the ADHD child to self-monitor and focus. They do not sedate; they normalise.

15. There is no controversy over this treatment, with over 150 reputable papers supporting the safety and benefits. Stimulants have been used with ADHD for over forty years.

16. Stimulants are used in conjunction with behaviour and learning programmes. Stimulants allow you to reach the child and, once you reach, you can teach.

17. ADHD is a strongly hereditary condition. Many ADHD children have an ADHD parent.

18. Adult ADHD affects about one per cent of the population. It causes clever adults to underfunction at work for intellect and behave unwisely in their relationships. Psychiatrists who treat adults with ADHD find the greatest problems come from impulsivity (impulsive outbursts, violence in marriage, unwise spending, accident prone, damaged relationships, work difficulties).

19. Many ADHD adults get big improvements with the same treatments we use in children.

20. ADHD can damage the relationships of parents with children, children with parents, children with peers and adults with adults. For this reason, early recognition and treatment is of utmost importance.

THIRTEEN

Sibling squabbles and competition

One day I was watching nature enthusiast David Attenborough, and he unlocked one of the great mysteries of life. In his hesitant tones I heard the answer to why brothers and sisters squabble:

> 'It seems that all little animals (with the exception of hedgehogs) love to trip, roll and fight. This quickens their reflexes, tones up their bodies and prepares them for life in the wild. A little lion that fights with his brother or sister is more likely to survive in the hostile adult world.'

Now, I am not suggesting we encourage teasing and squabbles, but it probably has some residual benefit. Athletic strength is built on all those taunts, tumbles and fights. Verbal sparring tunes woolly words into a razor-sharp response. Sisters who cope with an annoying brother will be better prepared for an irritating man in their later life.

Why siblings fight

Related but not identical

My brother always wanted to be an only child. It's not that I am particularly painful; we are just very different people. As he sat with his head in a book, I wanted to be out inhaling fresh air. My school achievements were average, despite hours of study and homework. He worked for ten minutes each night then won every prize and scholarship. We have always been emotionally close, but we are very different people.

Parents fall into the trap where they believe all brothers and sisters will have identical personalities and interests. For their convenience the parents encourage different children to do the same activities, which may not suit.

Age gap also makes a difference: children of similar age generally play better but compete more, and when ages are close, children often can't get on when they're together, but they can't bear being apart. The message for parents is to use no one programme, or no fixed expectation for all. Even identical twins are not identical.

Attention and boredom

Analysts interpret skirmishing as an unresolved power struggle, but most squabbles are due to boredom. Life slips into a quiet patch and a taunt generates a power surge of attention.

Sister is engrossed in her favourite TV soap, her brother walks over and 'inadvertently' blocks the screen. She hurls abuse, cries foul and protests to the referee. In the commotion the channel is changed and the power mysteriously unplugged.

Later, as he struggles with his homework, she brushes past, knocking a book to the floor. 'I never touched it,' she says. 'It just fell. Maybe it was the wind.' It was shaken by a distant earthquake!' Behind this protest of innocence, that twinkle in her eye registers the pleasure of victory.

After the age of twelve years, words become the main weapon. 'Gosh, that's a big zit'; 'Is that a dress or a tent?'; 'Have you ever wondered if you were adopted?'

It is tempting for parents to rush in like the United Nations at the first sign of trouble. They ask who started the fight and each child points at the other. Intervening may bring peace in the short term, but by rewarding with attention it encourages further fights. Parents must realise that a fight includes two combatants, and it's often hard to separate the good from the bad guys. Also, with the perversity of human nature, the one who complains loudest is usually the most guilty.

Life's not fair

The early school years are a time of competition, complaints and that constant cry, 'It's not fair, Mum.' Avoid being intimidated by comparative justice: 'When Jan was eight, you bought her a new bike'; 'When John got on the tennis team, he got a new racquet'; 'Jack does fewer chores but gets the same pocket money as me'; 'You're always doing things with Jane and do nothing with me.'

Equality is a worthy but impractical goal. You may love your children equally, but they will not end up with the same amount of attention.

The demanding, dissatisfied, intrusive child always insists on more of our time. In life it is always the one who shouts loudest who gets most. The sensible parents go for peace before equality.

Don't get into debates about justice – you never win. When told, 'It's not fair, she got more', acknowledge the statement but don't enter into the argument. I was in my twenties before I fully appreciated the unfairness of life. If your child gets this message at the age of eight, they will be advanced in their education. If they are really unhappy, suggest they take the matter to the Anti-discrimination Tribunal.

How to cope with sibling fights

The ways to cope with sibling fights involve:

- establishing limits
- encouraging conflict resolution
- learning to take the peaceful path.

Establish limits

Setting limits won't stop squabbles, but they let the combatants know where they stand. Rules should cover ownership, the use of joint property, personal space and acceptable behaviour. Join the Marquis of Queensberry and set down your rules for the ring, such as:

- This belongs to your brother. It cannot be touched without his permission.
- This shelf is for your sister's treasures. It is totally out of bounds.

- This bedroom is personal space. It cannot be entered without an invitation.
- Jointly owned toys, games and computers must be shared. If you are not currently playing with the computer, you cannot reserve it for your use.
- If you don't share, the toy will be put in time out for fifteen minutes.
- No disturbances are ever permitted during homework time.
- Broken belongings will be paid for from pocket money or one of your good toys will be offered in exchange.
- At dinner time there will be no touching, insulting or kicking your brother.

Encouraging conflict resolution

It's easy to become a referee in our children's battles but it is better they develop the basics of conflict resolution. Here's how to help them:

- When hit with complaints, don't adjudicate. Ask, 'How can we resolve this problem?'
- Suggest some options.
- Say you will come back in one minute to hear their solution.
- Use a three strike system –
  1. 'How can you both resolve this problem?'
  2. 'I expect resolution in one minute or you will both be sent to time out.'
  3. 'Both go to your rooms.'

Take the peaceful path

When siblings fight, parents have two options: to take the confronting path or the peaceful path. Some cynics suggest the complete ignoring approach: no parental intervention unless there is blood on the carpet. It doesn't have to be this extreme, but I still support the laid-back approach.

A final word

- Ignore minor squabbles.
- Keep bored bodies busy.
- Encourage cooperation by interesting the squabblers in a joint project.
- Suggest they move their battle outside or to another room.
- Remind all parties of the house rules.

- Ask them, 'Is this a real fight or just horseplay?'
- Give feedback for good cooperation: 'I love to see you two playing so well together.'
- Give stars and tokens for squabble-free hours.
- Put the disputed toy, computer or television in time out.
- The child who complains about getting hurt should be advised to keep clear of trouble.
- Don't interpret and apportion blame; just describe what you see and say what you will not accept.
- When nothing works punish both with time out in different rooms.

Occasionally one child is unacceptably vindictive or resentful to a sibling. This is more than normal sibling rivalry, and needs professional intervention.

Sibling squabbles

1. Siblings fight for a variety of reasons:
   - they may be related, but they're not identical – they are of different ages and have different personalities and interests
   - they are bored or want attention
   - by continually intervening parents are rewarding with attention

2. How to cope with sibling fights
   - set limits and rules so children know where they stand
   - encourage them to resolve the conflict themselves by asking them to suggest resolutions
   - use time out if the conflict isn't resolved
   - take the peaceful path of minimum intervention where possible

Shyness, making friends and strengthening social skills

The joy of belonging to the human race comes from meeting and relating. So parents are sad when they see their children as loners. They watch other youngsters gather friends around them like a Lottery winner at the bar, yet their child remains on the edge.

I am often asked if I can turn an introvert into a thick-skinned extrovert. There is no way to work this miracle but I can teach skills that help a shy child appear more outgoing.

Introverts and extroverts

Some years ago I was promoting my book *Toddler Taming* on the North American authors' circuit. Between studios I shared a limo with a

157

Manhattan psychoanalyst who had written a book on the interpretation of dreams. We were chatting about unrealistic expectations and how they caused so many emotional problems. With this she came out with a wonderfully wise statement: 'The world is divided into two sorts of people: extroverts and introverts. But there are very few true extroverts – just introverts pretending they are extroverts.'

Parents who were shy when young hope for a more extrovert lifestyle for their own children. But the parents' temperament may have passed through the genes, and their children's introversion is then increased by living with introvert adults.

We should respect our child's temperament and not try to change it. Look at it this way. The majority of adults have an intense fear of speaking before a large audience. You could push them on stage but they would be apoplectic and even more fearful in the future. In the same way, shy children do not need to be belittled, forced or hassled. For them socialisation comes gradually with time.

When your child hides their face and won't communicate, it's best to make a matter-of-fact comment: 'John is a bit overwhelmed. He will come and chat to us when he is ready.' If you say 'John won't speak. He's shy', the chances are John will fill the role you've set out for him.

Building friendships

There are two problems children have building friendship: some have difficulty making friends and others have difficulty keeping them. The first group are timid about asking people to play and get swept aside by the pushy hordes. The others boss and always want things their own way, or when a child comes to play they ignore their guest and go off to do their own thing. I see children who never get asked to a birthday party, and at school they are known by all but liked by none.

We can teach the timid how to approach others and ask them to play. Or we can resort to schemes that create opportunities for socialisation. For example, when we go to the beach, the zoo or out to eat we might invite another child. One parent told me how they built a swimming pool in their backyard just to attract the neighbourhood kids. It was an extreme effort to attract friends but it worked.

Changing the socially blind is much more difficult. Communication is like tennis; we read the other player's game and carefully direct our returns. As a doctor, when I talk to parents I watch their eyes, listen to the tone of voice and pick up on what they don't quite tell me. By tuning into their verbal language and body language, I know when to keep talking, when to slow down, and when to change direction.

Some children seem unaware of these subtle cues: they misread the game, hit too hard, return out of court and miss the point. In the past children learnt through the school of hard knocks, but nowadays we can teach some of the basics needed for social skills.

Teaching social skills

When social skills programmes were first promoted in the early 1980s, they seemed an exciting new way to help shy, inappropriate and ADHD children. Unfortunately, the follow-up studies were disappointing. It seemed that much of the success in the therapy room was not carried into the outside world.

Social skills training is neither easy nor particularly effective, but it is a move in the right direction. The formal programmes I have watched as an observer gave immediate feedback for good communication, pulled the child up for inappropriate communication and tried to get them to see how their actions affected others.

At home we can attempt something much simpler. We can:

- practise through role-play
- teach the basics of communication
- help children enter a conversation
- show them how to tune in to social cues
- show them how to finish a conversation
- show them how to join in play
- show them how to ask a friend home
- show them the tricks of negotiation
- show them how to use a common interest to help communication.

Practice through role-play

Role-play is useful but only in that small proportion of children who are prepared to play along. Role-play allows us to run through common situations, acting out the different ways we can respond. This provides a flight simulator to try out different approaches without crashing out when we get it wrong.

The basics of communication

Children don't need the painful handshake and trust-me eyes of a used-car salesman. But they must be able to greet and communicate. We can help them by showing them the basics. Good eye contact and a friendly smile show we wish to communicate. A slouching posture suggests we are disinterested while a slight lean forward shows we intend to engage. Heads nod and bodies move when communication is in harmony. Standing far apart signals a lack of confidence, while too close is an invasion of space.

Conversation openers

Even at my age I feel overwhelmed when I enter a room packed with strangers. As I struggle to start a conversation I find myself resorting to three well-tried techniques:

1. I ask a question – 'Is this your first time at this venue?'
2. I make a pleasantry – 'It's remarkably hot for this time of year.'
3. I comment on something of joint interest – 'What did you think of that speaker?'

Children can also be shown how to open up with a question: 'What are you playing?'; 'Do you live around here?' Or they can use a pleasantry: 'Gosh, it's windy today.' Or they can open with a common interest: 'That maths class was pretty boring'; 'Did you hear Jones call teacher a butthead?'; 'What did you think of last night's episode of "Neighbours"?'

These pleasantries are bland and boring, but they are just an opener. Once communicating, they can then get into something more meaningful.

Reading the cues

On returning home in the evening, a switched-on husband is quick to suss out the situation. They have something important to say, but as they see their wife's tired, tense eyes, they hold back for a more opportune moment. Some children have no idea about the right moment, while others can read their parents to perfection and know the exact second when the request for money or new clothes will score the greatest payout.

Reading the cues can be helped along through role-play. We demonstrate how the enthusiasm in another's eyes signals interest in our conversation. When bodies fidget and eyes glaze over our audience have had enough. Restlessness, rapid head nodding, throat clearing and flitting eyes signal a crisis in boredom and it's time to back off.

Conversation closers

It's sometimes easier to get into a conversation than close one without appearing awkward. But children can be taught the techniques used by us adults: 'I'd better get going'; 'See you later'; 'I should say hello to John'; 'I've some work to do'. Then, with a twinkle of the eye and a friendly smile, they move on.

Joining in play

Some children stand enviously on the side lines but can't pluck up the courage to ask, while others barge in, disrupt and act inappropriately. It's easier for us to help the standers than the bargers. The bargers continue to barge, whatever we say.

We can teach them that it's best to wait for an appropriate gap in the game then to try out some openers: 'This looks cool. May I join in?'; 'I'm Jane. Can I play?'; 'Do you need a hand?'; 'Can I join the next game?'

Unfortunately, children are capable of being extremely mean and may exclude all but the favoured few. When this happens the timid child has only three options: to get into a rival team, to play alone or start their own league.

Asking a friend home

You would think there should be no difficulty getting a friend over to play, but for some children this poses an insurmountable hurdle. To help, start by working out the basics. What day? What time? What to do? How to get here? Then ask! When procrastination and shyness prevent a child from asking, parents may need to deal directly with the other child's parent.

Negotiation

In life nothing ever goes quite to plan and to survive we must be able to roll with the punches and negotiate. Children who are socially smart learn this through life experience, but others struggle and need some help.

It may be possible to teach this through role-play: 'You can't join in our game now.'

'Well, could I play with you in the next break?'

Or, 'I'm not able to come to your house on Saturday.'
'Could you come on Sunday or the Saturday after?'
Or, 'You must finish your homework now.'
'I am so tired. Could I get up early and do it before school?'

A common interest

One of the best ways to ease communication and help mixing is to be with people who have similar interests. The boy may be a poor communicator, but he will talk continuously with fellow football fans. The horse-loving girl is mostly mute, but chats non-stop with other horsy types. The computer buff can talk megabytes to those with a silicone chip on their shoulder. The bike rider chats, rides a bit, chats more and feels close to their fellow bikers. When general mixing is poor, a common interest will encourage socialisation.

Strengthening social skills

1. Sensible expectations
   - the world is full of introverts trying to pretend they are extroverts
2. Conversation openers
   - ask a question
   - make a pleasantry
   - comment on a joint interest
3. Reading the cues
   - a welcoming smile
   - enthusiastic eyes
   - body movement
   - restless boredom
   - respect space
4. Conversation closers
   - 'I'd better be going.'
   - 'See you later.'
5. Asking to play
   - pick the right moment
   - know what you want
   - have a back-up plan

6. Negotiation
- be flexible
- regroup and try Plan B

7. Common interest
- football fans
- computer addicts
- sports or clubs

FIFTEEN

Increasing self-esteem

Self-esteem is how a child feels about themselves. When self-esteem is high, they are likely to be confident, positive, sociable, kind to others and more willing to attempt new tasks. When it is low, children may be negative, withdrawn, socially insecure and can even be quite paranoid.

Most writing on self-esteem places all the emphasis on the positive interaction between parents, teachers and children. But it's not that simple: children are also uplifted and put down by things like their academic abilities, social abilities and physical attributes and their temperament and resilience. Then all these elements form a picture that can be distorted by the child's perception, especially when they compare themselves to their or society's role models.

While there is no easy way of boosting a child's self-esteem, there are things we can do to help.

Factors that affect self-esteem

Learning, physical and social abilities and attributes

A child who has advanced intellect, ease in relating, strong work output, good looks and is talented at sport will start from a favoured position. On the other side there are many clever children with problems of attention, learning, language or mixing, who bust themselves and get nowhere.

In theory we live on a level playing field, but in reality, some children will always play uphill and against the wind. Our aim is to help them savour success, but despite our best efforts many will experience more than their fair share of pain and self-doubt.

Temperament and resilience

Each of us has been dealt an individual hand in the cards of life, but not all will react equally to the same hand. Some who are attractive, influential and intelligent still carry a monumental chip on their shoulder, while others with far fewer winning attributes plod on unperturbed.

How tough a child's temperament is will affect their resilience, which is then boosted or lowered by outside events. Resilience rises with stability, close support, a trusted confidant and the feeling of belonging. Children are better able to cope with adversity when they have an extended network of people who believe in them. This includes aunts and uncles, family friends and others in their close community.

A child's self-perception

Children have no direct measure of their performance, and they gauge this through feedback from those around them. This reaction from other people provides the mirror through which they see themselves. Unfortunately the mirror of life is fitted with side-show glass that distorts the image.

Even the most successful, clever and attractive children may have a poor perception of themselves. So a child may have an attractive, well-proportioned figure, but to them the reflection appears fat and droopy. Or the reliable, much-respected child may feel they are a social bore with no small talk. Those who are shy may believe they live in a world of extroverts, when in fact most of their friends are introverts pretending to be extroverts.

It's bad enough worrying about non-problems, but when there are genuine concerns about ability, appearance, body size or social skills, a child may distort these way out of all proportion.

Role models

As parents we would like our children to be as talented as a film star, as popular as a princess and as impressive as a much-admired public figure. These role models shine out from the pages of today's glossy mags, but when they are dead and gone their biographers reveal most of them to have been crippled with self-doubt, personal problems and an inability to maintain relationships.

It's important to set our sights and our children's on realistic goals. Our children are doing much better than they realise, if only they could see past the play-acting.

Encouraging self-esteem

There is no magic bullet to boost esteem, but here are some simple suggestions. Children do best when we listen, respect their feelings, appreciate effort and accept their mistakes. We can also boost their self-esteem by avoiding using words that wound, giving them some responsibility and helping them succeed at something. Teachers also can help boost esteem in the classroom. But it is important to start all this early.

Start early

Esteem is not something that develops at the age of six. Its foundation is laid in the toddler years. Young children are intensely dependent on their parents, and if we treat them as special, they feel special. But it takes more than having us around to boost esteem – we also need to be available. Littlies need a listener, a comforter, a responder, an encourager, an audience and a safety net.

An unhurried grandparent has special powers that boost esteem. They listen in wonderment as their tongue-tied granddaughter rambles on, making the little person feel like a wit, a raconteur and a legend in their own lifetime. This early feeling of security and importance sets the foundation for better esteem.

Notice and listen

School-agers can ramble, lose the plot or wallow in such trivia your brain starts to ache. They talk of non-topics such as teenage pop groups or some programme that would be better taken off the telly. But listening is important. If a child is to feel valuable, what they say should be valued. Show interest in their friends, work, hobbies, sports and words. Give feedback that lets them know you are with them.

Avoid the bland emptiness of 'Well done', 'That's good', 'You're clever'. Pick up on specific bits, as this lets them know you have a genuine interest. If we tune in to what our children do and say, obviously they must be worth noticing.

Respect their fears and feelings

All of us have our problems and worries: some are quite genuine, others are largely in our head. You can comfort the anxious air traveller with safety statistics, but five miles up in turbulence you might as well be telling Leonardo the *Titanic* is unsinkable.

Whether our worries are real or perceived, our bodies feel the same adrenaline upset and nothing others say will make much difference. School-age children may fear child abductors, germs, bullies, dirty toilets, the dark, spelling tests, talking in front of the class or being alone. It's not for us to reason why; our goal is to acknowledge, desensitise and give support to help them get on top. If we trivialise how a child feels, this affects their feeling of esteem. Children should be accepted along with their fears, feelings and frustrations. When they are hurt, acknowledge how they feel, then see how you can help. When they are upset with their results, let them know that they worked hard, then together work towards a better outcome next time.

It's okay to be wrong

The only people who don't do anything wrong are those who don't do anything. Children need to know that we all make mistakes. When a child makes a mistake or fears failure the problems appear bigger than they are and this eats away at their self-esteem. Children need to be encouraged to try, accepted when they fail and supported to try again. Explain that by making mistakes we learn from the process. Let them hear you say, 'I was wrong. I made a mistake. Next time I'll do it differently.'

Avoid words that wound

Children can be stubborn, defiant and intensely annoying. As parents we can accept this with a turn of the other cheek or give it back with all guns blazing. When parents are driven to the edge of mental destruction, it's easy to drop the nice talk and use words that wound: 'You've ruined it for all of us'; 'What's the point, you've destroyed the day'; 'Grow up'; 'Just go away'; 'Don't be so stupid'; 'Don't talk to me'; 'You know it all'; 'You just don't bother'.

Remember it is the behaviour, not the child, that we dislike. Even when they are merciless in their assault try to avoid using only negative words.

Use 'I' statements, not 'you' statements

Humans feel less criticised when they hear a statement about how you feel rather than how they annoy. So turn things around and say, 'I feel upset when we fight with each other'; 'I feel embarrassed when this happens in front of my friends'; 'I feel sad when I hear words like that'; 'I feel upset when my friends see this behaviour'. Also avoid the chill of passive-aggression, where the words are okay but the intonation is laced with poison.

Give them responsibility within reason

If I am to trust myself, I must feel I am trusted by others. Children need to experience independence, but they must also be kept safe. This balance between trust and safety is a tightrope we all tread.

Children can be slow, messy, unreliable and wasteful, but if we don't let them do real tasks, they will never learn. We also need to avoid constantly using negative words: 'Don't slice the bread, you'll cut your finger'; 'Don't run, you'll trip'; 'Don't touch it, you'll make a mess'; 'Don't climb, you'll fall'. Instead, turn the sentence around: 'Hold the railing so you're safe.'

The aim is to let our children hold the controls and fly as co-pilots with the captain sitting close by. Children need to feel trusted if they are going to trust themselves.

Help them savour success

Every human is made up of a mix of strengths and weaknesses. As adults we keep confident by promoting our attributes and camouflaging the rest. Many of the most impressive actors, artists and entrepreneurs of the moment are dyslexic, disorganised people, some with the attention span of a gnat. Yet they have risen to the top by moving the focus from weakness to strength. They may not read or attend but they are worshipped for their wit, creativity or humanity.

Every child needs to feel they have talent. Some get a great boost from team sports, while the lone spirits enjoy running, cycling, swimming or ascending some far-off peak. Craft, music, computers, drama and clubs are useful outlets. The aim is to move away from what our children cannot do to what they can do. For children to gain confidence they need to savour success at something, and it's up to us to find what that something is.

Aim for confidence in the classroom

The child who is strong socially and advanced academically will usually be confident at school, but those who underachieve find it hard to stay positive. Teachers boost esteem by making each child feel they are important and belong. So the child who struggles gets the same responsibilities and privileges as the potential Rhodes Scholar.

For example, a child who is weak in one area or socially insecure can be asked to tutor other children in their area of strength. With schoolwork, attempts are appreciated, mistakes are accepted and effort is acknowledged.

If homework is causing pain, set a fixed period during which they put in a full effort, then the books close and home life returns.

A final word

Over the years I have attended day-long seminars and read volumes on the subject of self-esteem. But much of the material was impressive-sounding fluff. I have no miracle methods, just these commonsense suggestions: start early, notice, listen, show genuine interest, recognise effort, be specific in praise, watch your words, accept feelings, give responsibility, show trust, accept screw-ups and allow each child to savour success at something.

Factors that affect esteem

1. Learning, physical and social abilities and attributes
   - held down by learning problems
   - held down by attention problems
   - social or mixing problems
   - physical problems – short, thin, fat, clumsy

2. Temperament and resilience
- some are created more resilient than others
- boosted by 'belonging'
- boosted by a close family
- boosted by a mentor or confidant

3. Self-perception
- you think you are the only one
- you see problems bigger than they are
- you worry over non-problems
- you believe that your role models are perfect

Encouraging self-esteem

1. Start early
- they need structure, stability, to know where they stand
- they need a close parent who is available
- they need grandparents who marvel at their cleverness

2. Notice and listen
- show genuine interest
- give specific feedback
- let them know they are worth listening to

3. Respect their fears and feelings
- fears are real – don't trivialise
- accept, support and help through

4. It's okay to be wrong
- accept mistakes, help them regroup, then try again

5. Watch your words
- avoid words that wound: 'You ruin', 'pest', 'stupid', 'get lost'

6. 'I' statements and 'you' statements
- state how you feel, not how they annoy

7. Responsibility and trust
- give responsibility within reason
- if we have trust in them, they have trust in themselves

8. Savouring success
- move the focus from failure to areas of talent
- seek out fun activities they can succeed at
- if school causes stress, build a fortress of outside activities

9. Classroom confidence
- to feel wanted and to belong
- responsibility and privileges
- tutor others in their area of strength
- homework with a focus on effort
- outside activities

SIXTEEN

Diet, weight and exercise

U ntil recently the word 'diet' meant a brief, painful period of depriva-
tion. Weight was something you lost before your high school reunion
and exercise was pounding the pavements or a six-month subscription to
the gym.

Now the secret is to establish a sensible diet, maintain appropriate
weight and adopt a more active, fitter lifestyle from an early age. And to
do it at a level that can be easily sustained over the next eighty years.

We can help set up our children for a healthy life by establishing a
sensible and sustainable balance of diet, exercise and lifestyle at the
earliest age. And that is what this chapter is all about.

A balanced diet

The energy that powers our children comes from the carbohydrates, fat
and protein in food. Of these, fat is by far the most potent provider of
energy. Such is the metabolism of young children, they need all the zip

they can get, and quite a bit must come from fat. After the age of six years, however, they need to gradually change to the low-fat, high-carbohydrate diet of the health-conscious adult.

Children also need iron, calcium and a range of vitamins.

A balanced diet of a small amount of meat, a substantial amount of dairy products and a variety of fruit, vegetables and cereal foods (such as breakfast cereals, bread and pasta) will give children everything they need to stay healthy and strong and to grow.

Children don't need lots of fizzy drinks or litres and litres of fruit juice. Good old tap water is a much better option.

Carbohydrates: quite complex

Carbohydrate is the main source of energy for parents, football players, athletes and children. It comes as simple, quickly digested sugars or the slower-released complex carbohydrate found in bread, breakfast cereals, pasta, rice and vegetables.

Complex carbohydrate foods contain varying amounts of dietary fibre. While fibre is not digested, it is vital to the long-term health of body and bowel.

Within reason, children can eat unlimited amounts of complex carbohydrate without increasing the risk of obesity. However, highly refined sugars do require some restriction as they are easy to take in excess, which can easily turn to body fat. Sugars also damage teeth. In an ideal diet at least two-thirds of the carbohydrate should be in the complex form.

Fats

If you were carrying all your provisions for a long Himalayan trek, fat would provide the most efficient source of energy. Children under six years need a high level of fat in their diet, but as they get older we should move them towards a diet that is lower in fat and high in complex carbohydrate.

Fat has over twice the kilojoules of carbohydrate so, while useful on a mountain climb, in normal life it tends to increase the risk of obesity and heart attack.

Today's new breed of cardiologist believes that the time to start preventing adult heart disease is not at the age of forty but at the age of six years. This is because studies have found that the earliest signs of coronary artery narrowing are commonly found in both young adults and adolescents. These fatty deposits in artery walls are laying down the foundation for future trouble.

The fat in our diet is intimately involved with the body's production of cholesterol. And cholesterol can cause the damage to arteries that causes heart disease.

A high total cholesterol is not necessarily a problem – it's the *type* of cholesterol that makes the difference. When fats are broken down they may produce 'good' cholesterol – high-density cholesterol (HDL), which reduces the risk of artery damage. But they can also produce 'bad' cholesterol – low-density cholesterol (LDL), which greatly raises the risk of heart attack and stroke. Those with the best chance of maintaining healthy arteries either have a low level of LDL cholesterol or an average LDL cholesterol, which is protected by a high HDL cholesterol.

Now this is where the fat intake and more specifically the type of fat eaten becomes important. Fat comes as saturated, polyunsaturated and monounsaturated fat. Fatty meat, butter, cream, many frying oils, cake shortenings and coconut milk have particularly high levels of saturated fat. When saturated fat is ingested it greatly increases LDL, the bad cholesterol, and lowers HDL, the good cholesterol. This raises the long-term risk of heart attack and stroke.

Until recently polyunsaturated fats were heavily promoted because they reduced the level of LDL cholesterol. Unfortunately, we now realise they also lowered the good, HDL level as well. This means they are better than saturated fats but they are still a problem. Monounsaturated fats are now promoted as the healthiest form of fat. They are found in olive oil, groundnut oil and canola oil, including spreads and 'butters' made from these. Monounsaturated fats raise HDL, the good cholesterol, and lower LDL, the bad cholesterol.

In practical terms you don't need to buy the most expensive forms of olive oil (extra virgin, first pressed, lurid green, etc). Switching to canola or groundnut oil is fine. Also use spreads which boast they are 'high in monounsaturates'. Remember:

- saturated fat increases LDL (the 'bad' cholesterol)
- polyunsaturated fat decreases LDL but also HDL (the 'good' cholesterol)
- monounsaturated fats decrease 'bad' cholesterol but tend not to affect 'good' cholesterol.

The ability to lay down fat in the arteries has a strong hereditary link: certain families seem relatively immune despite their diet while others who take great care may still develop heart disease. We can't change our genes but we can improve our children's chances if we lower the LDL and raise the HDL levels of cholesterol.

Protein, iron, calcium and vitamins

In this country the majority of children will consume more protein than they really need. If the majority of their protein supply is coming from meat, it will bring with it an ample amount of the best quality of absorbable iron. Iron is needed to make haemoglobin, which carries oxygen in the blood.

Milk and dairy products provide most of our children's intake of calcium. Establishing a good calcium habit is essential, as the mineral we set down in the first half of our lives helps protects us against brittle bones in older years. Statistics suggest that two-thirds of older women and one-third of older men suffer from osteoporosis, which is a lack of calcium and strength in the bones.

Where a family is strictly no meat and no dairy, they can easily run low on calcium and iron. If there is ever any doubt about the balance of a special food regime, discuss it with a dietitian.

Iron does not have to come from meat, and calcium does not need to come from a cow. There are alternatives, but sometimes it takes a mountain of other food to attain the correct levels of nutrition. The average ten-year-old requires 30 grams of quality protein, 7 milligrams of haem-type iron, 800 milligrams of calcium (girls need 900 milligrams) and 30 milligrams of vitamin C.

Vitamins can come as packs of pills, or through nature, by eating a wide variety of fruit and vegetables. The natural way has the added advantage of providing trace elements, antioxidants and other essential micronutrients.

In general, a child will have the right nutritional balance if they regularly eat small portions of meat, have a substantial dairy intake and enjoy a wide variety of fruit and vegetables.

Fruits and vegetables: the forgotten food group

While there has been much made of fats in recent years we seem to have overlooked fruits and vegetables. Survey after survey has shown that children are seriously short-changed in this department.' And yet it is becoming clear that these foods are not only brimful of vitamins and fibre but also umpteen other ingredients, such as antioxidants, which are now believed to play an important role in preventing degenerative diseases (heart disease, cancer, even diabetes) in later life.

Since this is a book on health, not chemistry, I will spare you the finer technical details. The main point is that children between six and twelve years need to get interested in fruit and vegetables and the wider the variety the better. While all this might sound like 'grandma knows best', it is worth taking seriously. Of course, most parents would give up their superannuation to get their kids to salivate over vegetables. But there are some tricks and, like superannuation, a small, early, regular investment gives good long-term results. Exposure is the key. Here are a few dos and don'ts:

Do

- Offer fruit morning, noon and night – and as snacks.
- Buy small amounts of many different kinds of fresh fruits and vegetables. Variety and freshness really help.
- Offer vegetables at every main meal – even in small amounts.
- Zip up the flavour by adding a little dressing to salads or a little margarine to cooked veggies.
- Remember: fruit with a little ice-cream is better than no fruit at all!

Don't

- Fuss, cajole or bribe children to eat vegetables.
- Despair if they say 'no thanks' with monotonous regularity; exposure is all-important here.
- Sneer at frozen or tinned vegetables.
- Expect children to eat vegetables that you would find tasteless.
- Give up. Fruit and veg are important for children.

Water: the ultimate health drink

The advertisement says, 'Diet Coke – less than one calorie.' But according to my research Diet Water has even less calories than Diet Coke. Water is a readily available, competitively priced drink. It should be introduced to our children early so as to establish brand loyalty.

Water is at its most boring when it splashes straight from the tap, but when chilled and served with ice or lemon it is much more appealing. For the ultimate presentation, put an empty glass in the freezer, then bring it to the table frosted, as if ready for the best French champagne.

Parents often overlook water and see fruit juice or milk as the main health drinks. The problem with juice is that it can be taken in excess. If one serving of orange juice contains over three oranges, after three drinks ten oranges are gurgling round, which can cause diarrhoea. While milk is the best source of calcium, when weight is a problem, it's wise to go for the low-fat varieties.

Some foods are better than others

'Health' foods

When your child goes to school with an all-natural health bar, while your neighbour's child has a slice of cake or a chocolate biscuit, you may not be providing any great health advantage. Some foods claim a healthy status due to the addition of yoghurt, carob, glucose or honey. But many, especially snack bars, may also contain too much fat and sugar. A muesli, carob or fruit bar may have half the fat content of chocolate, but that is still too much. Also, they are sticky, which glues sugar to the teeth and increases the risk of cavities. These bars certainly contain fibre, but only half what you would get from a banana.

Sugar is still sugar, whether it's called glucose, honey or molasses. Fat is always fat, whether it's called a health bar or not. Before you part with your money, read the label. The best health products for children are fruits, yoghurt, milk, bread, sandwiches and a wide variety of inexpensive, everyday foods.

'Cholesterol-free' food

Other snack foods that parents believe must be healthy are those labelled 'cholesterol free'. Yet, despite what is implied in advertisements, almost none of the cholesterol that damages our hearts comes from cholesterol we eat. The cholesterol that blocks arteries is mostly produced by the metabolism of fats in our diet.

You may buy a packet of crisps that is advertised as 'cholesterol free', but the crisps can still contain twenty-five per cent of an unhealthy sort of fat. Don't be fooled by misleading claims about cholesterol: read the label and establish the fat content before purchase. If you believe the manufacturer is trying to deceive, boycott their product.

Snacks: approximate fat and kilojoule levels

Note: Fat, especially saturated fat, is our greatest concern, not kilojoules.

Food	Fat content	Kilojoules
apple, large	0 g	400 kJ
banana, large	0.5 g	585 kJ
baked-bean sandwich	3 g	930 kJ
banana smoothie (full-cream milk),250 ml	10 g	1100 kJ
banana smoothie (half-fat milk), 250 ml	4 g	850 kJ
banana smoothie (low-fat milk), 250 ml	1 g	800 kJ
cheese,30 g	10 g	505 kJ
cheese cake (baked), average slice	55 g	3280 kJ
chocolate (fruit and nut), 6 squares	9 g	640 kJ
chocolate-chip cookie	3 g	225 kJ
carrot cake, average slice	42 g	2740 kJ
cup cake	6 g	760 kJ
doughnut (iced)	19.5 g	1425 kJ
Mars Bar, 63 g	11 g	1090 kJ
muesli bar	4.5 g	495 kJ
muffin (cake-bran)	8 g	530 kJ
potato crisps, 50 g packet	16 g	1050 kJ
quiche Lorraine, average slice	44 g	2400 kJ
yoghurt (fruit), 200 ml	4 g	740 kJ
yoghurt (low-fat), 200 ml	0.5 g	630 kJ

Fast food

The problem with fast food is not its speed but its fat content. What's more, it is usually the saturated, less healthy fats that predominate. A Big Mac and chips, half a Super Supreme pizza or a normal serving of Thai red curry would deliver more than a day's fat intake in one hit.

I don't wish to be a killjoy and ban these foods, but there must be sense in the servings. A Big Mac, eaten alone, has less than half the fat of a Big Mac, thickshake and medium fries. A Junior Burger and small fries has less fat than one Big Mac. One slice of pizza has half the fat of two slices. A half serving of that wonderful Thai curry has fifty per cent the saturated fat of a whole serving.

If weight is on target and the general diet is healthy, there is no problem in having one, or even two of these meals each week. Where weight is a problem or exercise limited, go slow on fast food.

Fast foods: approximate fat and kilojoule levels*

Food	Fat content	Kilojoules
Big Mac	24.6 g	2113 kJ
baked beans, one cup	1.5 g	715 kJ
bread, 1 slice	1 g	290 kJ
fried bread, 1 slice	12 g	840 kJ
chicken breast (baked, no skin), 90 g	3.5 g	470 kJ
chicken (deep-fried), 1 average piece	15 g	900 kJ
chicken nuggets, 6 pieces	17.7 g	1265 kJ
croissant	16.5 g	1150 kJ
fries (medium)	22 g	1702 kJ
ice-cream Cornetto	12 g	775 kJ
Junior Burger	8 g	1118 kJ
pasta bolognaise	20 g	1800 kJ
pasta carbonara	44 g	2750 kJ

Food	Fat content	Kilojoules
pepper steak	36 g	2250 kJ
pizza Super Supreme, one quarter	22 g	2140 kJ
rice (boiled)	0.5 g	915 kJ
rice (fried)	13.5 g	1490 kJ
sundae (hot fudge)	10.6 g	1318 kJ
sundae, no topping	6 g	772 kJ
sweet and sour pork	23.5 g	1925 kJ
Thai thick red curry	44 g	2220 kJ
thick chocolate shake, regular	9.5 g	1508 kJ

* *Nutritional Values of Australian Foods*, Australian Government Publishing Co, 1991; Leaflet, McDonalds Family Restaurants, 1998; Rosemary Stanton, *Fat and Fibre Counter*, 1993.

Weight and losing weight

It seems seriously unfair that some people eat enormously yet remain thin, while others go plump on the thought of a chip. In the past, it was thought to be quite simple: overweight was caused by overeating. But now we realise that fatness or thinness is greatly determined by genetic predisposition, which is then modified by the type of food consumed and the energy that is expended.

Studies suggest that if both parents are lean there is only a one in ten chance their children will be obese. When one parent is genetically over-weight, the risk rises to forty per cent, and where both have this problem, it rises to eighty per cent. Putting on the pounds is not all bad news: those people who do are effective metabolisers who are making the maximum use of what they take aboard. They're the family sedans with a fuel-efficient engine. So when the famine hits the land it is the plump ones who will survive, and the skinny supermodels will fade as quickly as you can say, 'Fabulous, daahling.'

The overweight baby or toddler will usually tone up and grow into an adult of normal size. But weight is much more serious at school age, because the fat child tends to become a fat adult. For this reason, if a child is an efficient metaboliser they will gain weight on an average diet, and will need to be committed to weight control all their life.

Adults find it relatively easy to maintain weight, but losing weight is many times more difficult. Fortunately, growing young children have an advantage: it is usually sufficient for them to maintain but not lose

Replacing fatty foods with low-fat foods

A child with a weight problem can be encouraged to cut down on fatty foods and to try some lower-fat alternatives. Here's a list of some popular fatty foods and some alternatives:

Cut down on these	Try more of these
fatty meat, sausages, salami	lean meat, chicken, fish (canned or fresh)
cakes, biscuits, snack foods (chips, etc.) pastries, croissants	bread, rolls, plain buns, plain crackers, pasta, rice
full-cream: milk, yoghurt, cheese, cream, ice cream	skim or semi-skimmed milk, low-fat yoghurt, low-fat cheeses, low-fat ice cream, frozen yoghurt
fruit juices, fizzy drinks, sports drinks	fruit, vegetables, water, diluted fruit juices
fried foods	grilled or baked food with little fat
butter, margarine, oil	low-fat spreads or butter substitutes that are light on kJs

Remember, the point here is emphasis and stealth. Few chubby nine-year-olds are going to relish an overnight abolition of their favourite foods, so gradually replace things in the left-hand column with those in the right. Even if you are only able to do this some of the time it will help.

weight. So as an overweight child grows in height their steady weight will gradually slip into a body of perfect proportion.

Losing weight for any child or adult must be approached as a long-term project. It is achieved by changing the balance of food intake and increasing exercise. So while we can't change our genes, we can change diet and exercise. As weight increases the ability to exercise reduces and that makes sensible food intake even more important.

The main target for weight reduction is to reduce fat. Get rid of fried foods, chips, sausage, pizza and fatty meat. Reduce the amount of butter, cream and the fat you add to bread, vegetables and pasta. Watch for the hidden fat in cakes, chocolate, biscuits and adding oil, butter or fat to normal cooking. Move from full-cream to half-cream milk and low-fat yoghurt.

Once fat intake is in control, target sweets, soft drinks and excessive amounts of fruit juice. The aim is to move from an over-sweetened, fatty diet to one that is high in the complex carbohydrates of bread, vegetables, cereal, rice, pasta and fruit. These by themselves need little restriction, but if they are greased up with butter and fatty spreads, the diet becomes a waste of time.

As well as diet there must be an increase in exercise. This starts by limiting television and computer time and getting children up and out. Increase the baseline level of activity by walking to school, going to the pool or getting on their bike.

Common drinks: approximate fat and kilojoule levels

Food	Fat content	Kilojoules
milk, 250 ml	9.5 g	675 kJ
milk (semi-skimmed), 250 ml	4.3 g	510 kJ
milk (flavoured), 250 ml	9.5 g	820 kJ
milk (soya fortified), 250 ml	8.5 g	800 kJ
orange juice, 250 ml	0 g	380 kJ
apple juice, 250 ml	0 g	440 kJ
cola, 250 ml	0 g	430 kJ
fruit cordial 250ml	0 g	350 kJ

Exercise

Don't expect that by attending school an unenthusiastic child will suddenly begin to enjoy exercise. The lead has to come from home. As parents we must set the right example by increasing, if necessary, the amount of exercise we do. The aim is to start them young and to develop patterns that we hope will last a lifetime.

With today's technology it is easy to be quite sedentary; in fact, you don't even have to move a buttock to adjust the telly. Previous generations had more fat and kilojoules in their diet, but they burnt them off with extra activity. As adults, we should try to walk instead of drive, use stairs instead of lifts and be more mobile in every part of our day. As for our children, we should walk with them to the shops, ride bikes and swim together. Television and computers should be limited and replaced with play. We should encourage them to play sport by being interested and supportive.

Regular exercise keeps muscles strong, helps our mental state and improves sleep. It controls weight and seems to lower the levels of the dangerous LDL cholesterol in the blood.

A final word

Good health in children comes from inheriting the right genes, having the right diet, watching weight, if necessary, and doing appropriate exercise. After the age of six children need a balanced diet that is relatively low in fat but high in complex carbohydrate. While we can't do anything about our genes, we can help a child keep their weight in check by eating well and doing exercise. Finally, the key to good health that lasts a lifetime is to *start early*.

Diet, weight and exercise

1. Diet
   - Up until the age of six, children need a diet high in fat. From the age of six, their diet should gradually change to one lower in fat and higher in carbohydrates.

- A balanced diet consists of a small amount of meat, a substantial amount of dairy products and a variety of fruit, vegetables and cereals.
- Water is the best thirst quencher.
- Children also need iron, calcium and a variety of vitamins. The best sources for these are foods, not vitamin pills.
- Children should be encouraged to eat a wide variety of fruit and vegetables.
- Like snack foods and fast food, some 'health' foods are high in fats and sugar.

2. Weight
- Fatness or thinness is greatly determined by our genes.
- Overweight school-age children tend to grow up into overweight adults.
- The best way to help a child lose weight is to reduce their fat intake by replacing fatty foods with low-fat alternatives.

3. Exercise
- Good exercise habits start at home: encourage your child to play sport, ride bikes or swim, and do some exercise yourself.
- Limit television and computer time.
- Regular exercise keeps muscles strong and improves sleep.

SEVENTEEN

A child's view of death, divorce and religion

A death or divorce in the family destabilises a child's world and reduces the emotional availability of those they depend on. The child's reaction to this situation will depend on their age and how well their custodians can come to terms with their own upset.

Religion brings support and values to many families. At the age of six, children will follow faithfully; by ten years they may start to question; and by adolescence they are beginning to plan their own destiny. This chapter looks at death, divorce and religion to see how they impact on today's children.

Children and death

Children learn about death through hearing their parents talk, watching the news and when Rover goes to the doggie kennels in the sky. Where a death is within the family, how the child responds will depend on how close they were to the person who died and how the death disrupts the equilibrium of their life. Also, a child's reaction to death varies greatly with age.

The under-six-year-old

At this age a child has no grasp of the concept of death. They respond to the disruption and perceived abandonment in their life but have no understanding of death and dying. When asked what happened, they repeat what they have been told, but they don't know what it means. To them there is no finality in death – the person might as well be on a long holiday.

This is an egocentric age where children are concerned about their own immediate needs, and don't grieve directly for the one who has died. They may feel angry that this relative has walked out as well as unsettled by the fears and tension that have overtaken the home.

The reaction of young children to the effect of death in their home can be intense and immediate. They become restless, clingy, difficult or they may regress. I am often asked to arrange counselling for an upset child following a family loss. But with these under-six-year-olds, it is usually the parent, not the child, who needs counselling. Once the adults find their equilibrium again, the child miraculously returns to normal.

When it is the closest and most important attachment figure who has died, it has an immense impact on a young child. Now it is an urgent priority to surround them with as much alternative and consistent support as possible.

The six- to eight-year-old

Though children aged six to eight are more mature, they are still predominantly influenced by the emotional state of their parents. They now have some slight understanding of death, but to them it may not really be permanent and their grandma may still be alive if they visit her home.

At this age a child may carry hidden worries and sometimes think they are to blame. For example, their brother may have died of leukaemia, and they worry they may have caused the death through resentment or jealousy. These secret agendas are at their most severe when parents retreat inwardly, bottle up their feelings and don't keep children informed.

The under-eight-year-old will ask copious questions. What they are after is reassurance, not a detailed answer. Their unsettled behaviour will resolve once stability and warm communication return.

The eight- to twelve-year-old

After the age of eight years a child starts to develop an almost-adult understanding of death. They see life far into the future and they realise that death is permanent.

Children will always be influenced to some extent by the stability or distress of their parents, but their grief is now their own. A nine- or ten-year-old will show the adult emotions of tears, preoccupation and periods of sadness. Some withdraw and become hard to reach. Occasionally their behaviour may be difficult, but this is more a sign of irritation with the world than a deliberate challenge to their parents.

To visit or not?

When a close relative becomes terminally ill, do we encourage a visit or preserve a happier memory? If the event is sudden, catastrophic and short term, there is little benefit in a visit. Where there is more time and the relative is still mentally alert, there is good reason to keep contact.

For children under the age of six years a visit brings no great benefit to their understanding, acceptance or adjustment. If they go, this is for the needs of their parents and the relative, not their own. After six years and particularly after the age of eight, a visit will allow the family to share together, gives a major life experience and provides a point for the older child to start their grief.

There is no right or wrong answer – just some guidelines. Personally, I would not involve under-six-year-olds. However, I would take a child over eight for all but the most major or short-term situations.

To view the body or not?

Viewing the dead is favoured by some families, and when it is the norm, adults and children should observe this practice together. It has no emotional advantage for the under-six-year-old, who will probably just ask endless, awkward questions. However, for the older child it is a moment they will appreciate being a grown-up and part of their family.

For me, the lid will be nailed and glued tightly shut. I want to be remembered as warm, enthusiastic and alive.

Children and funerals

A funeral is an occasion when adults can say their last goodbyes and start the process of resolution. A child eight years or older has the same need to grieve as their parents, and should be encouraged to attend. The six- to eight-year-old has less to gain, but while not essential, it's best to include them in the family group. The three-, four- and five-year-old has little understanding of death and gets no benefit from a funeral. At this young age it is parents and the expectation of others that influence whether a preschooler attends or not.

The need for open communication

Young children ask endless questions but don't have much interest in the answers. Adults often cope with these queries by hiding behind the jargon of death: 'We have just lost your grandma'; 'She is sleeping in wonderful peace'; 'She is happy up with the angels.' With explanations like these children may wonder where it was you lost Grandma or may see sleep as a dangerous occupation.

Adults also make the mistake of believing that the under-eight-year-old needs deep and detailed answers. But when a five-year-old asks an innocent question they will be happy with a few words of general reassurance. It is your availability and unflustered attention they want because this lets them know they are safe and secure.

The over-eight-year-old wants more information, and it's best to be honest and open. When Grandma is ill, tell the truth: 'Yes, we are very worried. She may die, but we are doing all we can to help.' If parents become stoic and non-communicative, children may bottle up their feelings, generate strange fears and get stuck in their resolution. But of course, it is hard for parents to talk openly and clearly when they are drowning in their own grief.

Divorce and separation

There are many similarities between a child's reaction to death and their reaction to divorce. Their understanding of the event depends on their age, and all children are immensely influenced by the stability and emotional well-being of their parents.

It is believed that the children of a hostile break-up suffer more deeply than a together family that loses their dad through a tragic accident. When a parent dies friends flock around, there is a funeral, then life slowly starts to get back on track. In a messy divorce friends have confused loyalties, there is no turn-around point and hostility can go on for years.

How children react

The under-six-year-old is all feeling and no understanding. They resent what has happened and react by clinging closely or responding with bad behaviour. They don't know what is going on but they hate the tension and disruption.

The six- to eight-year-old is also confused and disturbed by the disruption. They have a limited understanding, and are more unsettled than disruptive in their reaction.

The over-eights are more aware and they know that this event is forever. They may be confused in their loyalties. They often react with preoccupation, withdrawal and a reduction in academic grades.

Whatever the age, children do best when parents act amicably and maintain the maximum environmental stability. For more information on separation see Chapter 20, page 208.

Religion

Humans are at their emotional best when they see a future, a purpose and a meaning to life. Religious faith provides this for many families. Religion at its best brings values, a common goal, family strength and a supportive community network. At its worst, it can create fear and guilt and can legitimise inequality.

With my interest in the emotional welfare of children, I see the family strength and togetherness of religion as an immense advantage. And as one who studies child development, I wonder how much of a child's faith is the blind acceptance that is a normal stage in the young child and what part comes from a deep, personal commitment?

The development of true belief

The under-eight-year-old will totally accept the sayings, values and beliefs of their close family. At this age their parents are the most important source of learning, and they will repeat word for word what they have been told, without question.

The child over eight years ceases to take things at face value and may start to question their parents' beliefs. Though most will follow their family's beliefs and practices, they may start to have inner doubts and unspoken worries.

Eight years is an important milestone. At eight, children become less selfish and tune into the needs of others in the group. They start to compare, compete and worry that they are not as good or as giving as others. This new-found conscience and self-criticism brings the first feelings of genuine guilt. This kind of guilt is different from the pseudo guilt of the four-year-old who eats Mum's chocolates and looks guilty. The four-year-old's response is conditioned by the memory of the sore bottom they got the last time. But an eight-year-old's feelings of guilt come from conscience.

Guilt can be a catalyst that inspires humans to strive for self-betterment. On the other hand, feelings of negative self-worth have kept a generation of adult psychiatrists in business. But guilt does play an important part in some of the world's religions: it drives the wish to reach a higher plane and seek forgiveness. With extreme fringe groups fear and guilt hold the flock together, because to falter leads to perpetual damnation.

In adolescence, religion comes of age. These almost-adults challenge everybody and everything, especially the values of their parents. But this is the dawn of the development of abstract thought, when we work out our own values, causes and convictions. It is here, in the late teens, that true personal belief has its foundation. Now it is faith that comes direct from the heart.

Children and death, divorce and religion

1. Death
   - the under-six-year-old has no grasp of the finality of death
   - the six- to eight-year-old may have hidden worries, which can be made worse if parents don't keep them informed
   - the eight- to twelve-year-old is developing an understanding of death and needs to be allowed to grieve

- visiting terminally ill relatives can be a positive experience for older children but the under-sixes will benefit little
- viewing the body, if favoured, should be done as a family
- children over six can benefit from attending the funeral with their family
- children need to be kept informed, but don't give overly detailed answers to questions

2. Divorce and separation
   - under six years, children don't understand but will hate the disruption
   - between six and eight, children have some understanding and can be confused and disturbed
   - over eight years, children understand the finality of separation and may be confused about where their loyalties lie

3. Religion
   - religion can bring families together, providing values, a common goal and a supportive community network
   - religion can create fear and guilt in children
   - the under-eight-year-old accepts without question the beliefs of their close family
   - the eight- to twelve-year-old may start to question their parents' beliefs

EIGHTEEN

Sex education, sexual development and other sex-related issues

Children are created in two sorts: little girls and little boys. At the age of six years, their size and physical strength are very similar. Then, somewhere between the age of ten and fourteen years, the pubertal growth spurt will start. Girls are first to take off, and for a brief time are taller and more physically strong than the male of the species. After this there are considerable differences between the sexes, the male becoming larger and stronger, the female probably more mature and sensible.

Though adolescence is the age that causes most sexual concern for parents, the attitudes to sex that are important are laid down very much earlier.

Sex education

It's simple: start early, be open and address questions as they arise. Gone are the days when you waited until sixteen years to say, 'John, there is something I have to tell you.' Now, many sixteen-year-olds could educate their parents.

From the youngest age, address genuine questions when asked. If you sidestep and look flustered this suggests that sex is nasty, rude or taboo. Sometimes questions are asked to gain attention. I remember my boys asking their grandma, 'What's that word that begins with f and ends with k?' This got her full attention after which they continued, 'Ah yes. Fire truck.'

The biggest mistake parents make is being evasive or giving more information than is wanted. The under-tens need the simplest of answers, not the surgical details of breast augmentation, research findings on feromones or a summary of the Kinsey Report.

For the over-tens, if I were clever enough to get through to them, my sex education message would include the following:

- creating children without a stable relationship is rarely wise
- sole parenthood for the majority means poverty and loneliness
- trusting in luck is not an effective form of contraception
- both sexes are responsible for making children, and both sexes are responsible for contraception.

As for AIDS, I would quote a wise but politically incorrect Australian, the late Professor Fred Hollows: 'Currently in Australia almost all cases of AIDS result from two things: anal receptive sex and the misuse of dirty needles. If you're going to get serious about AIDS education, these must be the main areas to address.'

Sexual development

The first sign of approaching puberty is a sudden acceleration in height. For girls the average age that this happens is eleven and a half years (this ranges from ten to thirteen years). Boys get moving slightly later, with the average age being thirteen and a half years (the usual range is ten and a half to fifteen years).

As this growth spurt gets going, pubic hair appears and girls see the first sign of breast development. The breasts are fully formed by about fifteen years (this ranges from twelve to eighteen years). The first period occurs at about thirteen years, but with great variation – somewhere between eleven and sixteen years.

Sexual development often follows a family pattern. A mother who started to develop early or late may have daughters that follow the same pattern. But there is a considerable variation between children, which means there can be great differences in the height and maturity of children around this eleven to fourteen age group. If you are in any way concerned that puberty has arrived too early, too late or is unusual in any way, it's best to discuss this with your paediatrician. When they are undecided, they will ask the advice of a specialist in growth and endocrinology.

Other sex-related issues

Sexual interest and exploration

The under-eights have little worry about nudity, and at this young age there is no problem with communal changing. Five- and six-year-old boys and girls can bath together as can seven-year-olds with some supervision. But after the age of eight years our society expects us to segregate the sexes.

Children vary greatly in their maturity and wish for modesty, and we must be sensitive to their wishes. For parents it doesn't much matter what society expects – our aim is to protect innocent little people from hurt and exploitation.

Young children are fascinated by anatomical difference. It is quite common to find a four-year-old boy and girl, stark naked, checking out each other's assets. This is an innocent part of life education, which we calmly accept but firmly discourage. Six- and seven-year-olds are still inquisitive, and it's not uncommon for some superficial investigation and touching. At this age, and to some extent in the following years, our response should remain low-key, but rules must be clearly stated and the opportunity for repetition avoided.

Interest in the opposite sex is not unhealthy, and nudity, viewing and superficial touching are usually harmless. However, this depends on there being a mutual interest, no force and the children being of similar age. A ten-year-old investigating a six-year-old may be part of an isolated episode of innocent curiosity, but the inequality of age is potentially dangerous and should be guarded against in the future. Where one child demonstrates overtly sexual behaviour that is significantly out of keeping with their developmental age, this is of great concern, as it can be a sign of sexual abuse (see this chapter, page 198).

Using the correct words

Preschoolers can have pet names for private parts, but by school age it's best to stick to the correct terminology. Whether we like it or not, our children will be exposed to 'improper' words, because these are used in the real world.

One infants principal told me of his campaign to clean up the language in his school. There were no rude words allowed, and private parts were to be labelled appropriately. Then one boy was brought to his office after having called his mate a 'dickhead'. The principal decided to set an example, telling the boy, 'John, you are not allowed to use the word "dick". What is the proper name for what you have between your legs?' John seemed puzzled, then looked down and immediately saw the answer: 'It's the carpet, sir.'

Masturbation

Both boys and girls play with their private parts because it gives them pleasure. This was once considered an evil perversion, but now it is accepted as a normal, healthy part of life. Parents feel distress when a child self-stimulates, but our disquiet must not cause our child to feel guilty about this normal activity.

Little boys can get erections from the first day of life, and obviously this has no sexual relevance. Once their nappies are removed, boys and girls (predominantly boys), will frequently hold or touch. This continues to some extent throughout childhood, but with age, they do it with more discretion or in private.

The incidence of masturbation varies considerably from child to child. Occasionally we see early school-age children who rub against objects or are quite open in this activity. This is usually a sign of boredom or stress, and though it is extremely upsetting for parents and teachers, it is usually an innocent behaviour. If the child is persistent and does it in public, state the social rules, suggest they move to another room, give a subtle signal of disapproval and use a behavioural approach that turns the focus to fiddle-free days. Occasionally major masturbation can be a sign of sexual abuse.

Homosexual or heterosexual

It's amazing how attitudes change. In my medical student training homosexuality was seen as a psychiatric disorder. Homosexual men came seeking desensitisation therapy. Treatment involved the viewing of compromising pictures and when incorrectly aroused viewers were rewarded with an electric shock. But we have moved a million miles from that position, and homosexuality is now accepted as a common and unchangeable difference.

With such publicity and 'outness' from the gay lobby, parents may wonder whether their children might start to march to a different drum. In fact, most modern researchers believe that homosexuality and bisexuality are, to a large extent, in the biological make-up of the individual. They are certainly not caused by parenting style, homosexual assaults or mixing with the wrong sort of company. But how homosexuality might be recognised in the five- to twelve-year-old is much less certain.

Many normal ten- to eighteen-year-old heterosexuals have periods of attraction to those of their own sex, but their main interest will remain heterosexual. However, retrospective studies of adult homosexuals often report a more predominantly homosexual preference in childhood. While the majority of effeminate boys and tomboy girls are destined to be heavily heterosexual, retrospective studies again suggest more homosexuals come from these beginnings.

Though some homosexual boys are firmly oriented by the age of fourteen years, for most this realisation comes after some trial and error close to the age of twenty. For homosexual girls the realisation can often be somewhat later, even in the thirties, after marriage and children.

But gone are the days of shock therapy: you don't drive homosexuality out of the brain and body. And while it's common, it's probably less frequent than has been recently promoted.

Cross-dressing and gender dissatisfaction

Adults may cross-dress through their wish to be of a different gender (transsexual), their desire to attract a homosexual partner (effeminate homosexual) or as a fetish that gives sexual pleasure (transvestite). But these preoccupations are not in the minds of young children, and ninety-nine per cent of all cross-dressing and gender confusion in children is harmless, normal childhood play and of no concern.

Young children will often dress in their mum's or dad's clothes. This is quaint, normal and not a sign of perversion. It is best managed without undue comment or fuss. But where there is persistence and preoccupation rather than it being an occasional fun activity, it is wise to seek reassurance from a child psychologist.

It is quite common for a boy under the age of ten years to say they want to be a girl, and vice versa. This is usually entirely innocent and irrelevant. However, when a child overstates it and is persistent for over a year or more it's best to check what's happening by arranging a referral to a professional. Occasionally a psychiatrist may believe that some uncertainty in the home environment is the cause of gender confusion.

Parents: how intimate is too intimate?

Families who are open in communication and free from sexual hang-ups produce children who will develop the most appropriate adult attitudes. These parents are comfortable about nakedness, but they have boundaries between appropriate intimacy and overstepping the mark. The current emphasis on abuse has led many good parents to question the instincts they once trusted.

There is no problem with young children bathing, showering and sleeping with parents. There will be times when even a seven- or eight-year-old will ask about or even touch adult parts. This is common and best managed in a matter-of-fact way: state that there are social rules and that this is not appropriate.

With the tens to teens it's fine to be intimate, but quickly move away when anything happens that might arouse or lead to misinterpretation. Fathers can relate closely to older daughters and can be even closer when two parents are present.

We have to be particularly careful after a marriage break-up, however. When hostility continues after the break-up we need to exercise extreme caution, because the smallest incident can be misrepresented to the maximum malice. Take extra care when new companions, partners or potential step-parents are involved.

Concerns of sexual abuse

The statistics vary from study to study but, at the most conservative estimate, one in ten adult women and one in twenty adult men have suffered sexual abuse in childhood. The extent of this varies from an incident of touching to major repeated sexual activity.

The worst part of sexual abuse is that the perpetrator is usually a trusted adult or adolescent who is well known to the child. They can be a relative, family friend, stepfather or even father. In sexual abuse, power is inappropriately misused and children are made to feel guilty and frightened to speak out.

As a paediatrician, I find this an extremely difficult diagnosis to make. In its most clear-cut presentation, abuse shows as obvious physical damage or there is an unmistakable history. More commonly, the only sign is a change in behaviour. The child may withdraw into themselves, become angry or display inappropriately explicit sexual behaviour. When an astute parent sees this change they may pick up clues of the assault, but often the child is so guilty and confused they maintain a code of silence.

I often see another side to this when parents are incorrectly reported and investigated as abusers. In my experience this usually happens with children who have a major developmental problem that results in some disinhibited, inappropriate sexual behaviour. There is no evidence of abuse, just out-of-step behaviour that prompts the diligent child care worker to make the report. Often the families are already struggling to stay afloat, and while this assault on parents may be legally necessary, it is extremely destructive. Abuse damages children, but false claims of abuse can pull apart stressed families.

The main message for parents is to educate but not terrify children about the possibility of abuse, stranger danger and the importance of saying no. We need to know the whereabouts of our children and thus lessen the opportunity for misuse. We must listen carefully, especially when a girl becomes withdrawn or a boy becomes unexpectedly aggressive. We must be on our guard when there is any unexplained, inappropriately explicit sexual behaviour.

One of the saddest aspects of abuse is that the child can no longer trust the adults who are supposed to protect them. The sad part for me is that I probably diagnose only a small proportion of the children in my care who are abused.

Sex education, sexual development, and other sex-related issues

1. Sex education
   - start early
   - answer genuine questions clearly and simply

2. Sexual development
   - girls reach puberty between ten and thirteen years
   - boys reach puberty between ten and a half and fifteen years
   - how early or late a child develops may follow a family pattern
   - if you have any concerns about your child's sexual development, talk to your paediatrician

3. Other sex-related issues
   - masturbation is normal, healthy and usually innocent in children
   - homosexuality is probably part of an individual's biological make-up
   - homosexuals may not be sure of their sexual orientation until their twenties or even thirties, but they may show a preference in childhood
   - cross-dressing in children is normal and should be managed with minimum fuss, unless the child overstates it or is persistent for a year or more, in which case, see your paediatrician
   - families who are open in communication and free from sexual hang-ups produce children who develop the most appropriate adult attitudes
   - sexual abuse is most often committed by a known and trusted adult or adolescent

NINETEEN

Television, computers and the Internet

I worry about the current assault by television on both children and adults. I dislike the way it impedes conversation, reading, physical exercise and creative play. I resent the beaming of so much cruelty, horror, unhappiness and anger into my home. I don't wish to be a hermit or a Luddite, but there must be more control over this intrusive invention.

Computers and the Internet provide another screen. When they are used appropriately they can bring valuable skills and knowledge, but when they are misused, they can promote isolation, poor socialisation and glazed-eyed solitude.

The main thing to remember, whether it's television, computer time or access to the Internet, is that parents have control – they are not controlled by other people's transmissions.

Television

Today's television is so influential, parents need to take their children's choice of programmes as seriously as they would their diet or education.

We can't act like the KGB and jam all unwanted radio signals, but parents must take charge of the box. However, this can be extremely difficult, because marketing forces have raised some shows to the status of essential viewing. At school, the previous night's episode is the hot topic of conversation and those who missed out look like oddballs from a distant galaxy. Maybe it's time to join with other parents from your children's class and lay down some limits to resist these pressures.

Parents setting limits

At home you can start by establishing a rule that the television is turned on for specific programmes, but when the show's over, the plug is pulled. Parents need to set a good example: watch what is important to you and switch off the rest. Check programme guides and plan in advance what your children will and will not watch.

Television should be off during family meals in the hope that parents and children can rediscover conversation. Discuss the content of programmes and the tricks of advertising with your children. Children can learn that commercials rarely advertise what is essential or healthy: we can point out that there are few adverts for tap water, fresh fruit, or warnings against the fat content of fast foods or confectionery.

If you're watching the news clarify the stories for your children. They need to be reassured that most of what they see is happening at the other end of the earth and should not cause fear or concern in their own community. Unfortunately, young children under eight years don't always understand: to them, horror footage from central Bolivia might as well be happening at the end of their street.

I recognise there is a definite place for television and videos, but in overdose they desensitise and destabilise and may replace other useful activities like exercise, conversation, hobbies or even homework.

Television violence and fear

Studies of North American seventeen-year-olds find they have spent more time at the television than in face-to-face education at school. While this is going on, they will have been exposed to multiple murders, countless acts of violence, role models of dubious character and a stream of sadness and cruelty.

There are over 1000 reviews and studies that point to a link between TV violence and aggression in children, adolescents and adults. Organisations now exist in most countries that draw attention to this effect on our children. These organisations are concerned that cartoon violence and the mistreating of others on television distort the views of the very young child. They can show evidence that the stream of attractive, violent heroes we see on our screens influences the ideals of children and encourages aggression. They note that even violence mixed with humour can lead to desensitisation, so children fail to notice the hurt or suffering of others. They are especially unhappy with the current presentation of the news, which, through unnecessary images, leaves children and adults suspicious, frightened and with a scary view of their world.

I agree with these views and have special concern about news programming. To be high rating a story must promote controversy, discord, wallow in the suffering of others and be accompanied by graphic visual footage. News is driven by these criteria – not the relevance of the information.

In Australia I have to endure images of an irrelevant murder-suicide in California, a spectacular car accident in Ohio, or a helicopter hitting power lines in Luxembourg. This arrives in my home just because a Sydney TV channel has secured some explicit footage. It is no wonder that adults and children are afraid to walk the streets or see the world as hostile and without compassion.

Television viewing and violence

1. With current viewing habits, at the age of seventy years, each of us will have spent a total of seven years in front of the television.

2. In their first eighteen years of life, the average North American child will see 18,000 murders, observe 200,000 sexual remarks or acts and be exposed to 360,000 commercials.

3. Reports from the US National Institutes of Mental Health acknowledge a strong link between long-term exposure to television violence and aggressive, insensitive behaviour.

4. Children and adults can become numb and less compassionate with an overfocus on cruelty, injustice, discord and violence by watching too much negative television. This leaves people demoralised and fearful of a world that in reality contains much gentleness and good.

5. Even violence associated with humour disturbs, desensitises and increases aggressive behaviour.

Computers

Computers are a fact of life. We live in a world where knowledge of computers and how to use them is becoming more and more important. When today's children reach adulthood, many if not most of them will work with computers in their jobs. Most schools provide access to computers but, understandably, many parents feel that a computer at home will be of educational value to their child.

Supervision is the key

The trick with computers and children is supervision. Keep a close eye on your child's computer use. One way to do this is to limit their access to it. If you haven't already invested in a computer, before you do, decide how it will be used, for what and when, and make sure your child understands these 'rules of use'. Start your child on software that is 'beneficial', such as educational software. Most of these are now sufficiently game-like to grab the attention of the uninitiated for hours. Or, at first, you could insist that the computer only be used for school projects.

Computer games

Once children have been exposed to 'real' games, they are less interested in other types of software, and you'll probably be fighting a losing battle if you try to insist that the computer is only to be used for educational purposes. The best way to manage this is to limit access time and, as always, supervision is the key.

When you're buying a new computer, ask the hardware provider not to load games onto the hard drive. If games are offered as part of the purchase package, ask for the discs to be supplied separately. In this way, you have more control over what games your child can play.

Computer games do have their uses: they are a powerful source of behavioural modification and can be used as incentives or rewards. However, they have this power only if the child doesn't have free access to them at all times. By keeping the discs safely out of reach, you retain command.

Delete any 'adult' or violent games from your hard drive, even if you don't possess the disc for it and will lose it forever. Of course, your child may have access to unsuitable games at friends' homes. If you know that computer games are on the agenda during a visit, a quiet chat with the parents usually helps.

When supervised, computer games have their share of benefits. They can act as a tutor: word processing or a fun typing programme sometimes help even the most unmotivated with pencil and paper to become productive on screen. As well, computer games can help the disorganised to plan. Eye–hand coordination and speed of reflexes can be honed. High-quality graphics can incite creativity.

So the news isn't all bad: some experts believe that playing computer games excessively is unlikely to do most children harm, any more than playing other games. The key with computers is to retain control: you decide what the computer will be used for and when. It will probably be impossible to prevent your child from playing computer games. Instead, set limits and stick by them.

The Internet

Once you have a computer, you (or your child) will probably be keen to get online to discover the 'wonders' of the Internet. And the Internet can be wonderful: there are countless informative, educational and fascinating sites that can provide an excellent resource for homework and school projects (the Encyclopaedia Britannica site is one such site). But the Internet can also be incredibly time consuming, time wasting and sometimes inaccurate, and because anyone can set up a site about anything, a lot of sites are unsuitable for children.

The key, again, is supervision. Children should never have access to the Internet unsupervised, even if supervision is just out of the corner of your eye. Cyberspace can broaden general knowledge, help with assignments and homework, build self-esteem and provide opportunities to practise social interactions. But unfortunately it is also the gateway to online 'child predators' and unsound advice.

Before you decide to hook up to the Net there are some other things you will need to consider.

Cost

The Internet can be very expensive, so make sure you are connected by a low-cost phone call and that the Internet provider offers good value. Of course, the cheapest provider may not be the best if you spend longer on the phone line downloading pages.

Rules of access

As with the computer, you'll need to set out some firm rules of use. Perhaps your child is allowed on the Internet on only certain days or evenings. When there are two or more children jostling for access, you will need to set strict time limits for each child. When children are surfing the Net or zapping aliens in some computer game an hour seems to them like five minutes, so if there are any disputes, set up a timer.

Internet access can also be used as a reward, and loss of access as a punishment.

Where to go in cyberspace

If you are unsure of where your child should go, there are guidebooks to Internet addresses suitable for children. A hazard of even a harmless Internet address is that children may be able to access other tempting sites via advertisements placed by shrewd advertisers. These temptations are hard to ignore and are distracting to even the most tunnel-visioned adults. Agree beforehand that clicking on advertisements is taboo.

Remember too that not all the information available on the Internet is reliable or even true. It may not be evil, malicious or unsuitable for children but they may have to learn early that not everything that grown-ups tell them is correct and to check more than one source.

Avoiding unwanted sites

Recently a young boy in the United States bought a medical practice in Florida with his parent's credit card over the Internet. Even if you think your child is a budding doctor, you're probably not ready to invest in their first practice just yet. Shopping over the Internet is just one of a list of 'services' to which you'd probably prefer your child had no access. Luckily, there are sites on the Internet that provide programmes to screen out dangerous or unwanted information. For example, anything with a sex theme, drugs, gambling, alcohol, shopping (unless you want to lose a lot of money quickly!), cults, firearms, explosives and so on can be blocked off. There are also programmes to block online advertisements. However, be aware that blocking is not foolproof, as some unwanted Internet sites have innocuous names that belie their true nature. Also, bright children will always find a way around Internet 'walls' – or their friends will tell them. Again, supervision is the answer.

What are the don'ts?

Children should not give out personal information on the Internet. This blanket rule includes not only their or their family's real names, address and phone number but also credit card details. (In fact, children of this age should not have access to any lines of credit at all.)

A final word

Television is here to stay. But TV can become a negative presence in our homes when we are overexposed to it, leaving us no time for other enjoyable things (a chat around the dinner table, for example). As well, studies have found a link between exposure to violence on television and aggression in children and adults. The answer is to set limits: limit your child's viewing to one or two hours a day and certain programmes only.

There is no reason for parents to shy away from computers and the Internet. If we don't master them, we will be their slaves. Ignorance of computers or the Internet may be considered akin to illiteracy before long, so there is every reason for parents to take the first step.

Your children will spend most of their lives working with a keyboard and computers and should learn good practices early, such as typing skills and the importance of backing up homework. Learning keyboard skills now might prevent RSI in twenty years.

If children have learned to troubleshoot computer problems, how to save their work and housekeep discs, how to run a new programme from first principles without the manual and how to search the Internet, then time spent zapping aliens will not have been wasted.

Television, computers and the Internet

1. Television
   - Set limits: read the television guide ahead of time and allocate appropriate viewing.
   - When a chosen programme is finished, turn off the set.
   - Restrict viewing to one hour per day, with an absolute maximum of two hours per day.
   - Recognise the effect of excessive television viewing on fitness and obesity.
   - Don't watch television during family meals. Reintroduce talk and relating.
   - Many studies have shown a direct link between violence on television and aggression in children and adults.
   - Discuss the content of programmes to provide a reality check.
   - Limit news watching by both adults and children.
   - Discuss news stories to differentiate between what is happening in our local community and events far across the globe.
   - Television channels beam a signal; parents control the power supply.
   - The most important goal is to switch from constant bombardment to the watching of specific programmes.

2. Computers
   - Agree on limits of use in advance.
   - Supervision is the key.
   - Start children off with fun educational software.
   - Avoid exposing your child to adult or violent games.
   - Games can develop your child's learning and motor skills.

3. The Internet
   - Agree on limits of use in advance.
   - Supervise children's access to the Internet.
   - The Internet can be educational but teach children that not everything on the Net is 'true'.
   - Invest in an Internet screening programme.
   - Teach children that personal information must not be given out.

Separation, sole parent-hood and step situations: protecting our children

It is estimated that between one-quarter and one-third of today's children will be living with just one parent at some time before they have left school. No matter how positively we approach sole parenthood, it can make life immensely difficult. Even with the most amicable settlement there is usually a major change to the stability and living standard of the family. This chapter is not about the rights of parents; it's about children who are being hurt and how we can protect their welfare.

The games people play

Woody Allen fans are fascinated by the emotional tangles of the characters in his films, but these are nothing compared with the tangles of his own life. The Allen–Farrow break-up was fought with such bitterness that even in Australia I felt the anger. If I could sense it ten thousand miles away, what were the children feeling?

But their case is not unique. I frequently see children who have been used as a weapon in their parents' battle. Some couples spend thousands of pounds arguing in court what less angry people could settle in ten minutes over a cup of tea. I see access used to cause the maximum amount of hurt and disruption. Over the years I have come across abductions, bogus claims of sexual abuse, unjustified attempts to block access and countless demands for children to be kept away from a new partner. I have seen intelligent mothers try to change the child's name to their maiden name, just to punish the father.

Some fathers feel they have been given an amazingly raw deal, and it leaves them disheartened and sometimes quite dangerous. Other self-employed fathers hide their true income and, after the settlement, they live in under-the-counter affluence while their family sink into poverty.

Many custodial mothers come out of the break-up confused, isolated and depleted in self-confidence. When they start a new relationship, they're caught between the needs of the children and their need to make the relationship work. These two demands often conflict, especially when the new partner has an emotional inadequacy that motivates them to be over-possessive and jealous.

Frequently I see relationships like this, where a new partner cannot cope with any competition. They are intensely jealous if the children show any affection towards their natural father or mother, their grandparents or to people they have known for years. They cannot accept that children always have enough love to share. Sometimes the new couple will move to a far-off location. While this may be for genuine reasons, it is often to help the insecure adult avoid competition. But in the process, the children are deprived of much-needed support and love.

It's not fair

After breaking up, many parents feel they have been treated unfairly. Often this was a split they never wanted and it has been made worse by adverse decisions about property, custody and maintenance. But this is just the start.

Over ninety per cent of children will live with their mother. In the months following the break-up both partners' living standard may drop, but a year later there is usually a marked discrepancy in available money between the sole mother and the non-custodial father. Fathers generally lead a relatively free life, while the expense of child minding, the limited opportunity for part-time work and the restrictions on social life are more confining for the custodial mother.

Most custodial parents get the worst end of access. After a day of spoiling, the tired child is returned, accompanied by a pile of dirty washing. To add to the injustice, the child is unsettled and takes out their anger on the parent who gives most time and love.

The damage

It is not the break-up but hostility and ongoing instability that affects children badly. With **hostility** there can be so much tension before separation that the split comes as a relief. After this, there may be fights over property, possessions, custody and access. So children sometimes spend years in a chronic war zone, and it can leave deep emotional scars.

The impact of **instability** is usually underestimated. Most children live with their mother, and the majority of solo mums experience a dramatic drop in living standard. The problem is not just available cash, but a lack of funds can often result in frequent moves of home. This disrupts a child's life, with unnecessary changes of school and friends and

Divorce and sole parenthood: the damage

1. Unresolved hostility – ongoing anger, especially concerning access

2. Disruption and instability – move of home and school; move away from friends and local community

3. Lack of support – isolated from friends and extended family

4. Economic hardship – child poverty is commonly associated with sole parenthood; poverty affects the stability of housing and life

5. Unavailability – the parent may have to work unreasonable hours or is so stressed they are emotionally unavailable

6. New relationships – step situations cause difficulties, especially with older children

the loss of a sense of belonging to a community. Plus there may be new partners who come and go, adding further confusion for the children.

Our young ones are damaged by this mix of hostility, instability, frequent moves, and people coming in and out of their life. We counter this by aiming for an amicable settlement and the minimum of change and being particularly careful with new partners.

How children hurt

The under-six-year-old will usually be quite open in their reaction, with an immediate and often intense response to the break. They don't know what it means but they dislike how it feels. However, children of this young age recover quickly once the adults get their act together.

The six- to eight-year-old is in the middle ground where they almost, but don't quite, understand. They know this is a major event but may not realise that it is permanent. Children of this age may worry that they are in some way responsible for the split. They also worry about being abandoned and replaced. Their reaction and the depth of their hurt still depends on the stability and emotional resilience of the caring parent.

The eight- to twelve-year-old understands the implications of the split and understands it is forever. Often they will take sides and have confused loyalties. They may show bravado and a false disinterest, but behind this can be intense anger at what their parents have done. Most of their upset is open, but at this age they may bottle up emotions that can smoulder for years.

The adolescent: in the past it was thought that children of this age remained relatively unscathed by divorce but now it is believed they carry the greatest hurt. This is a point in life when children are fighting to make sense of their own personal relationships. Their confidence is shot when their role models screw up so spectacularly. Many worry that they may follow their parents' example.

How children react

There are three ways that a school-age child may react to major upset. They

- cling close,
- behave badly, and
- take it to heart.

Clinging close

Clinging is most common in children under the age of six years. They don't understand our adult antics, but they feel they have been abandoned by fifty per cent of those they trust. Clingy children hold tight to the remaining parent. They shadow their mum around the house and they're reluctant to separate at the school gate for fear that Mum may not return at pick-up time. At night they procrastinate about bed and many insist on sleeping with their mother.

The child's action makes good sense, but some parents are blind to what is happening. One mother told me how she split up with her boyfriend in the middle of the night so as not to upset their child. She then sounded surprised as she told me: 'I can't understand why her behaviour has become so odd since that night.' Of course, the little girl was now terrified to close her eyes in case she lost another parent.

Behaving badly

When a child feels stress they may transmit it back as bad behaviour. Younger children don't understand what is going on – they just react. Older children can be more vindictive and may single out one parent to abuse. Unfortunately, it is the parent who gives most love and care who usually gets the hardest kick.

Behaving badly is a particular problem when parents are emotionally fragile and intolerant of irritation. The child picks up on the stress in their home and reacts with irritating behaviour. The parent retaliates with anger, the child gets more distressed and their behaviour worsens. This starts a vicious circle, which, if not nipped in the bud, can escalate.

Taking it to heart

Though most children transmit their hurt outwards in the form of difficult behaviour, some older children bottle up their feelings and withdraw. Now the once-outgoing child appears distant, moody and lacking spark. School grades may slip, although occasionally a child may escape their unhappiness by overfocusing on study. Often they lose interest in friends and activities that used to give pleasure.

These children need to be able to talk about their feelings, but often their parents are so overwhelmed by their own problems they are emotionally unavailable when their children try to open up. Withdrawal is often the least recognised of a child's reactions and probably the most serious. It starts as grief but can slip into full depression.

Protecting our children

Amicable access

Visits are going to happen whether we accept the inevitable or create trouble. If you are interested in your own, and your children's mental health, make access as peaceful as possible.

Arrange the times in advance so that everyone knows where they stand. Don't send the child with a list of petty conditions that dictate what they must wear, where they may go and who they may meet. Accept that things will not always be done as you would like, but with joint custody, you cannot make unrealistic demands.

Stay in control of what you say. Children become confused when those they love are belittled and criticised. And don't ask too many questions – your children are on an access visit, not a spying mission.

Where a dispute threatens to destabilise a visit, try to sidestep trouble and address the problem at a time when the children are not present. If tension is running too high, arrange pick-up and set-down from a neutral place, or allow a friend to be an intermediary.

As children become older, they have sport and other commitments. These can interfere with a fixed pattern of access, but we need to be flexible to fit in with the needs of an eleven-year-old.

Unfortunately, even amicable access can confuse children. When Mum and Dad appear so civil the youngsters may wonder why their parents don't stop the nonsense and get back together. But civil it has to be –

when access is used to cause pain, children become acutely anxious or physically sick before the visit and it takes days for them to recover.

If separated by distance try to maintain communication by visit, letter, tape, photo and phone. Absence is said to make the heart grow fonder, but lack of communication dilutes the closeness between the non-custodial parent and their child.

Don't divorce the grandparents

At the wedding celebration there were guests on the bride's side and guests on the groom's side. At the divorce the relatives are still seen as being aligned. But little children don't understand the dynamics of a break-up; they have no interest in branding people as good guys or bad guys. They are unsettled by the change in their parents' life, and they rely on relatives from both sides to provide a vital safety net.

A wife may divorce her husband, but there is no need to divorce his parents as well. Legislation now guarantees grandparents access, but until recently I met grandparents who had lost all contact with those they loved. And this was at its most malicious when an inadequate new partner had come on the scene. Often the grandparents' phone calls were obstructed, letters destroyed and birthday presents returned.

One grandmother told how, after the separation, she had cared for the children every day for three years. But when the new partner arrived all access was blocked. Now the only time she saw the children was a glimpse from a passing bus or looking longingly through the bars of the school fence.

With break-ups children need the security of grandparents. If relatives are prepared to keep out of the politics and give support, they should have the most open of access. An amicable settlement involves being amicable to all friends and relatives who genuinely wish to help.

Consistency and stability

After an upsetting event some parents turn their back on the past and restart with a completely new life. The very strong may succeed, but for most it is an act of destructive disruption.

When the adults in a child's life have lost the plot, the child maintains stability through consistent people and places. They do best when they still have their school, their friends, their extended family and the security of their own home.

Until the dust has settled, make no move or change that is not essential. Try to remain in the same district, at the same school and, if possible, in the same home. It is tempting to run away from unhappy memories but your home community provides the best base.

Starting a new relationship

After a split children can become extremely possessive of the parent who provides care. Often the sole parent and child develop an unusually close relationship, which will be fiercely guarded if someone tries to come between them. There is no trouble when Mum has a superficial friendship, but when a new companion competes for love and attention, children see this as a threat.

Younger children (under eight years) are generally reasonably accommodating. But older children are quite clear; they already have a dad and they don't need another. They also know they have been hurt once, and don't want a second dose. Teenagers are usually obtuse in the extreme.

Success comes with slow steps and gaining confidence over time. Initially it is best to interact mostly outside the family home. Don't force the new partner on the children and don't call them Dad. State that this friend is important to you and will be around quite often. When children are threatened they may protect their patch with confronting, limit-testing behaviour.

Don't rush to get married or create more children. Though second relationships may be more satisfying than the first, statistics suggest that over half will have broken up within five years. As for new babies, they never bring a bad relationship together; they just create a mix of loyalties that only the most together parents can sort out.

Step situations

Most of the fairy stories I learnt when I was young were about abusive step situations. But while Cinderella and Snow White may have lived happily ever after, it is not that easy for everyone. A recent study of Sydney street kids showed the majority came from an unhappy step situation.

Step relationships can work wonderfully well, especially for the under-eights. But teenagers can react very badly. The Brady Bunch had Alice, but you just have unsettled kids jockeying for power. As with any new relationship, it's important to move gently. It can take years to gain the trust of your partner's children.

When there are difficulties with discipline, the natural parent should be the main enforcer. Often older children defy, ignore or verbally abuse a new partner. While they are not the main disciplinarian, at a certain point, the partner must take a stand. Where that point is, is anyone's guess.

When children from two relationships come together it is rare to have harmony. During visits keep them entertained, don't expect miracles and be pleased when things go well. You may like the children's father or mother, but this does not mean the children like each other. Step situations, especially with older children, usually cause great stress. When in trouble be quick to seek professional help.

Split, sole and step: protecting the children

1. The main priority is always the emotional well-being of our children.

2. With unresolved disputes, try to avoid the legal adversarial system, as this is expensive and deepens the wounds. Where possible use the mediation services, which aim at amicable agreement.

3. Never underestimate the detrimental effect of stress and hostility on children. Parents may feel angry, but that's their problem, not the child's.

4. You can't stop the break-up but you can ensure that it is as amicable as possible.

5. Children are unsettled by changes in housing, school, friends and the disruption of new partners.

6. Children need as little change as possible.

7. Children show their upset by clinging close, behaving badly or withdrawing.

8. Young children are open and intense in their reaction. Their behaviour settles when the parent's behaviour settles.

9. Older children may carry a more chronic but less obvious wound.

10. Children need to be told what is happening in a way that is appropriate to their age.

11. Don't draw children into adult battles. They don't understand the rights and wrongs; all they know is that it hurts.

12. Children need to know they will have two parents and both will continue to care for them.

13. They should know where they will live, where their non-custodial parent will live, and when they will see each other.

14. Keep close to grandparents and any extended family who genuinely wish to support.

15. You may divorce your partner, but your children do not want to divorce their grandparents.

16. Access must be encouraged and made easy. It's going to happen whether the parents make it enjoyable or a time of tension.

17. Don't spy on or slander the other parent.

18. When a child is out on access, it is up to the accessing parent what they do and whom they do it with. You can't prevent your child being cared for by a new partner.

19. Most custodial parents get a raw deal. No one said this is fair but that's the way it is, whether we accept it or not.

20. Children often react badly to a new partner. They do not wish to share their parent and they have already had enough hurt to last a lifetime.

21. The over-eight-year-olds are usually most difficult.

22. New relationships are best started outside the home and approached gently.

23. Children may attention seek, become defiant and rebel against the new partner's discipline. Initially the natural parent should be the main enforcer, though there should always be limits.

24. Blended families don't blend, they usually curdle. Don't be afraid to seek professional help when it's needed.

25. Children have more than enough love to share around. Never let a jealous partner obstruct the children's access to grandparents, parent or friends.

26. When a new partner spirits the children to the other end of the country, ensure that their motive is genuine, not jealousy.

27. Be careful of rebound relationships. The statistics show sixty per cent of second marriages fail within five years.

28. Beware of new pregnancies. It takes a strong relationship to cope with these changed dynamics.

29. The best we can do for our children is to provide peace and stability in their living environment while maintaining access to those they love.

An A to Z of children's health

This chapter covers A (abdominal pain) to W (worms). But before we hit A, let's address one of the questions that parents most commonly ask.

When should you call for help?

In our teaching hospital we train bright young doctors to become specialists in children's medicine. To pass their exams they need an immense amount of fine-print knowledge, but to be a good paediatrician they must also have that intuition to know when a child is sick or not.

Parents and paediatricians recognise the danger signs in a child's eyes. When these are bright, interested and alert there is rarely a problem. When dull, distant and the child's mind is muddled, alarm bells ring. Other symptoms also cause great concern:

- headache with neck pain and stiffness (possible meningitis or encephalitis)
- persistent localised abdominal pain (possible appendicitis)
- cold, clammy skin (shock or serious illness)
- rapid shallow breathing in a sick-looking child (meningitis, diabetes or other serious condition)
- unrelenting vomiting (possible gut obstruction)
- rapid deterioration (meningococcal or other major illness)
- following a head injury, drowsiness, confusion or change in pupil size (concussion or brain bleed).

Any of these require urgent medical attention. If in doubt always play it safe and go quickly to your doctor or hospital.

The key points: dull distant eyes, rapid deterioration, confusion and/or disinterest, neck stiffness, extreme vomiting or persistent pain, and any occasion when a parent feels worried.

Contents

Abdominal pain

This is one of the most common reasons for a parent to seek help from a paediatrician. Their healthy school child has vague abdominal pains that come and go. They start for no good reason and last between half an hour and six hours, after which the child returns to normal health. The pain may come back in a week, a month or somewhere down the track.

Pain is usually situated just above and just below the umbilicus. It has none of the fever, urinary symptoms or localising features of kidney infections or acute appendicitis. Between times, the child is happy, healthy and unstressed.

There is much debate about the cause of these periodic pains. Most believe they are an abdominal equivalent of tension headache or migraine. Whatever the reason, it worries parents, and unfortunately we have little to offer as treatment. If abdominal pain has been an occasional problem over months or years, and no medical cause can be found, it's a case of making a minimum of fuss and possibly giving some para-cetamol.

Adenoids

When your child says 'ahh', the tonsils are clearly seen on each side of the throat. The adenoids are similar to the tonsils, but you would need a little mirror to see them up the back of the nose. Both tonsils and adenoids have the purpose of fighting infection.

Adenoids live a quiet life, mostly remaining out of sight and causing no problem. The difficulty comes when they enlarge, which can affect the ears and the flow of air down from the nose.

The adenoids lie close to the tubes (the eustachian tubes) that equalise the pressure and allow drainage of the middle parts of our ear. If these become blocked, fluid collects, which can lead to hearing loss or repeated ear infections. When enlargement obstructs the nasal airway the child may breathe through their open mouth by day and snore by night. If the blockage persists the child may continue to breathe through their open mouth which can lead to an alteration of their bite.

Adenoidectomy is a simple operation, which can improve the drainage of the middle parts of the ears. It is usually performed at the same time as grommets (small tubes) are being inserted in the eardrums to release the chronic fluid collection of glue ear. Occasionally adenoids that obstruct the nasal airway are associated with sleep disturbance. Here a snoring child has restless, disturbed sleep leaving them sleep deprived and tired in the morning. Occasionally the child may briefly stop breathing in their sleep, which reduces oxygen levels at night. By day this can cause drowsiness or behaviour symptoms. In sleep apnoea, the operation of adenoidectomy will usually increase the flow of air through the nose. Children appear to show no adverse effects when we remove their adenoids.

Appendicitis

The appendix is a small, worm-like structure that sprouts from the lower part of the gut. Currently it has no known purpose, but presumably it was essential in the evolutionary days before man walked upright and ate today's refined foods.

This cul-de-sac of the bowel can become blocked and stagnate. If untreated it eventually bursts, releasing infected material into the abdominal cavity, which can cause life-threatening peritonitis.

The first symptom of appendicitis is a vague discomfort around the belly button that soon moves over the appendix (situated in the lower right part of the abdomen). The pain is sharp, causes difficulty standing straight and there may be fever and vomiting. When a patient has classic symptoms, appendicitis is easy to diagnose, but the picture can be much more confusing. Many who work in the emergency room eventually get caught out missing atypical appendicitis.

If appendicitis is suspected, call your family doctor or, if the situation seems quite certain, go straight to your local hospital. Surgical removal is a minor procedure and will be suggested if there are any reasonable grounds. A good surgeon will always play safe, which may result in removing some normal appendices. But this is preferable to risking the dangers of peritonitis.

Asthma

One in ten children have asthma. This is an allergy-related condition that causes spasm of the middle-sized airways in the lungs. The symptoms are shortness of breath and wheezing, especially when breathing out. Asthma is strongly hereditary, and many children who suffer from it have a mum or dad with the same allergy-asthma combination. Or, as a child, the parent may have suffered bouts of wheezy bronchitis and a telltale middle-of-the-night cough, but these were never recognised as asthma.

Most asthma is mild, occurring every few months in response to a respiratory infection, strenuous exercise or heavy doses of allergens (pollen or too many cats). These occasional bouts are treated with one of the safe, effective bronchodilator puffers (such as Ventolin (salbutamol)), which are given during the bad patch or prior to exercise.

Moderate and severe asthma used to cause immense trouble to children. When I was first a specialist paediatrician, some children spent half their year in hospital, while others missed months of school and were so breathless they never played sport. This has changed with the introduction of aggressive maintenance therapy. Now we do not wait for asthma to incapacitate; we keep it at bay with an everyday regime of inhaled steroids (preventers) and bronchodilators (relievers).

It is no longer acceptable for a child just to cope with their asthma – they must live life to the full. If this isn't happening, they should be in the care of a children's respiratory specialist. Allergy testing, air filters, avoiding milk and desensitisation are popular topics on the Internet, but they are not usually recommended by experts in asthma.

All chest specialists are united about the damage of side-stream cigarette smoke. It is hard to believe that, until relatively recent times, hospitals and ambulances had no restriction on smoking. In my days as a consultant paediatrician in Belfast, children were brought by ambulance to my clinic. The parents of one girl assured me she was well, yet at every review she was blue and in spasm. One day her mum innocently asked if the chain-smoking ambulance driver might be upsetting her asthma. Nowadays, to smoke in an ambulance would be viewed as an act of criminal negligence. But some parents still fill their children's home with the same pollution.

Bed wetting

At the age of five years, ten per cent of children will still wet the bed. Bed wetting (nocturnal enuresis) is due to a late maturation in normal bladder function. It is not in any way deliberate or of emotional origin.

Without treatment, the incidence will reduce every year, leaving approximately five per cent still wetting at the age of ten years. The majority of these children have never had a dry night (primary enuresis), though a few started with a period of full training, then relapsed (secondary enuresis).

There is debate regarding the difference between primary enuresis and secondary enuresis. In the past, we believed that those who slipped back had urinary infection or a major emotional upset, but experience shows this is rarely true. Nowadays we manage all children the same, whether a long-time wetter or one who has relapsed. The treatment of bed wetting involves the following:

Property protection

We don't want to upset the emotional sensitivity of our children, but parents must protect their property. This requires a waterproof mattress cover, a plentiful supply of bed linen and a smooth-running washing machine. Children attending school camps used to save their sleeping bags by spending the night in a large plastic garbage bag. Fortunately, drug treatment has removed the need for this assault on their dignity.

The 11pm lift

When a child is close to overcoming bed wetting they start to have a few dry nights. At this stage we can accelerate the process by lifting last thing at night. They go to sleep at 8pm, then at 11pm they are brought to the toilet. Some children stumble, half awake and happy to oblige; but a few are so stroppy that it's mission impossible.

Consider restricting fluid intake before bed

You don't need to be Einstein to realise that what goes in the top must eventually come out the bottom. For this reason it seems sensible to restrict fluid intake during the evening. However, despite the intellect of Einstein, there is no evidence that fluid restriction helps.

Alarms

The most effective treatment for bed wetting is a pad-and-bell alarm. A small sensor is attached to the pants or placed below the bottom sheet. When the flood arrives the sensor shorts out, sets off a buzzer and you have red alert. Often I am told, 'The alarm is no good. He doesn't wake,' but to be effective a mum or dad must struggle out, get John fully conscious and jointly remake the bed.

There are two essentials before starting this treatment: the child has to be motivated, and they must be completely awake during clean-up. Alarms can be hired from children's hospitals, some community health centres and chemists. The top enuresis clinics will claim an eighty per cent success rate, achieved within two months. But there are some relapses, and the alarm should stay in place until the child has stayed dry every night for a reasonable period.

Drug treatment

The antidepressant drug imipramine has been used for thirty years in the treatment of enuresis. No one knows how it works but a dose at bedtime has a high chance of producing a dry bed. Unfortunately, wetting usually returns once the drug stops. I would have thought that any safe treatment that dramatically reduced enuresis was worthwhile, but for some reason this drug is rarely recommended by today's doctors.

However, a new preparation, Desmopressin, is becoming much more popular. This is an antidiuretic hormone that acts through the pituitary gland in the brain and reduces the amount of urine released by the kidneys. It has a relatively short period of action so it is given last thing at night.

Initially Desmopressin was used to provide temporary protection for sleepovers and camps. But there is now a body of research that shows good results with no side effects for periods of six or even twelve months. As with imipramine, those who have not resolved spontaneously in this time will relapse when the drug stops.

Desmopressin is currently given by a nasal spray but an oral preparation will soon be released. The dose needs to be adjusted to suit the individual child, so it must be trialed well before the child departs for camp. Most but not all children get a good response.

Despite the interest in drug treatment the alarm is still the first line of treatment, because, when it works, it provides a cure. Desmopressin is useful for sleepovers and for the every-night treatment of the older child.

There are still a few psychological dinosaurs who interpret bed wetting as a problem of emotion. But I learned at medical school that the brain is located a long way from the bladder. Emotional upset does not cause chronic enuresis but chronic enuresis can cause emotional upset.

Body piercing: infection

Recently when I took a long-haul bus trip, it seemed that I was the only adult without a stud, ring or piece of metal through some part of my body. I know I have old-fashioned ideas, but I don't understand body piercing.

Still, whether I like it or not, I see a number of boys and girls with one or more studs and earrings. As bits of metal are foreign to the body, it is common for irritation or infection to develop in the days after the piercing is done. It's a bit old-fashioned but you can clean around the stud with methylated spirits in the same way you dried the umbilical stump all those years ago. If a minor infection develops get an antibiotic cream or antibiotic tablets from your doctor. When in doubt, get rid of the metal and restart once the body has returned to normality.

Bruises

A bruise results from by an injury that releases blood into the tissues. When a battered and bruised football player struggles to the sideline, his trainer hands him the freezing sponge or magic ice pack. The cool temperature reduces the blood flow, which lessens the blackness and swelling.

In the past, people used a steak to reduce the black. Using meat in this way may help your butcher recover from their mad-cow losses, but twenty minutes of cool compress is a better treatment for a bruise.

Burns and scalds

Having lived through the hazardous preschool years, parents are hyper-alert to the dangers of burns and scalds. These can be painful, disfiguring and potentially life threatening. In the school years the main risk comes from stoves, ovens, kettles, fires, fireworks, methylated spirits, petrol and lighting barbecues.

Any significant burn, especially of the face or over a joint, must be brought to a doctor or hospital. The first-aid for burns and scalds is, where possible, to put the affected part under cold tap water for ten or more minutes, then decide whether there is need for medical help. Blisters should be left intact as they give some protection and allow healing underneath. For pain use paracetamol.

Chicken pox

Chicken pox is an extremely common viral illness that can cause an unsightly rash. It leaves most children looking worse than they feel. This highly infectious virus is picked up from a friend, then incubated for fourteen to sixteen days before the first signs of illness appear. Chicken pox starts with small red spots and a slight fever. The spots get larger, fill with fluid, and then form itchy scabs. Though your grandmother told you, 'If you scratch that spot it will leave a scar,' the marks of chicken pox usually heal completely.

Chicken pox can be a very mild illness, particularly in young children. Sometimes you see a cluster of apparent flea bites, which would pass unnoticed except for the chicken pox contact two weeks before. When your child is covered in spots they are highly infective and should stay away from others. They will not be welcome at school until the last infective scab drops off. Calamine lotion is still the best treatment for itching.

Colour blindness

Most colour-blind children see plenty of colour; they just perceive things with a slight difference. It may affect their colour coordination when buying clothes, but most poor taste is a problem of dress sense, not colour blindness.

The main confusion comes with the colours red and green. At close quarters the colour-blind adult is quite clear when the traffic light signals stop or go, but a single light in the distance causes much more difficulty. This makes colour blindness a danger to train drivers, sailors and pilots.

An eye specialist, optometrist or school nurse can quickly test for this weakness. There is no treatment and the only down side is the obstruction to careers that run on rails, the sea or high in the sky. About five per cent of boys and a lesser number of girls have this difficulty.

Common cold

Colds come from a virus that gets into the nose or throat and can irritate the chest. After recovering from a cold there is some immunity, but it gives limited protection against future infections. Children are particularly susceptible to colds and 'flu viruses in their first year at school but this gradually gets better as resistance strengthens with age.

Colds are spread by droplet infection. We teach our children, 'Put your hand to your mouth when you cough.' Then we encourage politeness: 'Shake hands with the vicar.' Then in a moment of prayer his holiness pokes a nostril, and next week he splutters through the sermon.

Folklore suggests that Vitamin C prevents colds and 'flu but research evidence is not convincing. Medicines that dry the nose may help comfort but they don't speed recovery. Paracetamol is useful for aches and fever. A hot whisky does nothing for the child, but when taken by the parent it makes the child's symptoms seem less severe.

Convulsions, fits and seizures

When parents think of a convulsion, it is the generalised, tonic-clonic (grand mal) picture that comes to mind. The child suddenly loses consciousness, goes stiff, then jerks and convulses for some time. When they come out of the fit they are sleepy and confused and may have wet themselves.

This is a different picture to the simple faint. Here the child feels tingly headed, becomes unconscious, they are placed flat, the blood flows back to the brain, they pink up and come to. After this they may feel nausea but they don't wet themselves and are not confused or drowsy.

When a child has just one isolated convulsion, it may be a chance happening. When fitting is prolonged (over fifteen minutes) or repeated, it is of much more concern. The fever fits that were common in the toddler years are not seen at school age.

A major fit is a frightening experience for any parent to witness. Their child is out of contact and seems to be struggling to breathe. All we can do is place them on their side and position the neck in a way that helps breathing. Though terrifying for parents, our greatest concern is the fit that goes on and on (status epilepticus). If by ten minutes there is no end in sight, dial 999 to call an ambulance.

There are many other sorts of fit. One is the simple absence or petit mal seizure. This causes a brief switch off, the child stops, may blink their eyes, looks distant, then after five to thirty seconds they return to full awareness. There is no drowsiness or confusion but they are unaware of what happened in that time.

Teachers often send me a child who they believe has petit mal. Usually these are bored or attention deficit kids who prefer to look out the window rather than listen to their teacher.

If you have any concern about seizures, discuss this with your doctor. A brain wave test (EEG) usually, but not always, helps with diagnosis. A normal EEG does not totally exclude epilepsy, which prompted one cynic to write, 'The EEG is only reliable in diagnosing sleep and death, and there are easier ways to spot these.'

When anticonvulsant medication is prescribed it is usually continued for at least two years after the last episode. Children with reasonably controlled epilepsy lead normal lives, though they must avoid high climbing, bike riding on busy roads and swimming without supervision (as should any other school-age child). A good proportion of children grow out of their epileptic seizures before adulthood.

Cuts and stitches

Over the years the Greens' house has been like a field hospital for all the bumped, bruised and cut children in our neighbourhood. Often they come, wondering if a cut needs stitches. The first step is to clean with cold tap water, then the decision to stitch depends on the length and depth of the cut and whether it closes or gapes.

Stitches have mostly been replaced by thin paper holding strips (steristrips). These pull the sides of the wound together and have greatly lessened the volume of tears in our emergency department. Nowadays we also use tissue glue for many wounds. The edges are pulled together and the glue is applied. This keeps the edges close until the wound heals, after which the glue rubs off.

With deeper cuts be careful that no important nerves or tendons have been damaged. If the wound is on the face or there is ever any doubt, discuss it with your doctor. Cuts should serve as a reminder to check that tetanus and all other immunisation is up to date.

Dandruff

Commercial television has greatly improved since they stopped showing adverts about dandruff. This may be riveting viewing for some, but it holds my interest like a feature on piles, athlete's foot or country music.

As long as humans are alive new skin keeps growing and the old stuff must drop off. Most of us shed the dead skin as specks of dust, but some release it as large white chunks – dandruff.

Treatment is through regular hair washing, preferably with a medicated shampoo. The chemist will recommend one, but the ultimate choice is based on results. Treatment does work: it may not happen overnight but it *will* happen.

Deafness

We know that a tiny infant will respond to the voice of their parents, but despite this only a few of our severely deaf children are picked up before the age of one year. This severe problem is due to nerve deafness where sound does not get from the ear to the brain. Deafness is often a genetic condition, where we see families with more than one child affected.

The deafness we diagnose later at school age is much less major and sometimes can be hard to spot. A few children have a hearing weakness with only one frequency, usually the high tones (high-tone deafness). This causes problems in the understanding of spoken speech, where a conversation sounds flat, like a radio with no treble and too much bass.

If you have the slightest concern about your child's hearing speak to your health visitor or go and see your doctor as it is essential to get a high-quality test.

Fluid in the middle ear (glue ear) is by far the commonest cause of reduced hearing in the school-age child. The middle ear chamber, which usually resonates in air, becomes deadened with fluid. This reduces hearing by twenty to forty decibels (see this chapter, Glue ear and grommets, page 239).

Then, of course, there's selective deafness, when children switch off and leave parents looking like idiots. Scientists have now discovered a simple way to distinguish this annoying behaviour from true deafness. Parents should quietly whisper, 'Would you like Dad to book a trip to Disneyland?'

Developmental delay

This is a term used by paediatricians when worried about the developmental progress of a young child. Delay registers our concern but implies the probability that the child will catch up. When delay continues over some years the name changes to the more permanent diagnosis of developmental or intellectual disability.

Delayed children do move ahead but all other children are also moving and the gap between them may remain unchanged. When I assess a child of three years and note the development of a two-year-old, this child is one year behind, but more importantly, this is two-thirds of their expected level. At six years of age the same child may show four-year skills. Certainly they have moved ahead, but the same two-thirds fraction remains, and the diagnosis is now borderline or mild intellectual disability.

Formal tests of intellect become much more reliable as we get closer to school entry. Results indicate advanced, normal or low average ability and borderline, mild, moderate or severe disability.

Between two per cent and three per cent of children and adults have some degree of developmental disability, of which the vast majority are borderline or mild. In most of this less severe group, no cause is ever found, with birth, family history, chromosomes and the most sophisticated scans and X-rays all normal. Even with all our advanced medical technology most parents in my care never discover the reason for their child's slowness.

Dry skin

Most little children have skin that is smooth as silk. But a few inherit a dry, rough exterior, which will always need extra care. This dryness is often associated with eczema. Dry skins are easily damaged by long, hot showers, the high alkaline content of normal soaps and an overdose of sunshine.

Keep showers cool, which usually keeps them short. Baths can be longer, provided you use a commercial bath oil. Move from soap to a sorbolene or other mild cleansing preparation. Buy a jumbo jar of a cheap brand of sorbolene with glycerine skin cream. If the skin surface breaks into itchy red areas, particularly behind the knee or front of the elbow, suspect eczema (see this chapter, Eczema, page 233).

Ear infections

The ear has three parts: the external ear, the middle ear and the inner ear. The external ear goes from outside to the ear drum. The middle ear is that air-filled cavity inside the eardrum. The inner ear transmits sound to the auditory nerve and also adjusts balance.

The air-filled middle ear equalises the pressure with the outside atmosphere through two tubes to the back of the nose (the eustachian tubes). These are the channels we clear, with a yawn or nose blow as the plane descends. If the eustachian tubes get blocked, the middle ear becomes filled with fluid. The fluid in the middle ear may become infected (otitis media). If the fluid persists after the acute infection a condition called otitis media with effusion, or glue ear, may occur, interfering with hearing.

Outer ear infection (otitis externa) is an inflammation of the external ear canal. Otitis externa is a summer specialty for swimmers. As they dive, the canal fills with water, then they poke grot in the ear and then dive again. If the ear was kept dry there would be no problem, but there would also be no fun. Children can be taught to lie on a towel and drain one ear then the other after swimming.

Over-the-counter antiseptic drops help mild problems. Earplugs are useful but further prevent children from responding to our instructions, and the ear-plugged child can become intolerably noisy. If the canals are really sore a doctor will prescribe antibiotic drops or an antibiotic cortisone mix.

Middle-ear infection (otitis media) usually hits after a child has been stuffed up with a cold. The mix of blowing and sniffing with partially blocked tubes provides a fertile field for bacteria. The bacteria multiply in the confined space, drainage blocks and pressure increases to form an abscess. This can only resolve by natural immunity, antibiotics or release through a ruptured eardrum.

Otitis media can cause intense pain and some fever. When the doctor looks in the ear and sees a red, bulging drum, the diagnosis is made and antibiotics prescribed. When the ear is a reddish shade of pink the diagnosis is less clear.

Sometimes the middle ear fills with fluid but bacteria do not gain a firm foothold. This is glue ear, which knocks some decibels from the hearing and leaves the child open to recurrent ear infections (see this chapter, page 239).

Eczema

A child with eczema has dry, sensitive skin that can easily become red, itchy and weeping. Eczema often runs in families, and is closely associated with allergy and asthma. The rash can occur anywhere, but the main site in babies is the face, while in toddlers it is behind the knees and in the crease in front of the elbows. Children with eczema can be intensely irritated when they wear wool against the skin.

Treatment of eczema involves care for the dry skin with shorter showers, avoiding the usual commercial alkaline soaps and using moisturising creams, cotton underclothing and low-dose cortisone ointment. Eczema is generally at its worst in infants and toddlers. By school age the tendency is just to dry skin with the occasional flare-up.

Faints

It is called 'the passing out parade': children stand still for school assembly and gaps begin to appear in the ranks. Faints are due to a temporary shortfall in the blood supply to the brain. This is associated with getting up to stand, hanging around in heat, an unpleasant experience or being below par with some illness. With school children there is often a mix of heat, standing and an emotional overlay. On a school outing when one child keels over, others follow in quick succession.

Before falling, the child feels lightheaded and may be cold-sweaty and nauseated. Once they are down, the blood from the legs returns to the heart, which is quickly pumped to the brain. Getting flat or raising the legs is a matter of urgency.

A faint differs from an epileptic fit. It is short (under one minute) and there are precipitating factors. There is no convulsion, no incontinence, they respond to lying flat and their head becomes clear in a matter of minutes. Faints are quite common and generally benign. But if they are unexpected, repeated or unusual in any way, this needs to be looked into further.

Fever

When a child's temperature rises, this is a sign that things are running hot and out of balance. Fever tells us that our immune armies are rounding up some uninvited bug. The main invaders are the viruses that cause nose, chest, 'flu and gut illnesses, but any infection or imbalance can shift the body's thermostat.

Children and adults usually run at about 37 degrees Celsius (98.4 degrees Fahrenheit) and most fevers are 38.5 degrees Celsius (101 degrees Fahrenheit) to 39 degrees Celsius (102 degrees Fahrenheit), though I do occasionally see temperatures of 40 degrees Celsius (104 degrees Fahrenheit). You may hear parents claim figures of 42 degrees Celsius (107 degrees Fahrenheit), but this was either taken between sips of hot cocoa or they need a new thermometer.

The size of the fever is not proportional to the seriousness of the illness. A child with measles may have a higher temperature than one with deadly meningitis or peritonitis.

The most popular measure of temperature is a mother's hand on a flushed forehead. This is as reliable as a coin toss in the diagnosis of pregnancy. The face may be hot, but it doesn't reflect what's happening deep down in the corridors of power. Instead, fever should be measured by a thermometer placed beside or under the tongue.

When children are feverish, the main attention is to their comfort, fluid maintenance and to ensure we are not missing something serious. If they are happily snuggled under a rug by the television, let them have a little fluid to sip and leave them in peace. When I have the 'flu I don't want to be put in a tepid bath, sponged with cold water or left in front of a force-ten fan. If they are comfortable there is no need to give any medicine, but if necessary we can use paracetamol.

When I started paediatrics, any child with fever was prescribed aspirin. Then a pathologist who worked at our hospital, the Royal Alexandra Hospital for Children in Sydney, described a crisis condition that damaged the liver and brain (Reye syndrome, after Dr Douglas Reye). This was later linked to aspirin that had been given for fever. Though this syndrome is extremely rare and aspirin has only been barred in the under-twos, it is now fashionable to avoid giving aspirin to any child under the age of sixteen years.

The key points for fever are: keep comfortable, maintain fluid intake, use paracetamol if needed, remember that fever can be a sign of something more serious, and that fever fits are unlikely after the age of four years.

Flat feet

About one in every twenty-five school children have feet that are flat. These are often inherited from a flat-footed mum or dad. As the child stands the inner side of their foot, which should rise as a definite arch, lies flat to the floor.

There are two views on the management of flat feet: those who insist on jacking up the arch with shoe supports and those who let nature take its course. Parents generally prefer to take some action, even if it is unhelpful, while I favour the no-support option.

If the feet are strong, move fully and the child walks with style, flat feet are of no consequence. If there is an unusual range of movement or foot pain, that is the time to take it further.

Flatus: generating gas that smells

When I was a very junior doctor I put in some hard labour working in a busy emergency department. In those days we alternated between an 'easy week' of eighty hours on duty and an impossible one with sixty hours work and sixty more on call. Life was not relaxing, especially as I was in Belfast, which was then gearing up to self-destruct.

But there were lighter moments, one coming with the visit of a large US warship. A fit young officer appeared. 'It's like this, Doc,' he said. 'My job is in a deep-water mini sub. Me and two others are down there for ten hours at a time.' He then got embarrassed and said, 'Doc, I have a problem with farting! People don't want to close the hatch with me inside.' I understood the dilemma, but I didn't have an answer.

Everyone, from the queen to her corgis, will pass wind. This escapes in small amounts and passes without comment. This gas is generated by benign bacteria that consume carbohydrate leftovers in the large gut. If the sugars and carbohydrates we eat are mostly digested, gas production is low, but sometimes output hits overload. The main offenders are cabbage, beans, broccoli and lentils.

As parents we can bring some relief by simple modifications to the diet. After this we must teach our children the adult art of silent release and implicating others.

'Flu, or influenza

When adults have a runny nose and shiver, they often call this 'flu. But this is the common cold: true 'flu has fever, muscle pain, headache, sore throat, cough and major miseries. It lasts more than two days and knocks us flat.

Influenza is caused by a virus, and once we are infected, it provides short-term immunity. But when the virus returns it will probably be in a changed form and the previous year's infection gives partial or no protection. Sometimes we can go for years without 'flu, then suffer a devastating hit from some new strain.

A 'flu vaccine is available that is modified each year to reflect the change in virus. This provides about seventy per cent protection for that year, and some benefits for the next. Immunisation is not suggested for healthy children; it is only recommended for elderly or debilitated adults. Though I am not in either of these categories, I make sure I get my jab every year. Even if this gave a ten per cent chance of reducing the miseries of 'flu, it's worth it. With a seventy per cent reduction, it's a steal.

Treatment for 'flu consists of paracetamol, plenty of fluid and keeping comfortable. Following the virus of 'flu, bacterial invaders may get a foothold, causing respiratory, throat or ear infection. When 'flu hits a school it can decimate attendance. Children need to stay away for whatever time it takes to recover and feel strong enough to return.

Fluoride and teeth

I was brought up in a UK governed by post-war rationing. Sugar and sweets were a rare treat, I drank water, scrubbed my teeth and the result? A head full of fillings! But today most of the children I see have minimal or no decay. Many reach adulthood without experiencing the high-speed end of dentistry.

And why have things changed? Fluoride. It is clearly documented that adding fluoride to water has reduced enamel damage by fifty to seventy per cent. The addition of fluoride is supported by the World Health Organisation, as well as all the main paediatric policy bodies around the world.

If you live under an administration unwilling to take a stand against the anti-fluoride activists, give drops or tablets each day. The most important time for fluoride protection is while teeth are developing – from toddlerhood to twenty. Brushing with a fluoride toothpaste twice a day is strongly recommended. For under-eights use a toothpaste with a lower fluoride content; for over-eights use a normal strength toothpaste.

Then, just as you thought it was safe to get back into the dentist's chair, they introduced fluoride paint. This is one of those rare taste sensations that adds extra strength to the surfaces at risk.

Foreskin: how to take care of it

I wonder if some of the enthusiasm for circumcision comes from parents who don't know what to do if this cover is left intact. Ten years ago, when I wrote my book *Babies*, I took a strong stand against circumcision. At the time, I caught a lot of flak for this attitude, but things have changed, and mercifully the demand for circumcision is now in steep decline. If I were to mutilate any other part of my newborn with no medical justification, I would be charged with child abuse and probably lose custody. And now, as I write, there are adults suing their doctors and parents for an operation that was done without any benefit or proper consent.

The foreskin is designed to protect the delicate parts of the penis and is also endowed with sexual sensitivity. The foreskin is still partly attached to its underlying tissues and is not ready to be withdrawn until two or three years of age. Approximately fifty per cent of one-year-olds, eighty per cent of two-year-olds and ninety per cent of three-year-olds can easily retract.

The hygienic care of the foreskin comes from routine washing at the earliest bath times. This starts with cleaning and when ready a gentle easing back of the skin. The aim is to get this established by five or six years, because after the age of eight years, doors get locked and personal affairs become more private. Some prudish people believe that so much focus on this part will lead to over interest and self-play. But I believe that this fascination will happen whether a child is taught hygiene or not. Children play with their private parts because it gives them pleasure.

There have been recent claims that circumcision reduces the risk of urinary infection, AIDS and various cancers. However, when these studies have been analysed more scientifically, the statistics are unimpressive. Most top kidney specialists and paediatricians strongly discourage routine circumcision. If the foreskin does not retract easily by age four or despite adequate hygiene there are repeat infections, then discuss this with your doctor.

Freckles

These are part of that fair-skin, Irish-ancestry package that was never designed to be shown sunshine. Freckles are rare before the age of four years but after this those with the right skin type freckle quickly.

In the past freckles were seen as cute, but now they are recognised as a sign of sun damage to sensitive skin. Hats, shade and heavy-duty sun cream on every exit outdoors are the only way to protect skin from sun. The freckled adult is at greater risk of developing sun cancer than other fair-skinned individuals.

Giardia

This parasite hit the headlines when discovered in Sydney's water supply. Critics from other cities said they had no giardia, but most had never looked for it. At the time of writing it seems that the odd parasite in the water is not a major problem.

Giardia was well known to paediatricians long before this scare. The parasite is present in most countries, but while we are all exposed to the bug, only a few become sick.

Giardia inhabits the small gut where it has the potential to cause malabsorption, weight loss and diarrhoea. Over the years I have seen some very scrawny sick children with chronic giardia.

When Sydney's water was said to be impure, every ache, rash and pass of wind was blamed on giardia. But as the most reliable diagnostic test involves the collection of three fresh containers of faeces, few had their diagnosis confirmed.

Giardia is classified as a flagellate protozoan. As a flagellate it's not surprising that the usual treatment is the drug Flagyl (metronidazole).

Glandular fever, or infective mononucleosis

This is usually an illness of the adolescent and young adult, but sometimes it strikes school age children. Mononucleosis is suspected in the child with extreme tiredness, a low-grade fever and a throat infection that is slow to respond to treatment. The tonsils are large and of angry appearance, with neck and other glands enlarged.

As with many childhood illnesses, mononucleosis can be relatively mild or have a long, difficult course. It can be complicated by rashes, jaundice or even encephalitis. But not every throat infection is mononucleosis: the diagnosis can only be made by a positive blood test. As this is a virus it does not respond to antibiotics.

The drug ampicillin must be avoided in glandular fever, something I know to my personal cost. I once resuscitated a child critically ill with meningococcal infection. As this is such a dangerous bacteria I protected myself with the only antibiotic I had available – ampicillin. What I didn't know was that I was incubating glandular fever at the time. The rash was spectacular and the glandular fever not too pleasant.

Glue ear and grommets

Glue ear is a collection of gluey fluid in the middle ear. This air-filled chamber transmits clear, crisp sound from the eardrum to the hearing nerve. The middle ear is normally able to equalise air pressure and clear fluid through the narrow eustachian tubes that drain towards the back of the nose.

The cause of glue ear is uncertain but it may be the result of a low-grade infection and blockage of the eustachian tubes. It usually (but not always) affects both ears. Fluid in a drum is bound to reduce the transmission of sound (the Beatles would have been much quieter if Ringo's drums were full of glue).

Parents suspect glue ear when there is an even poorer response to requests than usual. The child's voice may be louder in the way we increase our volume when listening through a headset or talking over the sound of an engine. If the child does suffer from glue ear a diagnostic hearing test will show a twenty- to forty-decibel loss, and pressure studies will show little movement in the drum.

Glue ear can come and go, and for this reason it is usual to observe for a while before surgery. When the hearing loss is mild, some suggest a four- to six-week course of antibiotics in the hope of removing possible low-grade infection. There are also techniques to open the eustachian tubes, such as holding the nose while blowing up a balloon.

If the hearing loss is great or glue ear remains unresolved, treatment is through surgery. The child is anaesthetised and small ventilation tubes are placed in the eardrum (grommets). The fluid is cleared at the time of surgery and the tubes allow normal function to return. They stay in place for six months to two years and drop out when ready.

As grommets leave an opening to the outside world there must be care with diving and swimming. Parents can provide some sort of seal with earplugs, a nerd-like bathing cap or, in an emergency, blobs of Blue Tac.

Growing pains

This is yet another vague medical condition that we know exists but haven't a clue why it happens. Growing pains are certainly not caused by growth, which is as pain free as putting on weight or going grey.

The peak age for growing pains is eight to twelve years, and the main time is at night. The child wakes or can't get to sleep with discomfort or pain in the muscles and bones of their legs. Some associate these pains with exercise, while others believe they are part of the headache or abdominal pain response to tension. I wonder if this is a childhood variant of the restless legs syndrome of adults.

To diagnose growing pains we must first exclude a medical problem such as arthritis or injury. Growing pains have no known cause and no specific treatment. The best we can give is gentle massage to the legs, comfort to the child and possibly paracetamol.

Growth: too much or too little

The ultimate height of our children is usually predestined in their genes. Two basketball-playing giants should produce children who are taller than average. Two vertically challenged jockeys would expect smaller children with squeaky voices.

The pattern of growth is often a family affair. Girls with an early or late puberty are often like their mum. Skinny boys with a last-minute growth rush are often like their dad.

Height is also influenced by factors before birth. The baby who is full term (forty weeks' gestation) but starved in utero may be born small for dates and may stay small. We see this pattern with raised maternal blood pressure, placental problems and in some of our addict-created foster children.

The greatest concern for parents comes from growth that is too little, too early, too late or too much. When parents are worried we start by obtaining an accurate record of growth over a number of visits. We are not so interested in the centimetres on the day of the appointment but how this reading is keeping pace with normal patterns of growth.

Height and weight are plotted on standard growth charts (see Appendix I, page 257). The average child sits on the fiftieth percentile, which implies that half the population are taller and half are smaller. A small child might be on the tenth percentile, which shows that ten per cent are smaller and ninety per cent are taller. The tall child might measure on the ninetieth percentile, showing ten per cent are taller and ninety per cent are smaller.

A paediatrician would hope to see the short-statured child move along or rise above their initial percentile. They become concerned when an already low reading descends to a lower percentile.

Parents should talk to their doctor if there is an unusually early start to puberty, if height lags significantly for age or if height greatly exceeds expectations.

Paediatricians who specialise in growth give their opinion based on family history, rate of growth and the X-ray appearance of the growing ends of the bones. Occasionally children are found to be deficient in growth hormone, which is needed for linear growth. When this deficiency is diagnosed in the middle school years, treatment with synthetic growth hormone is both safe and effective.

Headaches

Life is full of headaches. When the child looks pale, below par and holds their head, the parents think, 'It's tension, eye strain, she's tired, it's something she ate.' But headaches come and go, even in the most relaxed, sure-sighted, well-slept child.

Some children get a few headaches, while for others they are a regular occurrence. These are usually vague, not too severe and settle quickly. Though migraine is much more common in teens and adults, it can occur in young children. In its classic presentation, migraine starts with disturbed visual symptoms followed by a strong, one-sided pain associated with pallor and nausea. In the young school-age child there is often a mix of abdominal pain, pale appearance and a less clear-cut headache.

Migraine is managed with paracetamol and rest in a quiet, darkened room. Where headaches become frequent or severe, a consultation with a paediatrician or children's neurologist is advised. As heads and brains are so important, be quick to seek help if there are any symptoms that are unusual or rapidly deteriorating.

Hepatitis vaccination

Currently the two types of viral hepatitis that cause most concern are hepatitis A and hepatitis B. Hepatitis A infection comes through the faeces–oral route, usually from infected food. It causes an unpleasant illness but one that will usually resolve completely. There is a vaccine available for hepatitis A.

Hepatitis B comes from infected blood and intimate body fluids. It can leave sufferers infective for years and carries a high risk of long-term liver damage. This problem of ongoing infectivity and liver damage makes hepatitis B a target for immunisation in some countries. However, in the UK the immunisation is only recommended for those babies and children who have a high risk of catching it.

Hepatitis A

In a country with clean water, good sewage disposal and interest in food hygiene, the incidence of hepatitis A is low. The main risk of contacting Hepatitis A is to adventurers who travel to places with poor water and poor sewage and food standards. Also at risk are some health and child care workers who deal daily with youngsters who are unreliable in their toilet training.

There is a safe and effective immunisation against hepatitis A, but it is only recommended for certain travellers, as well as health, child care and residential care workers.

Hepatitis B

Though AIDS is the most highly publicised blood-borne and sexually transmitted disease, hepatitis B is many times more infective, much more common and can also be fatal.

The greatest risk of infection comes from blood contact. Hepatitis B is almost universal in needle-sharing drug addicts. But such is the degree of infectivity that it also poses a risk through sporting injuries and normal sexual activity.

Hernias

Children have hernias, not from lifting furniture, but due to a slight congenital weakness. A hernia is a small opening in an abdominal muscle that should have closed during the normal developmental process before birth. Parents become aware of the problem when a small bulge appears, usually in early infancy.

An inguinal hernia may show as a groin swelling that comes and goes. There is a danger that this knuckle of gut will get stuck, blocked and possibly go gangrenous. The defect that causes an inguinal hernia always needs surgical repair. As this is inevitable, the operation should be booked soon after diagnosis. If the groin swelling ever becomes hard, red and swollen, the hernia is now obstructed and has become a surgical emergency.

Many babies are born with a slight bulge beside their belly button (umbilical hernia). Most resolve in the first year while a few remain until four years or five years of age. As these rarely obstruct, they can be given plenty of time to resolve. But by school age their time is up.

Hives, or urticaria

When I was a child my mother blamed my itchy hives on eating strawberries, but I thought our dog had fleas. Hives or urticaria means an allergic skin rash. It varies from a few red spots to large, itchy islands. At its most extreme, urticaria can block respiration and endanger life.

The skin rash is a reaction to something we ingest, touch or that stings us. Often the offending agent is quite obvious, such as penicillin. When this is recognised it must be totally avoided.

Unfortunately, urticaria can be much more complicated, especially when it is caused by something your child ate. You can give your child a food on one occasion and there is no reaction, yet two weeks later it covers them in hives. This is due to the cumulative effect. A little of the offending chemical may be contained in one product, then more from another, until finally the body is tipped over the edge.

If your child's urticaria is caused by a sensitivity to salicylate, they may fall victim to this cumulative effect, because salicylate is present in many fruits like oranges, tomatoes and strawberries. So last week they had a heaped bowl of strawberries with no ill effects. But today, they drank a glass of orange juice, had a rich tomato-based pasta then followed it with a serving of strawberries. As the last berry is swallowed, urticaria is appearing before your eyes. Come to think of it, maybe my mother was right all along!

Treatment involves avoiding problem products, the use of antihistamine to ease symptoms and a trip to an allergist when it all gets too difficult.

Immunisation

My blood pressure rises when I hear media arguments against immunisation. Every reputable scientific body in the civilised world supports vaccination.

In my paediatric career I have seen a tragic collection of children who have suffered greatly or died through the irresponsibility of refusing to immunise. I have personally managed one child who died of whooping cough. I have watched copious children debilitated with the spasms, whoop and vomit of this preventable illness. I have seen two children die a slow death of brain degeneration from the measles complication of sub-acute sclerosing panencephalitis. I have managed countless children, extremely sick, with the cough, conjunctivitis and unbelievably high fever of measles. Even in the last decades of the twentieth century I have witnessed one adult die of tetanus, and a child die of diphtheria.

I accept that every action we take in life is a balance between risk and pay-off but with immunisation the equation is so steeply loaded against the anti-lobby, it's hard to know how they have such power.

Unfortunately, our media is more interested in controversy than accuracy. When challenged they tell me, 'It's only fair to give equal air time.' The reality is that for each anti-immunisation activist, there are 1000 highly qualified professionals who support vaccination. If equality entered the equation we should hear 1000 statements of support to each one of inaccuracy.

In medicine there must be a careful balance between risk and benefit. Open-heart surgery probably kills one in twenty patients. Refusing the chance of surgery assures the death of twenty out of twenty. Car seat belts save thousands of lives every year, yet it is possible they might occasionally slow a child's escape from a burning vehicle.

At this point my position must be crystal clear. The current immunisation schedules are set out in Appendix II, page 262.

244

Itchy bottom

Though bowel training is established at two and a half years, bottom wiping comes much, much later. At age five years there may be a small forest's worth of paper product in the bowl, but it doesn't guarantee hygiene. An itchy bottom is most commonly a poorly cleaned bottom.

It's not just undercleaning, but also overcleaning that can cause itch. Some children react to the usual alkaline pH of normal bath soaps or even residues of detergent in the underclothes. If in doubt use a product for sensitive skin (see this chapter, Dry skin, page 231) and make sure that clothes are well rinsed after washing them with detergent.

A classic but rare cause of itch is an infestation of worms. These wrigglers lie in the large bowel then crawl out at night to lay eggs around the bottom. This causes itching, which is diagnosed by examining what is happening by night and watching the toilet by day (see this chapter, Worms, page 255).

Left-handedness

It is said that one in ten children are left-handed. In the past the left hand was associated with a weakness in reading, spelling and learning but now the only proven problem is the mechanism of writing. English goes from left to right, making it mighty awkward for the left-hander. Their work will be obstructed and smudged unless they write with a bizarre, hooked hand.

Hand dominance develops at about the age of two years and is firmly established by the age of four years. It is usual for the right-handed child to be strongly right. A number of lefties are less certain and are able to use both hands.

When there is weak or no dominance it's best to be right in a right-handed world. Thankfully, though, we have come a long way from my school days when you wrote with your right hand or 'God's representative' tried to change brain dominance with a ruler.

Measles

Measles causes a major illness with cough, conjunctivitis and extremely high fevers. It is one of the nastiest of the common childhood conditions and one that would not occur if the recommended vaccination schedules were more generally accepted.

Measles has a ten- to fifteen-day incubation period. The illness starts with a bad cold, cough, sore eyes and moderate fever. After about three days a red rash sweeps all over the body and the temperature soars to up to 40 degrees Celsius (104 degrees Fahrenheit). At this point most children are a picture of misery, with discoloured skin, conjunctivitis, a crusted nose and nasty cough. After this peak the rash and fever start to settle, leaving a weak, coughing child.

No child needs measles or its complications of bronchitis, pneumonia, ear infection, encephalitis and the slow degeneration of sub-acute sclerosing panencephalitis. In the years between 1978 and 1992, 164 Australians died of measles. Don't procrastinate – vaccinate.

Meningococcal infection

Meningococcus is one of the most feared infections of the moment. Out of the blue a child can embark on a devastating downhill course that often leads to death or disability. Despite its viciousness this is one of the easiest bacteria to kill, responding to the most basic 1940s brand of penicillin.

The meningococcus bacteria is a relatively common fellow traveller in the community. Why it infects some people and misses the majority is unknown. The bacteria enters the body, initially causing a mild illness that can move on to a rapidly expanding blood infection (septicaemia) or meningitis (an infection of the tissue that covers of the brain). Most children I have treated had both the septicaemia and meningitis. The presence of septicaemia is suspected in any extremely sick child with an almost-bruised-type skin rash that increases every minute. Meningitis is considered in the child with headache and a stiff neck.

A doctor can easily be caught out, seeing a vaguely sick child in the morning, giving reassurance, and sending them home. But some hours later the infection becomes all-consuming, with the child crashing onto the downhill course.

If any child looks sick and is dropping fast, this is the most urgent of urgent emergencies. The situation is even more serious if there is neck stiffness, rapid shallow breathing and a bleeding skin rash. The only way to prevent death and disability in meningococcus is a quick diagnosis, immediately followed by that first dose of life-saving antibiotic.

Mumps

You suspect mumps when your child has some fever and an obviously swollen face. Often mumps is so mild it is not suspected but in most it causes some fever and a characteristic swelling of one or both of the parotid salivary glands. These glands lie below and forward of the ears. The submandibular glands, under the jaw, may also be enlarged and tender to touch.

This virus has a variable incubation period, averaging out at about eighteen days. Mumps is infectious for two days before the swelling and until the glands return to normal.

Nursing a child with mumps has a strange effect on fathers. They cross their legs and maintain good distance, as they have heard the tales of swollen, sore testes that can occur in twenty per cent of adult males. Fortunately, mumps is not the most infectious of childhood illnesses and epidemics are much less common since the introduction of the measles, mumps and rubella vaccination.

Though mumps is not usually a serious illness, immunisation is recommended as it can occasionally cause deafness and more commonly a mild encephalitis (infection of the brain).

Nits

When two adults put their heads together they come up with a brilliant idea. But when kindergarten kids get together they catch nits. Nits are the tell-tale eggs of head lice. They show as hard, white flecks cemented to the hairs. Nits are an extremely common part of life for many children in the early school years.

The lice spread by direct contact or from shared hats and clothes. Head lice are probably more common than in the past due to our insistence on hats for sun protection. In the early school years hats may lie in heaps and many are tried before the child finds their own. Often the bug is not seen but an experienced infant teacher can spot a nit at twenty paces.

Once the diagnosis is made your meticulously cared-for child returns home like a leper, one hand clutching a note: 'Dear Mrs Smith, Your daughter has nits. Please treat before she can return to school.'

Treatment involves a special head lice overnight lotion and shampoo, which is readily available from every chemist. The rest is all those clichés of nitpicking with a fine-tooth comb.

Nose bleeds

Not all nose bleeds are the result of injury. Some children seem created with delicate nasal blood vessels that just bleed from time to time. For others, this is part of their allergic nose problem. Then there are bleeds that come as part of an upper respiratory viral illness.

Treatment involves a bit of boy scout first-aid. First have the head held still then, if needed, compress the soft part of the nose just below the bridge. Continue compression for ten minutes and see what happens. When bleeds keep recurring it's time for an appointment with an ear, nose and throat specialist. Any acute bleed that won't stop needs a trip to casualty.

Nose block

The nose is the first-line filter that screens air heading for the lungs. If allergens are about, it's the nose that sniffs them out. When one looks at the major problems listed in this book, a blocked nose seems pretty trivial. Yet nasal allergy is unpleasant for the child and sniffing is intensely irritating to the parents.

The allergy-troubled nose may run, but more often it is chronically blocked. The child breathes through their mouth, which affects their tone of voice, enjoyment of food and snore-free sleep. What's worse, an open mouth projects a vacant expression that makes the clever child look impaired.

The offending allergen can be demonstrated by pinprick skin testing. In my experience this usually shows that the child is allergic to most pollens, house dust and house dust mite. Desensitisation treatments are time consuming and reasonably unreliable. The preferred management of the allergic nose is the regular use of a cortisone-based nasal spray or antihistamines if symptoms are acute or severe.

Passive smoking

I recently spent some transit time in Bangkok airport. There the authorities forbid smoking in public areas, restricting the nicotine-starved traveller to a small, sealed-off room. Here they puff and pace like agitated goldfish in a glass bowl. Every so often a mask-wearing attendant mucks out the enclosure and quickly retreats. It may seem that I am an anti-smoking extremist. The truth is – I am!

248

I own a life insurance policy. As I am a non-smoker I pay a premium that is reduced by fifty per cent. Now, I am no mathematical genius, but to my brain, this suggests that smoking can't be good for you.

A child spends the first eighteen years of their lives stuck in the atmosphere we provide. There is now a lot of evidence that it is not just those who smoke, but others who inhale their side-stream who are at risk. The list of dangers includes chest infections, cot death and asthma, to mention just a few.

If parents wish to reduce their life expectancy by fifty per cent, I suppose that's their business. All I ask is that they don't damage their children's health in the side-stream.

Rubella, or German measles

Rubella is a mild childhood illness. It is very different from the high fevers and extreme sickness of measles. Many children and adults have such a low-grade infection they are unaware they have carried the virus and are now immune.

Rubella has a fourteen- to twenty-one-day incubation period, which is followed by a slight fever and a faint pink rash. There is often a characteristic enlargement of the lymph nodes at the back of the neck (just above the hairline). For most children rubella is a vague unimpressive illness.

The main danger of rubella is its risk to a pregnant mum. When an unborn baby is infected, especially in the first three months, this can cause deafness, blindness, intellectual disability and major heart defects. In the first eight to ten weeks of gestation there is up to a ninety per cent risk of major foetal damage.

To protect the unborn babies of the future it is now recommended that all children receive rubella immunisation, through the triple vaccine (measles, mumps, rubella). This directly protects girls for their child-rearing years, and by immunising boys, we reduce the risk of the virus entering the community.

Women who are planning to become pregnant should have a blood test to check their rubella vaccine is still protecting them.

Snoring

It's not just Grandad who snores. The sleeping child can produce equally good vibrations. Snoring may be associated with the nasal airway obstruction of the common cold, allergy, enlarged adenoids or big tonsils. The nose blocks, the throat relaxes with sleep and the airflow resonates.

One much-promoted condition of the moment is sleep apnoea. Here a sleeping child has a marginal airflow, which reduces oxygen levels in the brain. They usually snore and the next day feel acutely under-slept. The effect of low oxygen can also cause problems with mental function and behaviour.

Occasional snoring is of no concern; just roll the child over to sleep on their side. When there is chronic snoring or any hint of sleep apnoea, discuss this with your family doctor, paediatrician or ear, nose and throat specialist.

Suntan and skin damage

It may seem impossible to establish sun sense in children, but bigger battles have been won. When my bike-riding boys were at school only nerds and epileptics wore helmets. Attitudes were hard to shift, but a few years later, bike helmets are fully accepted.

The secret of sun protection is to start early. Protection is not a maybe – it is a must. Hats, shirts, avoiding peak hours and high-factor creams have to be an accepted part of everyday life.

If hats are to be worn they must appear 'cool' to the child. There is a difference between those favoured by a bald octogenarian and the hat of an iron-man or 'Bay Watch' babe. During the summer, a pump pack of sun cream should be kept in a prominent place. Small containers that fit in pockets can be filled from this central vat.

Once skin is burnt, no expensive after-sun treatment can reverse the damage. The best we can do is keep it moist with an economy softener such as sorbolene with glycerine cream. After excessive sun exposure keep fluid levels high as this can cause dehydration and sunstroke.

Teeth: what to do if one is knocked out

Children should be encouraged to wear a properly fitting mouthguard for all stick-swinging and contact sports. Despite this advice, about one quarter of all children will have tooth trauma before the age of fifteen. Many of these injuries will involve the permanent upper front teeth being completely knocked out. In the past, once dislodged, the permanent tooth was lost for life. Now dentists can save many of these permanent teeth if we follow a few simple rules.

Retrieve the tooth and, if dirty, rinse gently in milk, saline or the child's saliva **but do not scrub**. If possible put the tooth back in the socket and hold it in place. Otherwise preserve the tooth in a cup of milk (not water) and get to your dentist. They will reimplant and steady the tooth with a small splint. After about ten days the dentist will remove the splint but it will be six to twelve months before you know whether the reimplantation has been successful.

Testes: undescended or retractile

Ninety per cent of newborn males will have both testes present and easy to demonstrate. Most of the other ten per cent appear in the early months. But those not down by one year rarely make it without help. Surgery for undescended testes is now recommended at age two to three years.

Some school-age children have retractile testes, which are hard to locate on routine medical examination. If a tense child is met with a cold hand the testes may spring for cover, but an experienced doctor can easily demonstrate that these testes are present and correct.

If a testis is still undescended by school age and you have not already consulted a paediatric surgeon, this should be arranged now. An intact testis will function to some extent in any position but it works a lot better in those cooler climates of the lower latitudes.

Tonsillitis

The tonsils are two patches of lymph tissue situated on either side of the throat. These, along with the adenoids and other defences, act as the first line of protection against invading infections. When they are fighting some invader they may be enlarged and red with associated involvement of the lymph glands in the neck.

The tonsils are seen as two sentries guarding the entry to the lungs. But this exaggerates their true importance, as no one has shown any reduction in resistance following removal of tonsils and adenoids. Presumably these are one small part in a long line of defence.

Any cold or upper respiratory virus will cause some inflammation in the throat, which will generally leave it red. True tonsillitis specifically involves the tonsils, which will be swollen, red and flecked with infection. A generalised viral action requires no treatment. Tonsillitis is usually caused by a bacteria, and will be treated with an antibiotic.

Occasionally, glandular fever presents with a severe tonsillitis of viral origin. Though usually a problem of adolescence and young adults, it can occur at this school age (see this chapter, page 238).

Tonsillectomy

There was a time when it was said that any child old enough to open their mouth would lose their tonsils. Certainly this operation was overused, and its results were sometimes quite hazardous. This caused a major backlash, so most paediatricians then counselled against tonsillectomy. Around that time of overreaction I met many children who had been refused treatment but who had a dramatic turnaround in health, school attendance and quality of life after I referred them to a sensible surgeon.

At present, there is a more accepting attitude towards tonsillectomy, and if you feel that your child is disadvantaged by repeated genuine bouts of tonsillitis, insist on referral to an ear, nose and throat expert.

As a rule of thumb, tonsillectomy is considered if there are three or more infections each year for two or more years, or five infections in any one year. A wise surgeon interprets these with flexibility, taking into account the degree of the distress and the general health of the child.

Tonsillectomy is usually accompanied by the more minor procedure of adenoidectomy. The tonsil operation may be reasonably straightforward, but the post-operative care needs skilled nursing and good and regular pain relief. There is a small but real risk of life-threatening haemorrhage in the hours and days following surgery. For this reason most operations are now performed in hospitals experienced in the post-operative care of children.

Removal of tonsils and adenoids does not lessen a child's ability to fight off future viruses and bacteria.

Tummy upsets

A common problem for parents is the child who is off their food, feels sick, vomits or has diarrhoea. Parents usually blame this on 'a bad sausage' or 'an off prawn', but these are rarely the cause. Most upsets come from whatever virus is at large in the community. As viruses do not respond to antibiotics, we treat the symptoms, not the cause.

World-wide, more children die of dehydration due to gut problems than any other illness. Most upsets are relatively mild, but we must never lose sight of the danger of dehydration.

When a child is feeling sick, they don't need building up with solid food; they require clear fluid that stays put. With an uneasy gut, go for small sips, taken regularly. The contents of a sherry glass every fifteen minutes will achieve quite a load in a day.

Ten years ago we encouraged parents to rehydrate with flat lemonade. But today this is thought to be dangerous, and now we recommend one of the electrolyte solutions like Dioralyte. If lemonade is used it must be diluted to one part lemonade with four parts of water.

It's not the number of vomits or toilet trips that indicate the severity of a tummy upset. What matters is the fluid balance in the body. If eyes are bright, skin is moist, mind is clear and urine is flowing, this would seem safe. Dull eyes, a distant brain, dry skin and little urine spell danger and the need for immediate hospital help.

The key points are: hydration with small frequent amounts of clear fluid, special electrolyte solutions or lemonade, but only if diluted; when the child becomes distant and dry, this is an emergency.

Warts

Warts are unsightly raised areas, and are mostly on the hands and sometimes the feet. They can be single, multiple or almost in a crop. They are caused by a virus, which is eventually defeated by the body's immune system.

Warts last for months or years but disappear quickly once immunity arrives. This has helped generations of gypsies and wart charmers who know that the virus is on a short-term lease. Warts are more unsightly than painful. Plantar warts appear on the sole of the foot and can be tender when walking.

The best treatment is to be patient until the arrival of immunity. If you can't wait, try a wart-shrinking paint or get a skin specialising doctor to freeze with liquid nitrogen. Freezing is painful and may require a number of applications.

Whooping cough, or pertussis

Whooping cough is a long, unpleasant respiratory illness. It is caused by a bacteria that is relatively unresponsive to antibiotics. There is a seven-day incubation period, then one or two weeks of vague upper respiratory illness, and after this comes the cough. This bursts through in characteristic spasms. The child coughs until totally breathless, then fights for air, which rushes in with an inspiratory whoop. Often the spasm ends in vomiting and the child is terrified of anything that may set off another cycle. The cough reduces and finally clears in four to twelve weeks.

Whooping cough is of greatest risk to infants who are too young to immunise, yet have little natural immunity. When epidemics hit, it is the young baby and unimmunised toddler who is at the highest risk of serious illness or death. Little children are much safer when the reservoir of wild infection in the community is reduced by general immunisation.

But with fewer children being immunised, school-age children and adults are currently contracting whooping cough. In the years 1993 to 1996 in Australia, almost half of the cases of pertussis occurred in children over the age of nine and adults. There are some failures, but immunisation gives eight-five to ninety-five per cent protection.

The whooping cough vaccine of the past was not without side effects. There were some relatively minor reactions but there was also concern over an extremely rare risk of acquired brain damage (encephalopathy). In the late 1970s this possibility was promoted in the media, with the result that immunisation rates dropped to under one-third. In the following epidemic that swept the UK over thirty children died from whooping cough. It is engraved on my memory: one child who could not be resuscitated was under my care.

The link between vaccine and encephalopathy is presumed but not proven. Research puts the risk at between zero and ten cases per million of those who are vaccinated. In an epidemic the risk of contacting pertussis is between seventy per cent and 100 per cent. Of these, the risk of encephalopathy caused by natural whooping cough is seven per 1000 cases. That is, 7000 per million may contract encephalopathy from whooping cough, while zero to ten per million may contract it from the vaccine. This puts the worst possible estimate of vaccine damage at one-thousandth of the risk of the natural disease.

But immunisation is not only about saving lives; it protects all those children from weeks of fighting for breath, choking and vomiting.

Worms

The most common villain is the threadworm, which lives in the lower end of the bowel and usually produces no problems other than the occasional itch. The female worm crawls out in the dead of night and lays eggs around the bottom. If observed at this time, little worms may be seen and all this wriggling causes itch. Children scratch, get eggs under their fingernails, and that's how reinfection occurs. Threadworm is not always easy to eradicate. The whole family needs an antiworm treatment, followed by special emphasis on well-washed hands and hygiene.

Infection with other worms is possible but unlikely. Worms do not cause tooth grinding or nightmares.

Height and weight charts showing normal growth

BOYS: 2 TO 18 YEARS HEIGHT PERCENTILE

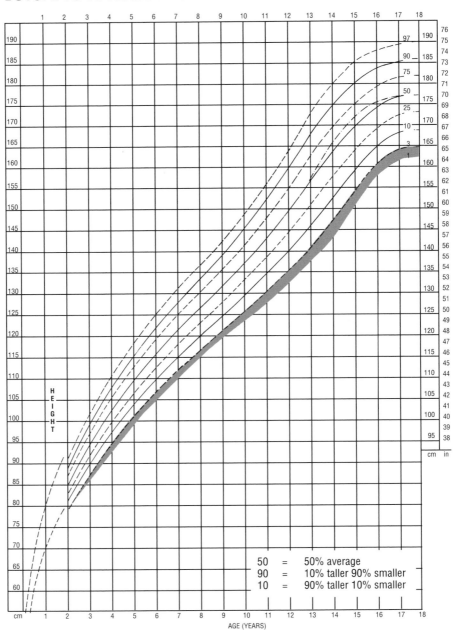

50	=	50% average
90	=	10% taller 90% smaller
10	=	90% taller 10% smaller

AGE (YEARS)

(Standards appropriate to Aust., UK & Nth America)

BOYS: 2 TO 18 YEARS WEIGHT PERCENTILE

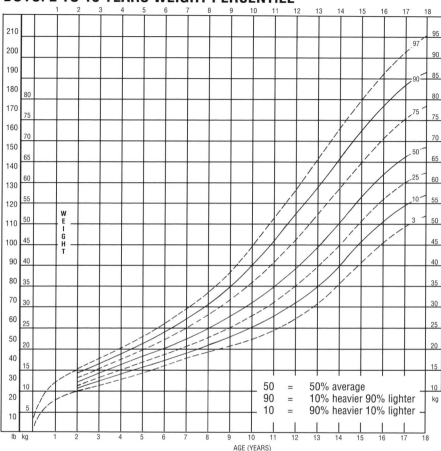

(Standards appropriate to Aust., UK & Nth America)

Boys' height chart

- 50% equals average height
- 90% means 10% of boys will be taller; 90% will be shorter
- 10% means 90% of boys will be taller; 10% will be shorter

Boys' weight chart

- 50% equals average weight
- 90% means 10% of boys will be heavier; 90% will be lighter
- 10% means 90% of boys will be heavier; 10% will be lighter

GIRLS: 2 TO 18 YEARS HEIGHT PERCENTILE

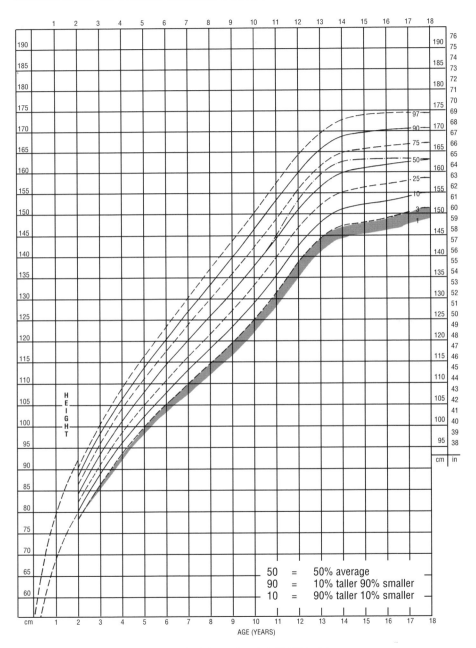

50 = 50% average
90 = 10% taller 90% smaller
10 = 90% taller 10% smaller

AGE (YEARS)

(Standards appropriate to Aust., UK & Nth America)

GIRLS: 2 TO 18 YEARS WEIGHT PERCENTILE

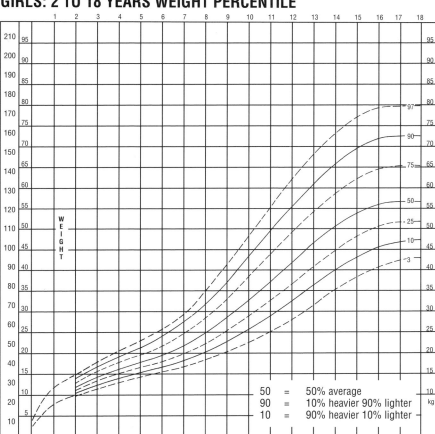

(Standards appropriate to Aust., UK & Nth America)

Girls' height chart

● 50% equals average height
● 90% means 10% of girls will be taller; 90% will be shorter
● 10% means 90% of girls will be taller; 10% will be shorter

Girls' weight chart

● 50% equals average weight
● 90% means 10% of girls will be heavier; 90% will be lighter
● 10% means 90% of girls will be heavier; 10% will be lighter

Standard vaccination schedule*

Triple Vaccine Diphtheria, tetanus & whooping cough (D/T/P) and polio and HIB (haemophilus influenzae Type B)	1st dose 2 months 2nd dose 3 months 3rd dose 4 months
Meningitis C	2 months
Measles, mumps, rubella (MMR)	12–18 months (can be given any age over 12 months)
Pre-school booster D/T and polio	3–5 years
MMR – second dose	Usually given with pre-school booster
BCG (tuberculin)	10–14 years or infancy
Booster tetanus and polio	13–18 years

* Recommended by the Department of Health

Permanent teeth: age of eruption

central incisors	lower	6th year
	upper	6th to 7th year
first molars		6th year
lateral incisors	lower	7th year
	upper	8th year
canines	lower	10th year
	upper	10th to 11th year
first pre-molars	lower	10th to 11th year
	upper	10th year
second pre-molars	lower	11th to 12th year
	upper	11th year
second molars	lower	11th to 12th year
	upper	12th year
third molars (wisdom teeth)		20th year

Helping coordination*

Children with coordination difficulty will often have problems swinging a bat, throwing and catching balls, tying shoelaces, riding a bike, running with style and assembling things with their hands. When children see themselves as clumsy they can lose confidence in themselves, and when playing with other children they can be made to feel left out.

Parents can help to some extent, but no amount of practice will turn the poorly coordinated child into a top tennis player, football legend or star of the ballet. To help, take the pressure off them and avoid competitive sports, unless they enjoy them. Here are a few simple suggestions that should be followed in a fun way:

Throwing and catching

Throwing can be practised by aiming at a large target such as a rubbish bin, then gradually decreasing the size to an empty milk carton. With catching, arms can't coordinate quickly enough to trap the ball. Practise with a large ball such as an inflatable beach ball, gradually working down until the child bounces, throws and catches a tennis ball with reasonable reliability.

Hand movements

Manipulation can be improved through simple activities such as paper weaving, threading paper clips and clay work. Construction sets should be encouraged, starting with large pieces and working towards those that are smaller. Simple craft suggestions, such as hammering nails into a piece of wood and weaving string designs, help coordination. Have a desk set up with reams of paper permanently on hand.

Bicycle riding

Some children find it hard to master a two-wheeler bike. They go quite well until the trainer wheels are removed, then after this it's hard work. Find a bit of open space where steering will be unimportant, and the surface not too tricky. After this there are no short cuts: it takes hours of parents running behind holding lightly to the saddle. If this gets too hard put the bike away for a few months and then try again.

Swimming

Some children find it easy to kick, easy to move their arms but extremely difficult to kick, move arms and breathe all at the same time. Be reassured that all these children will become proficient swimmers as long as we don't turn them off water along the way.

Swimming lessons that involve a lot of sitting around waiting to participate generally fail. A teacher who insists on perfect style rather than safe swimming may also be unsuccessful. When lessons are unsuccessful children do best splashing around the pool having fun with their mum and dad. This is better than a whole academy of swimming instructors.

* These ideas come from Neralie Cocks, Occupational Therapist, the Child Development Unit, Sydney.

Helping handwriting*

Proficient handwriting is not a skill that comes easily to some children, so be patient. Aim for legibility and content, not calligraphy. Spend short periods practising these ideas, and keep it positive and fun.

Check posture

Make sure the child is sitting in a chair that supports their back. The table must not be too high or too low, as this results in tense shoulders and slouched posture. Elbows should rest comfortably on the table and feet flat on the floor. It helps if the child leans slightly on the non-writing arm, which stabilises the paper and allows the writing arm to move freely across the page.

Check pencil grip

Some children develop a tense, awkward pencil hold that slows down written work and tires the fingers. A thicker pencil or special plastic grip can help reduce this tension.

Circular movements

Practise anticlockwise and clockwise circular scribble patterns across the page. Use a large sheet of unlined paper working from left to right then repeat using wide-spaced lines. Eventually introduce the lined paper that is used at school.

Individual letters

Start with letters formed in an anticlockwise finger movement: a, o, c, e, s, d, g, q, u. Then move on to the clockwise letters: r, n, m, h, k, b, p. Now string together a continuous row of n's and u's.

Curvy letters

Move on to letters with a curvy movement, such as v, w and y. As you go, check the sitting posture at the table and pencil grip. Praise and keep practising. If teachers are still concerned, ask an occupational therapist for help.

* These ideas come from Neralie Cocks, Occupational Therapist, The Child Development Unit, Sydney.

Index